MORE THAN MUSCLES

— Mr. USA —
Mind, Motives, Mentors

Joe Troccoli

iUniverse, Inc.
New York   Bloomington

More than Muscles
Mr. USA—Mind, Motives, Mentors

iUniverse books may be ordered through booksellers or by contacting:

iUniverse
1663 Liberty Drive
Bloomington, IN 47403
www.iuniverse.com
1-800-Authors (1-800-288-4677)

ISBN: 978-1-4502-5241-6 (pbk)
ISBN: 978-1-4502-5243-0 (cloth)
ISBN: 978-1-4502-5242-3 (ebk)

Printed in the United States of America

iUniverse rev. date: 9/16/2010

Contents

Preface

I audaciously believed that grandiose bodybuilding achievements were attainable while maintaining my morality. Such desires presented many personal and public debacles in my life. My dilemma became even more complex as I struggled to understand and overcome my apparent imperfections. Many of us cannot be satisfied with mediocrity or the lowest common denominator. Striving for our own perfection may be the manifestation of complex internal consequences or something as simple as passion. Either way, for those of us afflicted with the obsession to transcend ourselves, good enough is never good enough. Thus, satisfaction or gratification may be as elusive as the mythical unicorn. This issue influenced many of the conflicts within this publication and, in essence, was the driving force behind this work.

We all have never-ending internal battles between our positive sides (good) and our negative sides (evil). Many times, I failed miserably in my conduct and competitions, proving that even "a wretch like me" can be saved and find success. And what exactly is success? Its actuality may not quite match the definition you presumed. Mine certainly did not! It is my hope that each reader walks away with a better understanding that struggle is an essential part of life, making us stronger, more compassionate toward others, and more appreciative of the truly important aspects of being human. Hopefully, by exposing my own private encounters, clashes, and torments, I can help others realize that we are not so different after all. In fact, we are not as isolated or insulated from each other as we may have thought.

Who was I, the offspring of poor, uneducated folks from the wrong background, to dare to want more than my upbringing allowed? As a small child in New York, I was blessed with little more than loving parents and grandparents. But the many emotions associated with such an abundance of love proved to be a profound catalyst in overcoming so many other unfavorable odds. Inspired by tough mentors never to fear hard work, I learned that fortitude and perseverance lead to overachievement. Without overreaching, I would have allowed my life to be dictated by negativity and the status quo.

After a short stint in journalism, I found one of my callings as a firefighter/paramedic. The service side of me provided aid and comfort to others, while the gladiator in me scratched my way to the top of the sport of bodybuilding. Throughout this seeming paradox lifestyle, I tried to be the best father, husband, and son I could be. As you will read, my ideals and principles were tested often and quite severely.

Another strong motivation to complete this memoir was to immortalize some of the incredible characters who served as my mentors. While far too many people have assisted in my personal growth to include herein, Giuseppe Bencivenga and Father Donald O'Brien have been extraordinarily instrumental. Before either of their spirits left this world, their indelible chivalry, morality, and dignity exalted my life and inspired me to do far better.

A point of interest prior to engaging this story: I deliberately attempted to keep every chapter brief so that each reader may pause for his or her own reflection and interpretation. Certain portions, however, are packed with a full spectrum of human emotions. It is my hope that the brevity of the more poignant sections allows them to be fully explored and pondered, rather than caromed over. Additionally, as our obligations from living in such a fast-paced society inhibit our leisure time, such a format was designed to fit within those time restraints.

Lastly, every effort has been made to prevent harm or scrutiny upon anyone casually mentioned or featured within these pages. The omission of those personalities or sections would have jeopardized the accuracy and factual nature of this work, thereby removing integral and fundamental aspects of my story. In spite of my best attempt to put everyone in the best light possible, reality sometimes is neither flattering nor pleasant to accept.

Introduction

In his most famous speech, titled "What It Takes to Be Number One," Vince Lombardi said, "Winning is not a sometime thing. It's an all the time thing. You don't win once in a while; you don't do things right once in a while; you do them right all the time. Winning is a habit. Unfortunately, so is losing."

On my long and sometimes winding road to my Mr. USA victory, many challenges tested the implementation of such mandatory habits to which Mr. Lombardi alludes.

In the sport of bodybuilding, the Mr. USA and the Mr. America titles are the sport's equivalent of an Olympic gold medal for a gymnast, a Wimbledon championship in Tennis, or a NASCAR Daytona 500 win. But unlike most other sports, bodybuilding has two separate but equal "Super Bowls" per year. It gives prospective competitors two chances at immortality annually. The Mr. USA competition traditionally takes place during the summer, and the Mr. America Championships are in the fall. Many fantasize of tasting such sweetness, but few ever savor the extraordinary pinnacle of accomplishment. The prestige of any sport's highest title places one within elite ranks, with the associated respect of his rivals and peers. I endured many obstacles, battles, and personal losses to fulfill my destiny. During much of those peaks and valleys, I also carried the distinction of being one of America's Bravest, a professional firefighter. From the euphoria of my national title to the life-changing illness I sustained as a firefighter, I view Vince Lombardi's oration as far more than rhetoric.

Like many citizens of the United States, I am a product of foreign-born lineage. My ancestors believed that America stood for individuals being at their best. That was, and still is, the premise and promise of Uncle Sam's greatness: ordinary people doing extraordinary things. I so revered the sacrifices made by my forebearers that I felt profound guilt that they had forfeited so much for my benefit. My firsthand knowledge of the hardships they endured, to hand me a better world, hijacked a tremendous amount of pleasure from my triumphs and achievements. However, through much self-analysis and retrospection, I finally realized that my genealogy did not assure my success or relevance in this world.

Additionally, I carried much shame and regret for not having had the power to alter the fate of some loved ones' final moments. I had stigmatized myself with blame over those critical times in their lives. My self-doubt and remorse caused so much unnecessary emotional pain. But was it truly unnecessary, or were those agonizing times crucial in formulating my understanding and perspective of this world? Either way, I had to learn how to rise above my greatest nemesis: myself. Indecision and self-doubt are common impediments to many of us—particularly when we have ambitious goals. Most of the time, those elaborate plans require bold steps. And daring steps are difficult to forge out of average talent or capacity. There are no freebies or handouts.

Understanding that the world is unyielding and complicated, how can we obtain the cherished summit where so few have dwelled? That revelation, illustrated in one ordinary man's implausible story (which you now hold in your hands), smolders within each of us. My story is synonymous with those of so many others who've had grand ambitions. While each person's journey embarks in his or her own unique direction, the eventual destination usually exists where we least expect it. If we are willing to forgo our excuses, we can foster the winner that is waiting to flourish in all of us.

Whatever our individual hindrances may be, overcoming them will require the courage to delve into the darkest corners of our subconscious. While I am not a psychologist, nor do I pretend to possess the patent for the secrets of life, my experiences have taught me how essential it is to brave temporary discomfort in order to deliver long-term tranquility. In the course of fulfilling my objectives, there were times to savor the good, the unavoidable humiliation of accepting the bad, and the disgrace of admitting the ugly. You, just as I, must have the stamina, determination, and perseverance required to pick yourself up one more time than you fall. Eventually, such persistence begets a lifestyle where we control our own destination.

Along the pathways to our goals, finding the fortitude to defeat our tendencies to surrender can be difficult, although possible. All of us can develop the psychological and emotional tenacity to overthrow our intimidating angst and cowardice. First, we must overcome our fear of failure because our missteps may be essential toward winning. Many have paralyzed themselves into a state of idleness due to their phobia of falling short. Therein lies the real challenge for mankind: "No guts, no glory!" Most of us understand that we will not achieve successful results with each and every attempt. However, by raising the white flag before exhausting all means, we guarantee our own defeat. On many occasions, great accomplishments come at a high price. We must understand that bumps and bruises litter nearly every path to achievement.

My scars surely run deep and are plentiful. While I am no Winston Churchill, I can connect with his precedent of fighting on. He endured more than his share of vices and downfalls. But his optimism prevented his imperfections from sabotaging his place in history. He is worth remembering because when tribulations affronted his private and public life, he did not adopt the path of ease. And while his flaws were legendary, his heroism helped alter the story of a continent. Not even he would have predicted the direction that his life would lead. His sentiments were much like mine, for he offered, "Success is not final, failure is not fatal: it is the courage to continue that counts." This is the crux of this memoir. The central idea is that losing as a habit is not always the result of inferior genetics but of a mind-set with deep, often unrecognized roots. Winning, then, is a habit—not always the result of superior genetics but of a mind-set that can be cultivated.

Our attitudes will either help us or hurt us. By choosing associations and influences wisely, our futures can be viewed by the present company we keep. The mind-sets, motivations, and mentors we embrace will ultimately determine our characters. And our characters are who and what we really are—not our reputations or ability to slant public opinion. While I was fortunate to have been blessed with a nurturing family, it was my choice to adhere to their values and spiritual examples. There have been positive and negative role models to emulate, but my self-imposed discipline and standards veered me away from mimicking false heroes. Was there luck involved? Quite possibly there was. But if so, it was to a small degree. I've come to suspect that we actually create our so-called "good luck." Actually, the culmination of a litany of virtues proved to be the ingredients required to transform me from an insecure and fragile child to a tenacious and purposeful adult.

It all starts within our minds. That is where our passion delivers us to our own versions of success. Without genuine zeal, a utopia cannot exist. Absent such fervor, transient and inconsequential pleasures are all that we can attain. The material rewards that the world promises are deceptive and lack a lasting or prolonged impact. True happiness, or victory, is an intrinsic state of mind that we can only experience once our characters have been thoroughly tested. Therefore, consummation of our internal crusade becomes even more satisfying than the initial conquest we sought. The accuracy of my premise is especially true when our integrity remains despite the temptations that confront us. That, then, is the ultimate form of gratification.

Please retrace and explore with me the calamities, exhilaration, and escapades that have culminated in my own extraordinary tale. Hopefully, you will then appreciate Vince Lombardi's conclusion to his great motivating lecture even more: "But I firmly believe that any man's finest hour, the greatest fulfillment of all that he holds dear, is that moment when he has worked his heart out in a good cause and lies exhausted on the field of battle—victorious."

ONE

Oh My God

(Pain is a great motivator)

Why are some losses so devastating that we never fully recover?

Las Vegas was as beautiful as I remembered from my visits before my disability. The vivid cobalt sky rested upon the surrounding horizon's red mountains. Humanity endlessly converged at the gateway of excitement's gleaming epicenter, the famous neon Strip. It remained the very zenith where mundane conceded to extraordinary and hustle replaced boredom. Spring breakers utilized the perennial "two hours and a shower" tactic as their rite of passage before the albatross of responsibility took over their lives. A two-hour power nap and a quick shower were the only interruptions for the partying faction before reengaging in anarchy. While only six months before an historic presidential election in which "change" meant the first African American leader, the cyclical choices of each generation remained the same.

Was there a better environment to replenish myself with essence since my strife had taken root? It was my wife's and my first travel since my profession's most common derailment was diagnosed. Two years earlier, my scarred lungs chose to surrender after a quarter century of inhaling toxic environments. The inhalation of harmful poisons during my career as a firefighter/paramedic had left me vulnerable to the one major insult that would overload my recuperative abilities. Thus, my slow-burning fuse had been lit, and such a provocation or breaking point proved to be inevitable. While *the* 9/11 occurred eighteen hundred miles north of me, *my* 9/11 had its genesis in more subdued circumstances. Like hundreds of 4:00 am calls in every firehouse across the country, the ever-present Zetron alarm system whisked our crew at breakneck speed to serve the public. That particular dawn rewarded me with lasting memories of second-guessing and labored breathing. Fate's injustice saw to it that a chemical explosion in a confined business force-fed me the overdose of virulent substances I could least afford.

The two years that followed my disability's culmination left me stagnant from medicinal side effects, attempts at rehabilitation, and the limitations due to my oxygen-dependent body. My dormancy caused me to yearn for the glowing and lively Nevada nights. But this trip was not for me. It was intended more as a countermeasure or antidote for my wife's grieving heart. Since the loss of her mother one year earlier, unshakable depression had replaced her serenity with turmoil. She needed this trip to awaken her once-powerful zest for life. While I was barely able to provide active companionship for Amy, our leisure pace fulfilled its purpose. Our romp may have appeared, compared to our robust surroundings, to have been more like a Geritol commercial. Regardless of its geriatric-like tempo, it was therapeutic, and we appreciated it. After four days of reacquainting smiles to Amy's bereaving frown, we returned home on the late evening flight and wearily dropped into bed.

Checking my caller ID in the morning, I was perplexed to find that Don O'Brien had called around eight thirty in the evening, while we were still in flight. First, that was late for him; he was one of the few people whose bedtime preceded mine. Additionally, we had been communicating with each other earlier on that day of the curious call, and he knew I would not be home until midnight. I believed it was a simple mistake. Also, even though he never liked leaving messages on answering machines, the absence of his voice made me a little uncomfortable this time. Surely, I rationalized, his ever-pleasant "penthouse" phone response would welcome my inquisitive morning call, as always. My numerous ignored calls, however, prompted me to go to my friend to investigate.

There must be a reason he's not in his room. He's usually back from his walk by now. Surely it wasn't his blood sugar because we calculated his meals perfectly before Amy and I left for our Las Vegas trip.

These and a myriad of unpleasant fears galloped through my adrenaline-filled system as I raced toward Don's place. The drive felt as if I were on a boundless treadmill. Every traffic light taunted me like an obstructed hourglass. The previous multitudes of visits had been much less stressful. Anger at myself, for leaving Padre without medical help, grew with every unanswered cell phone call. My palpitations hopefully would prove to be unwarranted. As Don's motel finally appeared, two versions of me simultaneously battled for dominance. The paramedic side had cardiac algorithms flashing through my stale mind, while the compassionate portion had me incapacitated with culpable fear. Stepping out of my car onto teetering legs made it apparent which Joe prevailed.

The Tides Motel is a vintage 1960s two-level oceanfront motel. There are three wings surrounding a pool, with the building-less side facing the sandy beach. It is located in Hollywood, Florida, just steps from the pristine Atlantic Ocean. The motel is owned and operated by Germans, and consequently, it caters to Germans. Father O'Brien called it "God's Country." It was his yearly reprieve from frigid Boston. Donning Red Sox paraphernalia brought out his devious childlike side. He relished the fact that his beloved Red Sox had actually won the World Series, instead of my New York Yankees. Ever since my frantic call in dire need of confession some thirty-two years earlier, our friendship was replete with fond bantering. In addition, since his first heart attack and diabetes diagnosis, he had grown more dependent upon my medical skills. "Padre," his self-titled moniker, was a pillar of advice and moral virtue. His array of intellectually potent conversations never led to boring exchanges. Our trust and respect for each other over the years blessed our friendship with shared devotion. Not even his decade-long reassignment to Boston from South Florida broke our bond.

With each unanswered knock below the number 110 on his door, I tried to convince myself that Padre had been called back to Boston to tend to parish business. As soon as my fearful question of his whereabouts to the heavily accented office fräulein left my lips, her countenance jarred me before she uttered a word. Her eye-to-eye laser-like grasp of my senses drained all hopes of any pleasing explanation. That horrifying interlude drove me past purgatory and into the flames of hell with instantaneous emotional agony. I cannot recall her first words—I only remember that both of our eyes swelled with the desire to unleash the deepest of horror. Once she composed herself, she provided the explanation that no decent person ever relishes sharing. I slowly and painfully dragged my worn-out remains to my car. Rather than my life flashing before my bloodshot, saturated eyes, my alliance with Padre flickered in my mind like a historic 8 mm presentation on an episode of *Biography*, narrated by Mike Wallace. Every utterance, every shared resolution for the world's woes, and every nuanced characteristic of Padre skipped before me as if the two of us were reminiscing our friendship one last time. The overwhelming sentiment that ached in my soul was that of profound regret.

While the drive to The Tides had stretched each second into a forever, the trip home was a blur. My foggy mind compressed over three decades of interpersonal friendship into less than thirty minutes. Each relived scenario reinforced why his passing hurt me so deeply. He'd baptized my children and cheered at my bodybuilding competitions. He'd taught my boys how to play chess and enthusiastically attended my parents' fiftieth wedding anniversary party. When a momentous event occurred in my life, Padre was always there. He first experienced the "terrible twos" by watching my children pulverize mollusk remains at the local crab restaurant. He proudly boasted about my U.S. Bodybuilding Championship to anyone who would listen. When he had his first heart attack, I was immediately notified.

The Monday night in 1978 when his Red Sox gained a fourteen-game advantage over my Yankees, we were together. He immortalized that moment (to my dismay) by snapping it with one of his beloved 35 mm cameras. He cherished that photo and dusted it off every season to rub my nose in his finest moment. His giddiness was short-lived, as I would always remind him of Bucky Dent's Green Monster clearing blast. There was the time we went to Everglades National Park, and he joyously took me on an airboat, only to have his toupee shift into a yarmulke position. Oh, and "the trip" to Disney World—surely his most embarrassing moment! Of course, I strategically brought it up whenever the situation called for unfair tactics in reversing a losing debate into victory.

Neither one of us had thought to check the weather before our day trip to the Magic Kingdom. As Murphy's Law would play out, monsoons coincidentally greeted our Orlando arrival. Ever the optimist, Padre converted our mouse-eared expectations into a chess challenge. Having earned the rare and honored rank of chess master, he always had his chess set handy. A local six-dollar-a-day roach-filled motel offered the perfect environment for such an impromptu event.

A fistful of frustrating checkmates and several thunder-filled hours caused me to seek other forms of entertainment. As Padre watched television, I neurotically engaged in my obsession of sit-ups, push-ups, and various other exercises. Gloating in my pumped physique, I summoned Padre to sit on my lower back so I could pump out some "donkey calf raises."

Donkey calf raises are a bodybuilding calf exercise made famous in the Arnold Schwarzenegger movie *Pumping Iron*. The bodybuilder relies on an assistant to sit on his lower back for added resistance. The individual exercising bends ninety degrees forward at the waist and, resting his upper torso on a bench or dresser, flexes his calves up and down. The assistant "rides" the back of the bodybuilder, similar to riding on the back of a donkey. Easily embarrassed, Padre sheepishly placed his overweight body onto an imaginary saddle on my back, and I triumphantly forced my calves to contract against gravity's helper. Just as a rhythmic pattern developed, our motel room door swung open without notice.

Gasping to comprehend her unnerving discovery, a rotund maid's bulging and distended-eyed gawk made it apparent that she had never watched *Pumping Iron*. Her exaggerated sclera and repetitious scream of "Oh my God!" convinced us that *Candid Camera* would have loved this moment. Our adipose maid continued her high-pitched phrase while waddling down the entire length of the hallway.

Padre's animated cherry red face quickly ran about the room collecting his traveling chess set and car keys as if preparing to make a Bonnie and Clyde–style escape. Realizing what graphically distorted thoughts the maid's ignorant eyes convinced her she had witnessed, I laughed so hysterically that I was paralyzed in amusement. Our ride home was marred with humiliation interspersed with bursts of uncontrolled howls and giggles.

Similar to a magician's trance-ending finger snap, the reality of losing Padre sobered my momentary bliss at those fond memories, thrusting me back into the pain of the present. Once additional details of Padre's passing became available, it was clear that his eight thirty call the other evening was the estimated time of death. There was instantaneous elevation of my grief upon realization that he'd reached out to me in his most dire time of need—and his plea went unanswered by his potential savior. This was the third time in my existence when someone I sincerely professed to hold dear called upon me, while confronting mortality's moment, and was forced to succumb alone. I prayed aloud for forgiveness and wished that I had the opportunity to turn back time and change his darkest hour. If only I had known! My soul-searching led me to attempt to trace each statement he'd made during our last visit at The Tides. Was there a clue that I neglected to pick up? While no profound epiphanies jumped out of my hazy faculties, I vaguely recalled several references to his mortality. Eerily, it seemed too similar to the last encounter I'd experienced with my grandfather many years earlier, making it impossible just to dismiss.

My mother's parents had lived with us for most of my younger years. That was a common practice for first and second-generation Italian American families. My final college semester exam was scheduled for a Monday morning. On Sunday, my grandfather, who was usually a man of few but meaningful words, had a sudden inclination to converse about seemingly unimportant subjects. Feeling the pressure of the next day's scrutiny, I was much less amiable than usual. I cut off his numerous pursuits at small talk and attempted to isolate myself in my room. His frustration was eventually replaced with the acceptance that this day's mingling would not be fruitful. While I was absorbed in my textbook, his parting statement would live to haunt me forever: "If something happens to me, please take care of Grandma." He passed away the next day. The knowledge that our last interchange was highlighted by my compassionless egocentricity still pries at my core. How could I have ignored such out-of-character foreshadowing when his fragile health was so conspicuous? His well-known ailments should have taken priority over my neurotic desire for academic perfection.

Now it had happened again! *Why?* I wondered. So much was discussed during my last visit with Padre that surely it would shed some light on this. Unfortunately, the clarity of my thoughts was beclouded by the anguish from the day's upheaval. My oxygen-deprived mind constantly struggled with anterograde amnesia since the onset of my medical issues. Remembering names and recent events had become like piecing together a jigsaw puzzle while blindfolded.

As I climbed into bed that night, I turned up my oxygen concentration to counteract my grieving heart's irregular rhythm. My chassis grew heavy as my mind raced. Each time I dozed, my body would spasm as if to rebel against the inevitable subconscious pilgrimage. Retrogressing farther and farther into my childhood, I recalled flashes of an odyssey long ago forgotten. Visions of my youth, interspersed with Padre's final images, transformed into a kaleidoscopic mix of faces and flashbacks. My last cognizant thought was about Padre's firm handshake and something about a promise to …

Upon awakening the next morning, I raced to find a pen and paper. For the next three days, I feverishly jotted down bullet points of chronicles from my half-century migration. This divinely conspired ammunition led me toward a destination that was unknown to me. I became little more than a conduit through which acute reproductions of conversations and experiences were transposed through me onto a keyboard. Within one month, my convictions and motivation to keep my word to Padre emerged as a memoir that seemed to capture the essence of who I am … and why.

Personal responsibility and introspection can give us answers to questions we didn't know we had.

TWO

Gold-Lined Streets

(The origins of my soul)

When and from where do we derive our consciences?

WE ALL REFLECT ON CERTAIN defining moments that personify our versions of events. By most standards, 1968 was a tumultuous year in the United States.

I originally approached this day's truancy from school in a lighthearted way. Its historic value, I innocently thought, was similar to our visits to a museum or landmark. It quickly became apparent that this day was different, much different. I had grown somewhat numb to the profound loss that Dealey Plaza's echoes caused well over four years earlier. My vantage point, standing on the rear trunk of my grandparents' Mercury, gave me the vicarious tachycardia my family was experiencing. At the age of seven, this elevated view of my mother's eyes taught me that from the abyss, life can be resuscitated. To her left, my normally emotionless grandmother mirrored the array of sentiments that this "revival" drew from her daughter-in-law.

With each cheer of the crowd, the tears flowed more intensely. The stream of emotions corresponded to the collective jubilation of the thousands of Democratic faithful. Camelot was reawakened after 1,700 days of gut-felt mourning. I sensed the insatiable craving for nirvana while awaiting the arrival of my mother's messianic speaker. Such joy had been vacant since Walter Cronkite had placed his black glasses on his famous visage, wiped his upper lip, and proclaimed, "President Kennedy died at one PM central standard time ..." No wonder so many people tried to rekindle their dreams by symbolically resurrecting the president through his younger sibling Bobby. The innocence of so many Americans was erased at that bleak moment in history, but few had the wind taken from their sails the way a young Italian American Catholic woman from Mount Vernon, New York, had. She was naive beyond description yet full of life and vigor. Each tear seemed to represent a moment of tranquility forever agonizingly removed, and each cheer from the believers was the equivalent of maternal snuggling.

"Bob-by! Bob-by! Bob-by!" Reverberated chants emerged from every direction, filling every ear with tantalizing strength I could have only related to the time Mickey Mantle hit a home run at Yankee Stadium, before my idolizing eyes. While few of the would-be commander-in-chief's words were audible through this wave of spellbinding imagery, I knew that the depth of understanding transcended normal communications. This environment bonded generations, genders, and, for the first time since Martin Luther King's recent assassination while on the Lorraine Motel's balcony, races. Dark faces and light ones created a backdrop that must have made the campaigning dignitaries proud. If for only one moment in this year of the Tet Offensive and Kent State, Americans felt united and positive. I recall trying to comprehend why all races could cry and revel together only on this day.

I was confused as to why my best friend from school, Russell Rivers, and I could not enter each other's apartment buildings. We were able to play baseball and army men in the aqueduct between our buildings, but a whispered rule disallowed us from entering the segregated halls of each other's adjacent brick dwellings. The one time that curiosity caused me to disobey the unspoken rule and venture into the "wrong" building, I was met with inquisitive stares and the tantalizing aromas of unfamiliar cooking. I convinced myself that collecting for UNICEF would be the perfect excuse to taste the forbidden fruit. Betty, the ever-present heavy woman in the colorful muumuus, who lived on the second floor of Russell's building, quickly reminded me that UNICEF "ain't gunna stop your mama from spankin' ya." I never had a second odyssey into those tabooed hallways.

Returning to our remarkable moment, love was the overriding sentiment, and I was safe from any reprimands. According to my mother, I was watching "the next president" as he promised to make the country a better place for everyone. "He is so handsome and young," my mother said into my grandmother's straining ear. "He makes me feel good when he talks!" she screamed into my face.

Long after the speeches ended, we sang, danced, and mingled among the masses for hours. When we finally made our way home, my baptism in hope had the alternate effect of actualizing how bad the world truly was, all while slipping under my innocent radar. I felt such shame and guilt for all the awful mistreatment of the "Negroes," as African Americans were called. My mother had always told me to smile at them and be nice to them. That day, with persuasive convictions, I understood why. Pity and compassion were the motivation, and I promised myself that I would always follow that mantra.

As the four o'clock alarm rang the next morning, my first thought was to offer that day's mass as a sacrifice for all of the persecuted people in the world. I especially intended my prayers for the "poor Negros" in the world. Monsignor Scanlon was not aware that his prayers and mass would already be spoken for. Being an altar boy had its advantages. As I offered the ritualistic "gifts," I believed that this celebration was divinely inspired. A sense of peace awakened my drowsy eyes with the knowledge that God loved me and interceded in my hope's fulfillment. As I viewed the three attendees of the mass, I remembered the verse in the Bible that read, *For wherever two or more are gathered together in my name, there I am in the midst of them* (Matthew 18:20).

Surely, my mother, who always drove and took part in mass when I served, was requesting the same spiritual intervention for the mistreated and less opportunistic African Americans. Her tightly clinched eyes, bowed head, and interlocked fingers were all the affirmation I needed to assure our collaboration. Tranquility descended upon my cassock-covered heart because I knew God would deliver. Though certainly not of privileged stock, I would later grasp that my parents' gift of spirituality was a great equalizer throughout my life. I did not need expensive possessions to fulfill my internal quest. I was so satiated from my sincere faith that at times I'd get choked up when I realized how lucky I was compared to most. Never for a moment did I wonder if I was loved or where I'd spend eternity. I was truly the luckiest child ever born. With all the flaws my parents had, they surely surpassed any standard of nurturing excellence. Could I ever live up to their example?

For each mass over the next five years, my mother and I cooperatively dedicated our prayers to God. It was rarely discussed but knowingly shared. There were even times when we urged reinforcements such as my father and both sets of grandparents to mass with us. *After all*, I thought, *the more transcendental an intervention, the better.*

My maternal grandfather was especially difficult to get to church. He was one of the toughest men, according to most relatives. Like a stone crab, he was as hard as a rock on the outside, but if you could tolerate the effort of breaking through the shell, sweet insides awaited. At seventeen, he had the desire to emigrate from fascist Italy for the promise of freedom in a new continent with "gold-lined streets." As Il Duce ruthlessly assumed dictatorial powers and dissolved political dissention, Giuseppe Bencivenga made his move.

Under intense political scrutiny, this Naples-born immigrant came to America with little more than the clothes he was wearing. As he so often told it, he was also brutally persecuted in an Irish-dominated New York. With no skills, he labored on the docks of the city for all the rotten bananas he could eat and literally nickels in pay. Too proud to admit he was cold and unable to afford a jacket, he selflessly labored every waking hour to send his pittance back to retrieve his family, one member at a time. With the prejudice of the time, his Italian accent prevented him from attaining tolerable living quarters. After a period of living under discarded blankets and boxes on the docks, he and a group of equally shunned Italians boarded together in a one-room slum apartment. With his eye on the target of a family reunion, he feverishly continued his regiment in spite of frostbite and severe lower back pain. Proving mortal, a lack of proper nutrition and hypothermia led to his loss of a kidney. Still, however, he never complained, as if there was someone or place to which one could complain.

Stoic and proud, he stood as an example of strength and sacrifice for all who were fortunate enough to have known him. His most valued possession was his United States citizenship. While never one to deny his roots, he absorbed himself in the desire to assimilate as an American completely. He loved Old Glory so dearly that he constantly reminded me that there was no other nation as great as America. Unfortunately, he was illiterate and had to struggle to learn how to read so he could fulfill his dream of reading the U.S. Constitution on his own. While some may have considered his goals simplistic, he dauntlessly taught himself to read, and he kept a copy of the Bill of Rights close to his heart. He went on to devote his newfound literacy to other Italian Americans by teaching them the merits of America's founding principles and documents. Surprisingly, he held no malice or bitterness toward those who made his continental transition more difficult. Quite the contrary:

he was grateful for the bananas and blankets that others left behind. He would always say with apparent experience, "One man's trash is another man's treasure."

Fellow Mount Vernon citizens, who knew little of his adventures and struggles, mockingly referred to him as "the proudest American." While unsophisticated by today's superficial standards, he was more man than most could ever conceive, let alone emulate. Ironically, his gentle nature with his grandchildren was legendary. On several occasions, just moments after punching a stranger who had the gall to disrespect one of us, this dichotomy would comb our hair with absorbed intent or wipe ice cream from the edge of our mouths. Never has a human asked so little of those around him yet gracefully offered so much.

As with many transplanted Italian American families, gluttonous orgies of daylong ethnic feedings were coupled with well-intentioned conversations. Most gatherings were highlighted by intense emotions. A casual observer would conclude that the louder voice tended to present the winning argument. However, once the verbal darts hit their intended targets, a combination of elevated insulin levels and genuine love warmed the room's chill. A day's thematic conclusion was usually stated, and the hugs, cheek pinching, and backslapping would continue. All the elder females, who had pubescent male–like mustaches, cooked, cleaned, and interjected from the exile of the kitchen. My uncles, who I honestly thought were born with wine on their breath and were served by their spouses like kings, were all content. Worldly treasures, to them, were the cracked and faded photos of their immensely respected lineage. They had little else. Each "old-country" relative was spoken of with the type of reverence usually reserved for royalty. When factual conversations occurred, the actual peasant-like pauper existence of those honored and deceased relatives became apparent. Still, their lofty status was believed to be worthy of homage. My elders were all products of 1929's short sale of stock and the following decade-long Great Depression. To some of them, Joseph Kennedy was the equivalent of an Antichrist. It was their understanding, albeit limited, that his manipulation of the markets contributed to the "crash," and reciprocally led to his financial fortune. They trusted no organization, be it a bank or government entity. Outside of their bloodline, skepticism was rampant.

My mother's idealistic wide-eyed gullibility was in direct contrast to most other family members. Her perspective was that all humanity was well intentioned. Her older brother, Carlo, was more astutely aware of the harsh penalty inflicted upon anyone not conforming in our Democratic Party–controlled city. When my grandfather lectured us on the Mussolini-like tactics of Mount Vernon's political machine, my uncle became agitated at such despotic domination. My mother leaned toward baking fresh lasagna or manicotti for the mayor to demonstrate her lifetime of allegiance to the Democratic Party. The knowledge that my grandfather would be fired from his job if he did not register as a Democrat and actively campaign for the party was the impetus for Carlo's lifelong rejection of the Democratic Party, big government, and political dynasties.

My father left the bantering for those less consumed with earning the family's salary. The sole earner in our home, his approach was pragmatic and rooted. "If you don't work, you don't eat," was his philosophy. He never deviated from this role, which left him little time or energy to engage in deep or fluffy conversations. Grease beneath his fingernails and calloused digits were symbols of his commitment to his niche. Our meals were validation enough that he loved us. To him, words were fleeting and inconsequential. Besides, real men could and should never show emotions or vulnerability. If the previous statement is true, then my father was the symbol of macho.

The dynamics of survival from the perspective of many Italian American families resembled ours. Friends from dissimilar backgrounds were mostly isolated to school and outside activities. Growing up as a young toddler devoid of actual multicultural family influences led me to believe that Ozzie and Harriet were simply a Hollywood-contrived family, while reality was Giuseppe and Giuseppina. I assumed that everyone was raised exactly the same way I was.

Every noble journey begins somewhere, and some origins happen to be more humble than others.

THREE

Attila the Nun

(My New York state of mind)

Can seemingly ruthless behavior trigger future success?

IF IGNORANCE IS BLISS, THEN one could say that I spent my early youth in a frolicking dreamland filled with Christmas morning memories and oblivious contentment. When confronted with an unfamiliar predicament, there was no doubt that my resolution skills would raise a few eyebrows. Such was the case during my first outing at Tibbetts Brook Park for a summer dip in their enormous swimming pool. It would be pacifying to blame my flaws on my uncontrollable excitement, but that would be misleading.

In the midst of my frolicking, Mother Nature decided that a pause was appropriate. So I scurried my tender feet across the searing landscape to ask my father for directions to the restroom. Gazing across the horizon assured my father that the parched pavement and the substantial distance from the men's room required an alternate plan. He whispered to me, "Just go in the pool." Several seconds later, collective screams of displeasure from the cavorting patrons in the crowded pool must have reminded my father that his youngest child was not quite ready for prime time. Turning toward the pointing and scattering crowd, my father did his best to pretend he had no affiliation with the young child by the lifeguard stand. That young boy had his swimming trunks pulled down to his ankles and was "tinkling" a fountain-like stream into the pool. My parents' obvious embarrassment imparted upon me that the statue-like water feature I simulated was not exactly part of the cunning master plan.

During my early school years, I was surrounded by cousins and a brother who were all my nonintellectual equals. One afternoon, my cousin found a strange new "firecracker" tucked in his mother's closet. The meeting of our two vacuous brains concluded that we were one match away from our own Independence Day celebration. As we placed our improvised device on a rock pile, we labored to ignite the stubborn "wick" that was affixed to our fascinating pyrotechnic toy. Eventually, we recruited an older, and apparently wiser, relative. My more experienced cousin destroyed our inventive delusion with a weird explanation of female menstrual cycles and the need to prevent bleeding. His giggling use of the word "tampon" apprised me that I was not to mention this dud firework to anyone. Moreover, it was my first sortie into the world of fire science.

Each relative's home was within walking distance of my own, and the same doilies protected similarly undeserving secondhand sofas in each of their homes. Yet smiles filled our well-fed and clean faces. Our spongelike minds observed the uneventful and the historic. Long before Michael Jackson and his siblings glided across stage, the original "moonwalkers"—Neil Armstrong and Buzz Aldrin—etched within me the idea of aiming high.

I was ill prepared, however, for the enlightenment that Catholic school would encroach upon my gullibility. While stepping from the rusted door of the car my father had pieced together from junkyard parts, I witnessed my classmates having their shiny Cadillac doors opened by "the help." The first few weeks dazzled me, as I heard my fellow classmates' personal accounts of world travels and unfathomable escapades. While outwardly casual about my classmates' statuses, I quickly withdrew when asked about my upbringing. Previously unaware that Sts. Peter and Paul served the Bronxville upper bourgeoisie, my indoctrination was swift and enlightening. It was my initial and personal experience of a societal pecking order, and I truly comprehended that I was not a Rockefeller. What separated my early years from true ghetto status was a possible dispute over degree, but that difference was minimal. While proud of my parents, I shunned opportunities to flaunt my relatives at school-sponsored assemblies and sporting events. The same mothball odor seemed absent from my classmates' relatives' jackets. The rips that came with hand-me-downs never showed up on their cloakroom garb. Thank goodness for school uniforms. I was able to disguise my identity in my blue blazer and gray pants.

Once the awe of inadequacy became manageable, I was initially jolted by the academic demands. The New York public school system never prepared me to transfer to Catholic school. I was especially not equipped for Ms. L.'s classroom. She was a matronly ex-nun who should have doubled as a U.S. Marine drill sergeant on her days off. To say she was strict is like saying the Grand Canyon is big. A typical homework assignment in one subject was about ten pages of math problems. Then each hour, as we changed subjects, she'd continue to expand her nightly directives exponentially. And God forbid one of us would make her angry! She'd turn to her "special" books, containing esoteric and complex assignments, which she reserved for punishment. She'd tear out pages with the ecstasy of Josef Mengele with a fresh scalpel. When such assignments were "earned," one could be sure that little sleep would be had that evening.

My life belonged to Ms. L. In class, we were subjected to a nonstop barrage on the limits of the brain's attention span, and at home, I was relegated to the nightly battle against fatigue and the clock. Her religious order's ex–hit man (we mockingly referred to her religious order as the "Sisters of Satan") even possessed my dreams. I had recurring nightmares about being on an island where Satan moonlit as gatekeeper. Lucifer would allow me to leave once I finished putting together a building made of tens of thousands of bricks. Every single night, as I'd get close to finishing my task, the devil would viciously knock it all down and merrily command me to begin again. My only salvation from those fantasia ordeals was the morning alarm clock, warning me that Ms. L. was waiting.

On several occasions, her actions so created collective fear that all of us were mesmerized in horror. A soft-spoken and sweet girl named Anna once neglected to meet Ms. L.'s standard for a homework assignment. Anna's father was petitioned to assist in her penance. Poor Anna was paraded to the front of the class and manhandled across her father's lap. What followed was the turning point in Anna's fledgling confidence. Ms. L. pulverized Anna's exposed buttocks so many times that I lost count. The repetitive and revolting cracking sound echoed in my ears long after the onslaught ended. Once her beaten bottom was methodically walloped, a reclusive and withdrawn Anna emerged. After a year of steady and obvious decline, she was forced to withdraw due to personal issues.

Another time, a happy-go-lucky kid named David mispronounced a word during a chalkboard chore. He was copying and pronouncing words out of a textbook. The word none of us will surely ever forget was "nowhere." David mistakenly said "now here." As Ms. L. stomped toward David, a tense atmosphere became tangible. She challenged him to repeat what he had just said. David had no idea that he had mispronounced the word. Ms. L. positioned her spitting-mad lips barely one inch from his. As the same mispronunciation left his unsuspecting mouth, Ms. L.'s open palm made a thunderous deposit across David's pale left cheek. Over and over, Ms. L. demanded that David repeat what he said. Each time, his innocent attempt to please Ms. L. was regretfully met with Mike Tyson–like precision. As each blow found its mark, his survival instincts succumbed to his trepidation to disobey our taskmaster. Ultimately, even Ms. L. realized that David was punch-drunk and totally unaware of what instigated that drubbing.

The stress was smothering and relentless at first. Eventually, a robotic and emotionless separation served as my coping mechanism. I became numb to all of Ms. L.'s oppressiveness.

When Ms. L. was not physically asserting herself, she was forever lecturing on "time management, pushing beyond your comfort zone, and demanding more from yourselves." Her booming voice would constantly point out that she was not there to bring smiles to our faces or make us like her. But I realized that her goal was to instill "drive, fortitude, and the ability to overcome obstacles." She stressed, "Long-term success is my only concern." That was for certain because there was definitely not any instant gratification in her classroom. In the beginning, I only wanted her lectures because I considered them a reprieve from getting homework assignments and a hiatus from writer's cramp.

With time, though, the words began to take root. Ms. L.'s moralisms found their intended target. Strangely, a previously unknown component of my personality was awakened by the unrelenting sermons and pressure. The thought of giving up or quitting angered me. It somehow required me to have my back against the wall to find the spark and fighting spirit that I never knew I had. I discovered my abhorrence for failure. Such demands and adversity stimulated an internal drive that came to know very few boundaries. My desire to surpass expectations and outside commands began an underlying process that transformed me into the ultimate overachiever. Good was never again acceptable. I sought to outdo myself constantly. I actually surprised myself and began to excel academically. In an unexplainable way, I began believing that I was more capable than I had given myself credit.

Although too puerile to appreciate fully what my temperament would evolve into, I did distinguish that my disposition was quite different from Anna's and David's. I had been an extremely shy child who suddenly discovered my voice and opinion. It was my first experience with what I later identified as an elevated level of self-esteem. Satisfaction with mediocrity, from that point forward, became as evasive as a dangling carrot that was always beyond this horse's reach. My parents saw the frustration I initially encountered and offered to place me back in the public school system. I refused because sacrificing short-term pleasures for long-term goals became my routine and ritual.

The security that I took for granted and clung to at home would be tested also. As earlier stated, my home was constantly inundated with extended family looking for an excuse to celebrate the day's sunrise or party because there were seven days in a week. Anything was an acceptable reason to feast and raucously play cards as if hell had frozen over. My grandparents lived with us also, which often brought about visits from my grandmothers' nine siblings. Most of our relatives' almost-daily visits were more than welcome. One exception was an older aunt who suddenly decided to foster two teenage sisters from Puerto Rico. Innuendos and mumblings hinted that the girls had been "abused" and it was our duty to make them feel welcome.

At first, the sisters were shy and aloof. With time, they became comfortable and gained confidence. I was intrigued by their accents, fascinating mocha complexions, and relative maturity. Then they began instigating recreation in our basement. The activities were innocuous at first, and I began to enjoy their company. Ultimately, the "games" became confusing and uncomfortable. By virtue of the amount of times they "examined" my body, they should have earned PhDs in medicine.

It was always the same scenario: little JoJo, my childhood name, was the hospital's emergency room patient. I had just been involved in a car accident and was not allowed to move. Of course, as any experienced physicians would do, they removed my pants and underwear. My prepubescent body caused me embarrassment, especially when my "physicians" felt the need to examine me with *their* pants off too. While one sister engaged in *hands-on* training, the other one watched and craftily "scratched" her developed genital region. As soon as the non-examining observer let out a curious moan that was seemingly caused by that vigorous "scratching," they switched places.

These episodes sparked both mortification and interest. While totally outwitted, I certainly knew my "medical treatments" were erroneous, and I would come to understand some years later that such self-pleasure was unconventional for medical professionals. I began praying arduously and ended these shenanigans by constantly claiming to have stomachaches or other ailments that prevented further basement predicaments. With the knowledge and assimilation of these sins of the flesh, I internalized tremendous guilt and disappointment in myself. I lost my sense of solace and slipped into an apathetic daze.

Simultaneously, as the probing from the sibling interns ended, my incarceration at the hands of Attila the Nun also concluded. Ms. L. taught one more year before the public learned of her antics and she was dismissed. Miraculously, my perseverance and disdain for failure bolstered me in my weakest hours. While I was truly miserable during that period, I would later come to discern the importance of those lessons.

The next several years at Sts. Peter and Paul were the antithesis of the first. The teachers actually greeted us with pleasantries. Twenty-four-hour days were once again long enough to participate in sports. As the weight of the world lightened, I regained the bounce in my step. I felt the sincerity of my once-contrived smiles return. Intellectually, I was convinced that I belonged with Bronxville's best. In my beloved sport of baseball, I was no longer an effortless out in my team's lineup. Opposing teams could no longer disregard the short guy with the number one on his jersey. I had chosen to use the number one in honor of Bobby Murcer, one of my boyhood idols.

The first game of the season was my awakening. Leading off the game, and my new life, I drilled the first pitch over the center field fence. Rounding the bases, my chest grew like the Grinch's heart as he danced around Whoville's Christmas tree. As I stepped on home plate, clocks ceased and silence harkened the screaming bleachers. Through the mass of blended facial features, a beacon of light drew my galloping eyes directly to my father's tear-filled stare. His pride grasped my soul and elevated my delight. Mr. Macho actually had a chink in his armor! It was one of only two times that he ever outwardly shed tears. It would take a near-death experience and years before I'd witness another tear from my father. This, though, was a joyous moment. My celebration was multifaceted. First, the taste of public success was intoxicating. It was especially satisfying on the heels of so much humiliation and closeted self-doubt. Second, I felt free and invigorated as I recaptured my childhood euphoria. Mostly, though, the tangible proof that I brought such pride to my parents provided enough joy to make the past year's remorse instantly vanish.

That year, I went from being a dugout wallflower to one of the team's most counted on contributors. With such high expectations and consistent clutch performances, I saw my future. I would play center field for the New York Yankees! I was so convinced that my destiny was in the hallowed confines of The House That Ruth Built that I began to profess it matter-of-factly. The more effort and dedication I invested into academics and baseball, the greater and more fulfilling the rewards were. They fed on each other. Success bred confidence, and the more positive I felt, the more I escalated focus and expanded labor. I was in the zone.

Once again, I found myself thankful toward God. During my dismal times, I had a tendency to question the existence of spiritual help. Now I was constantly praying and talking to God. During one of my deeper devotionals, I recalled thinking that if it had not been for the trials and tribulations of Ms. L.'s class, I would not have developed such persistence and determination. What was originally considered a negative and anger-inducing trauma was, in fact, instrumental and essential for my personal growth. While the loving relationships from family members clearly influenced the overall person I would eventually become, Ms. L.'s tartness forced me to adapt, giving me the strength needed to handle the unpleasant side of life. The hostility and self-pity were immediately replaced with understanding and appreciation. I understood that although Ms. L.'s style temporarily overshadowed her substance, she was directly responsible for some of my work ethic.

As young students, we were not enlightened enough to comprehend that Ms. L. had inadvertently taught us self-esteem through accomplishment instead of sugarcoated insincere compliments. It was obvious that Ms. L.'s methods and approach were not for everyone. Later in life, I would witness the fraud of repetitiously declaring last place kids as "winners" and watering down trophies as nothing more than proof of participation. Those whose egos were stroked without deserving achievements often carried a vanity and narcissism rooted in entitlement or conceit. However, those fortunate enough to have the tenacity to survive Ms. L.'s boot camp regimen blossomed into self-reliant citizens with genuine self-worth and pride. Thus, she gained my appreciation for her role in my life. Many times in my future, her influence would prove invaluable.

My new confidence and courage opened me up to expand my boundaries and relationships outside my family and neighbors of similar socioeconomic status. My new friends broadened my perspective. I regularly joined large groups of kids from every background to engage in huge baseball, football, or basketball games. During balmy July days, dozens of bodies would emerge on the local baseball field like locusts migrating toward a new year's wheat harvest. When snow blanketed our neighborhood, multiple interlocking trails of sleds raced to the bottom of our gradient roadway. Imagination and camaraderie were our pastimes. We'd talk and mingle until our well-obeyed curfews. Life was simple, and relatively deep bonds developed. We all respected our own and others' parents and never considered breaking the law or testing the system. Conformity was cool, and recalcitrants were avoided.

Some within my close-knit family began to scatter to different cities and states. A few departed for employment purposes, others for health reasons. My mother's parents spoke often of moving to Florida because my grandfather had one kidney and a debilitating heart condition. His doctor believed that the cold New York weather was detrimental to his heart and remaining kidney. He explained that the shifting of massive amounts of blood to my grandfather's core from low ambient temperatures put too much strain on already weakened organs. After many discussions, my parents decided to move to Florida with my grandparents because they needed our assistance. The fact that my grandparents were such an essential influence upon me made me welcome the continuation of living with them. Unfortunately, a southward move would end many of the friendships I had established since I had blossomed with confidence. Nevertheless, we packed our belongings for the sunny shores of South Florida.

No matter how bad things are, we can overcome them with tenacity and desire.

FOUR

Southern Hospitality

(What you don't know can hurt)

Are all childhood dreams simply fantasy, or can they come true?

AROUND THE TIME OF DON Shula's coronation as the only NFL coach capable of claiming perfection, the Ides of March welcomed some new Florida residents. Symbolic of a fresh new beginning, the humidity drained our pores of the past's unnecessary load. All-encompassing excitement bounded within our psyches.

My father would be laboriously repairing appliances and air conditioners in the tropical region. My mother hoped to re-create the homey environment to which we were accustomed in New York. My grandparents set out to continue their retirement. And my brother, Tom, and I would attend a southern public school during a time of racial unrest. We would all learn a new word: "Watergate."

After years of donning me in school uniforms, my mother relished the idea of dressing me in outfits that suited her tastes. While it pleased her tremendously to witness her youngest son in white shoes, a matching white belt, and loudly colored double-knit bell bottoms, someone forgot to check my new classmates' apparel preferences.

This "city boy" immediately noticed that the term "southern hospitality" did not exist at Olsen Middle School in Dania, Florida. While ethnic diversity was an unheard of concept at Sts. Peter and Paul School, my array of friends in my old neighborhood traversed all racial lines. I was positive that I would be prepared to blend in ... until I met Tommy C. Tommy was about six inches taller than I, even without his massive Angela Davis Afro. As he approached me, I was certain that he would be the first of many new friends to greet me. With my unfeigned smile, I extended my hand with the anticipation of matching warmth. Somewhere between the time that Tommy's clenched fist attempted to unite my belly button with my spine, and his two associates did their best to remove my mother's favorite white footwear, I diagnosed my naïveté.

A secondary lesson that Tommy and his accomplices schooled me in was the proper use of derogatory racial insults. I had never heard the terms "honky" or "cracker," but I quickly realized that Tommy was not using such terminology as endearing references. Did I mention that my freshly parted Vitalis-drenched hair was also an object of Tommy's disapproval? Battling a physical as well as verbal assault, I was in the midst of one of life's many lessons—whether to fight or flee. Tommy and his gang's attack left me on the ground, gasping to inflate my lungs with the air that Tommy's fist had removed. They were victorious and gloating over their Pearl Harbor tactics. Believing it was over, I anticipated that they had walked away. But they summoned a circular barrier of even more hostile dark faces around me, and I knew that round two was coming.

Suddenly, an unknown defiant voice bellowed within my angered nucleus, and I envisioned punching five feet of rage into Tommy's flared nostrils. Somehow, beneath my fury, my mother's voice seemed to temper me with the words "Be nice to them." As furious as I was, my empathy for African Americans and fear of hurting him handcuffed a full-fledged retaliation. Still, I staggered to my feet and tackled Tommy, pinning him to the ground. I was immediately heaved to my feet by a gym teacher, Mr. Hamilton. While I was still gasping for air, Mr. Hamilton carried me into his office and unraveled the mystery of racial relations in the South.

Once the overstated version got around school about how I valiantly fought back against Olsen's resident bully (and I underwent a thorough wardrobe adjustment), an acceptable reputation was dispersed about me. Tommy and his allies gradually became more hospitable and even referred to me as "Mighty Mouse." The clear message was that the weak would be abused, and only power was respected. Furthermore, as my athletic prowess became known, I was afforded a level of courtesy and admiration that my white shoes and belt almost denied me.

Within a few months of my welcoming committee's indoctrination, I discovered girls. Or, more appropriately, they discovered me. While I had normal teenage desires, I was neither ready nor willing to embark on dating. I was much shorter than most boys were, and young teenage girls tend to develop earlier (oh, how I remembered from my "emergency room" visits!). A very tall neighbor named Lisa, who was a year older, began expressing interest in me. I reluctantly agreed to go to see the movie *Billie Jack* with her. While walking to the movie, she startled my barely adolescent hormones with, "I wore a halter top so you could feel me up." For a moment, I thought Tommy C. had punched me in the gut again. My uneasiness must have been tangible because I immediately withdrew into my shell. Once at the theater, any chance of a second date was eradicated with my attempt to save money. Thinking I was quiet and stealthy, I requested, "One child and one adult ticket." Yes, I saved money. But Lisa quickly lost interest in me and turned her affection toward my older brother.

A few months later, we moved to a neighboring town in South Florida, and suddenly I felt at home again. Similar to our Mount Vernon neighborhood, a bounty of young teens transposed boredom into bedlam. These individuals were absolute characters. The synergy of the mix created wholesome havoc. Among this new group of friends, I met a teen who was hysteria compressed into a compact package. Dennis was brash and bold and could have easily been nicknamed "Dennis the Menace." He'd hastily "moon" a stranger driving by, and the next minute he'd dress like Igor from *Young Frankenstein* and impetuously knock on an unsuspecting neighbor's door. Unlike me, he oozed confidence with girls much older and more mature than we were. His tactless clowning was daily entertainment for our group. No one was immune from Dennis's ridicule and keen ability to imitate everyone's quirks. The lasting effect of Dennis's friendship was that I gained appreciation for his satire and parodies, which became ingrained into my personality.

Together, Dennis and I first experienced the lore of lifting weights. From the moment my paltry hands wrapped around a barbell, magic transformed my ambitions. Bodybuilding became my drug of choice. The more I touched dumbbells, the more I wanted to work out. As my frail frame felt the rush of coerced blood engorging latent fibers of muscle, a man emerged where a boy had once lived. It seemed so natural to my craving muscles. Uncanny results occurred with such rapidity that Dennis decided that the pace and gains in strength were beyond him. At this time, I learned the importance of genetic predisposition.

One evening, my father showed me his tattered high school yearbook. Due to his involvement on the tumbling team, his body displayed uncharacteristic development for his time. So much so that he was voted "best physique" as far as high school superlatives.

Every day brought new exercises, and each day's toil stoked my fledgling fire. Every other goal became secondary to my passion. My garage became my dungeon, and my body was tortured to its daily limits. Within my torture chamber, I read every bodybuilding magazine about past champions and replicated each workout with the precision of a diamond cutter. While I unearthed my Xanadu, I still comprehended the importance of education and responsibilities. I quickly rationalized that my many activities, pastimes, and enterprises would require resourceful manipulation of time. Once again, Ms. L.'s endowment saved the day. My years of altar boy service and early morning homework sessions aided me with this notion: *While others only dream, I'll work and scheme.*

In part, a lifetime of achievement was made possible by my fateful decision to utilize early mornings to work out. Regardless of the era or schedule confronting me, my predawn barrage would serve as the day's stimulus.

I received a great deal of attention because of my blossoming body, especially from the wrestling coach. He approached me to help his team. Never one to deny a request, I tried out and joined the team. Even though I excelled, I still preferred the weight room to the mat. As fate would have it, a higher calling would quickly end my season.

My father's younger brother had been diagnosed with multiple sclerosis. I had always remembered him as a brawny and powerful man. His diminished state was ghastly and dispiriting. Worse, for reasons beyond my scope of understanding at that time, the elevated support and attention that his MS stricken body required exceeded his wife's caretaking abilities. He had nowhere to turn, and my parents welcomed him warmly. As had always been the case, my parents displayed a level of altruism that defied description. Emulating their empathy, my daily duties involved stretching his contracted body, twice-a-day Icy Hot topical heat rubdowns, carrying him into and out of the bathtub, and generally assisting his needs. Daily rosary sessions, which I had engaged in since my youth, were now devoted to his recovery and improvement. My difficulty lay in my high opinion of him. Why would such suffering and burden afflict such a kind and superb man? I actually tried to alter fate by pleading with God to give me the multiple sclerosis instead of such a dignified uncle. His life, like my father's, had been arduous and thorny. I was blessed from infancy with cradle-like security. It made no sense and I grew resentful at my Lord.

Through his Veterans Administration hospital visits, we learned of an experimental electrical stimulant implant to be awarded to the winner of an essay competition. The surgery would be performed in Miami. Understanding the magnitude of his destitution, I penned my most candid feelings for the benefit of Uncle Butch, whose real name was Joseph. When we learned that the hospital chose my essay from the thousands of entries, it was my devout belief that his slavery to MS was over. Unbeknownst to me, though, was his principal desire for close proximity to his immediate family. That longing supplanted his physical requirements. He so much wanted to be close to his family that he actually refused the surgery to expedite his trip back home. He eventually confided, "It's better to die near my family in New York than to live away from them in Florida." Knowing his decision to relocate to a veterans hospital close to his New York family was akin to a death sentence, we reluctantly granted his wish. His dream of reincarnating his family unit gave him the initiative and guts to subsist in institutions for quite a while. Eventually, though, his institution-induced depression and advanced disease progression devitalized any remaining impulse to survive. His final heartbeat mercifully ended his torment on a somber July day.

Fate, however, dealt him a kind twist after his demise. While his wife sadly and unexpectedly passed away within seven months of Uncle Butch's passing, it touched off a series of events that delivered the closeness my uncle yearned for when he was alive. Both of their remains were ultimately laid to rest, together, in a beautiful veterans cemetery close to Las Vegas. Even though his final resting place seemed heavenly, the pain of his tragic ordeal caused me much grief.

Some lessons drive a wedge deep into our serenity. I became bitter and somber and boiling over with profound guilt. I wondered aloud how I was so lucky … and how others could be so unfortunate, through no fault of their own. Uncle Butch seemed like a great man, and I was just an average kid with so many unearned blessings. The luster was once again dulled from my light. I absorbed my sorrow into prayer.

One evening, with eyes fixed at my popcorn ceiling, I implored my Maker for soothing words. My stereo unapologetically interrupted my meditation. Irritated, I stretched to cease the clamor. Flashing through my reposed ears was a melody and lyrics that arrested my attention. The voice! The words! The arrangement! They were meant for me. Elton John's "Daniel" introduced my emotions to therapy at a level my teenage conflicts screamed for. Bernie Taupin's words seemed to capture the frustrations of my fourteen-year-old self better than the adult mentors often surrounding me. So enamored by this remedy, I sought every morsel of information about his music. The more I absorbed myself into the collaborations of Bernie Taupin and Elton John, the more complete I felt. The placement of words to represent human emotions was an art form with which I became obsessed. What began as discarded napkin scribble slowly and methodically progressed to complete alliterations representative of my being. Whenever life dealt me a body blow, I would lyrically re-create my pain. Any failures I may have experienced now had a positive outlet. My overloaded schedule once again had additional conquests to compress. Writing lyrics was the missing ingredient that completed my recipe. There were days when I only had time to write a verse or two, but by corresponding with elevated distress, my lyrics would dramatically increase. I owned every legitimate and bootleg Elton John album available. Whether isolated in my room, working out in my garage, or staying up after hours to catch a glimpse of Elton John on Don Kirshner's Rock Concert, Elton John's ballads filled the void around me. My love of music propelled me to crave its company constantly.

A career in writing lyrics replaced my childhood fantasy of taking the place of Joe DiMaggio, Mickey Mantle, or Bobby Murcer. As my collection of personal ballads expanded, I heard about a new radio station in Hollywood, Florida. My considerate mother drove me to the offices of Y-100 to introduce me to the music world. There seemed to be an instant connection, and Y-100's personnel director hired me on the spot. I was like a kid in a candy store as the popular personalities behind the voices welcomed me.

If you open yourself up to the world, it will transform you.

FIVE

Don't You Dare Stop

(Rising above the fray)

Why do some people refuse to quit?

RUBBING ELBOWS WITH THE NUMBER one radio station's disc jockeys would be cool for any fourteen-year-old. For a relatively unsophisticated wide-eyed dreamer who was looking for acceptance, it was magnificent. I received copies of all the latest and most desired albums from my new colleagues. Along with the albums, I had access to all forms of pop culture's spoils. My collection of rock star shirts was the envy of my school. My prized gift, undoubtedly, was a life-size Elton John cardboard cutout. For years, I pompously displayed that cardboard "Captain Fantastic" (Elton John's nickname for his alter ego) in my bedroom. I became associated with the hottest music of the day. I relished my tasks and quickly developed a good reputation among my peers and supervisors. Responsibilities increased, and my time cards suddenly had important-sounding job titles printed on them. I began by simply answering request lines for the station and quickly moved into the powerful position of calculating the standings for the top forty songs on our playlists. My name gained significance when it was articulated from the famous disc jockeys' vocal cords.

Additional assignments such as running our annual Fourth of July beach bashes and arranging the disc jockeys' community engagements placed me in the public domain as a representative of Y-100. Unfamiliar fans naturally gave me credibility because of my employment and association with South Florida's number one radio station. Numerous times, music's elite, such as Olivia Newton John, Isaac Hayes, and Minnie Riperton, graced our studios. Naturally, an impressionable teenager viewed each exclusive rendezvous with reverence. A few disc jockeys included me among their inner circle. Conversations turned into phone calls, and before long, they spontaneously extended dinner and party invitations to me.

One crimson-haired DJ, CH, saw to it that my schedule mirrored his on-air time. Weekends at the station differed vastly from the crowded halls and sales crew–filled offices during the week. Two adjacent broadcast studios were off limits to all but the on-air talent. However, CH authorized and orchestrated my paperwork session in the second studio. I was truly in rock 'n' roll heaven as I immersed myself in some of my favorite Elton John hits, enjoyed via studio-quality headsets. However, one particular Saturday afternoon, my heavenly tingle quickly turned into a shiver running down my spine. As Elton's brilliant and exalted voice penetrated my auditory canals, and atrociously caustic noise left my lips in the form of song, a hand other than mine drove itself deep into my shorts. My impromptu operatic transition from bass to soprano, along with flailing appendages, undoubtedly showed CH that his groping was unwelcome. After bouncing off the surrounding desk like a pinball racking up points, my spasmodic movements thrust me onto the floor. Pulling the rotated headset off my eyes, I caught a glimpse of CH's brisk escape. Furious and embarrassed, my instincts painted a picture of my hands crushing his trachea. However, as CH entered the on-air studio, my desired retaliation lost out to paralyzed and uncooperative limbs.

Instead, I contacted my supervisors at Y-100, and they laughed at my complaint. They treated the incident as a joke and even commented, "Everyone knows that CH wants you." They explained that they allowed me into the on-air studios because CH wanted me to be close to him. No matter how much I expressed my anger at that occurrence, it proved to be entertaining to the managers. I refused to return to work under those conditions and exited Y-100 for the last time.

Several days later, CH called me and apologetically offered to pay my salary out of his pocket. He took full responsibility for the incident. He explained that he had never had anyone else treat him with such warmth and kindness unless he was gay and cruising for a "pickup." He'd misunderstood my courtesy as a form of covert sexual attraction. His insistence that he believed his attraction toward me was mutual convinced me that he meant no harm. The ensuing months brought me several more phone calls from CH, begging for forgiveness. He disarmed me with horrific and raw accounts of a childhood radically different from my storybook rearing. Somehow, my ear and advice became the cleansing that my assailer sought.

Years later, I learned that CH isolated and pathetically lonely, died from a new disease called AIDS. The saga of CH taught me that we are all searching for the same primordial desires. The most basics among them, love and acceptance, had deserted him. I was fortunate to have been raised by a family that had always cherished and embraced me. CH ached for the very relationships I took for granted, and years of rejection had left him anguished. It was clear that regardless of sexual preference, we all laughed and cried, and we all deserved consideration and compassion.

At fifteen, I purchased a motorcycle, and those wheels expanded my world. The lone headlight chaperoned me to McDougal's Gym before the city's coffee brewed. Belonging to a gym introduced me to the sweat, grunts, and smells of hard-core training. Although I was small, I was overflowing with enthusiasm, and it paralleled me perfectly. I intensely observed every musclehead's routine and sponged information like a freshly baptized cult member. Sniffing out the minutest details of each movement, I quickly learned who was informed and who was wasting time. I gravitated toward the burliest and was befriended by most. Before long, I weaseled into workouts with behemoths much more advanced than I was. I pledged to myself never to quit and always to exceed their efforts.

The first time I gained the privilege of training my legs with McDougal's resident stud, I felt honored. Dave had just won the teenage Mr. Hollywood Bodybuilding Championship and had incredibly developed legs. I had never seen such muscularity in person. My legs looked like twigs next to his sequoia trees. When I flexed my hairy Italian American legs, they simply straightened at the knee joint. When Dave contracted, snakelike interlocking granite formations collided and battled for dominance. If I had an ounce of common sense, I would have known that I was out of my league. Much like a bumblebee is unaware that his shape should prevent flight, my rosy fervor blocked all self-preservation instincts. In my garage gym, there were few leg exercises at my disposal, so I was in for a distinct experience.

I followed Dave's initial light set of leg extensions with my best imitation of his slow, controlled explosions. *Not bad*, I confidently thought. His second set, while doubling the weight, was performed with equal precision. A few repetitions into my next set, I sensed that my brash thoughts might prove to be premature. A few more sets of leg extensions and my numb legs begged me to listen to the modicum of intelligence that I had so artfully hidden. As he pounced onto the hack squat machine, my alien legs dragged slowly behind. He exalted my efforts by loudly using slang terms to call me private parts of the female anatomy. Such uncomplimentary metaphors for felines had a distinct sting to them, and they caused uncontrolled laughter among the gym's members.

I wanted Dave's approval. I needed his respect! Living up to my promise never to quit, I foolishly followed his exact directions. In the middle of the second set of hack squats, tremors within my stomach advised me that there would be consequences. My quadriceps had checked out, and the guts that were allowing my futility were fighting to escape. Choking down my protein shake, excess saliva and tunnel vision signaled a looming launch. Still, I fought on. Somewhere between the hack squat machine and the leg press, my stomach's contents forfeited their privacy and divulged themselves with a *splat* sound that turned every head. The gym's owner, Joe, heartily laughed and proclaimed, "Whoever heaves it cleans it." Still convulsing within my defeated stomach, I scrubbed the stained and foul-smelling floor. As I teetered to my feet, all expected an unconditional surrender. Instead, I placed a mop bucket next to me and slithered back onto the leg press. Everyone stopped working out and astonishingly watched the vomiting idiot prolong this Bataan Death March. By the time I finished quadriceps, hamstrings, and calves, there were two more gut-bursting interruptions into my trusty bucket. Somehow, in a senseless stupor, I dragged my ruins onto my motorcycle and drunkenly rode home.

Waking up the next day to tortuous stabbing pain definitively proved that yesterday's stupidity was to be today's problem. As if I had casts on my legs, movement was out of the question. Rigor mortis and softball-size bruises converted my twigs into anguishing anchors. I made Herman Munster's stride seem fluent and graceful. This pathetic imitation of walking continued for two full weeks. I later learned that Dave and a host of other gym rats had secretly planned to annihilate my legs, believing it would be the last they'd see of me.

However, with bucket in hand, leg workouts became the focal

point of my training. I became so engrossed in proving my mettle that many vomit-interrupted workouts blazed my trail. I threw up so many times that Joe McDougal painted my name on a bucket and demanded that it accompany me at every workout. Over time, the twigs that brought me consternation would slowly show promise. Many of those entertained by my initial calamity would learn that persistence compensates for most shortcomings. It came to be a lesson for all. I reached into my bygone standards and once again appreciated Ms. L.'s impact on me.

Meanwhile, high school presented very little academic challenge. The advanced level taught in Catholic school placed me way ahead of my peers. While they were learning most subjects for the first time, these lessons had been drilled into my memory years earlier. Absent were the challenges that triggered me to push to higher levels. Though I continued to employ my excellent study habits, I grew complacent and bored. School was a breeze. The only thing that regressed was my confidence around girls. Though I had many female friends and was quite comfortable conversing with them, I was intimidated by the thought of intimacy. I was raised to believe that premarital sex was a sin, and the very notion prompted uncomfortable recollections of my New York basement. Therefore, I shunned circumstances that could present such temptation. Some girls commented about my excessively long eyelashes and even called me cute, but I always seemed to have an excuse that kept things platonic.

After completing a workout early one morning, I instinctively rushed toward the gym's shower. It was a tiny plastic cubicle the size of a phone booth—barely large enough to fit one adult. "Great-Leg Dave" had one of the female members squashed against the rusted pipes, lamenting as if she were dying, yet begging him not to stop. As my startled mind comprehended what this entangled commotion meant, Dave turned his head toward me and generously asked, "Do you want some of her?" The female coitus participant invitingly smiled toward me, and I used the excuse that I'd be late for school. But as much as my modesty and conscience rejected my potential participation, I was envious of Dave's cool brashness. I was never able to look at that female gym member in the eyes again, and none of us ever mentioned this proposition to each other.

Although my frame was not ready to enter a bodybuilding

competition, my strength had increased radically. Some of the gym members coaxed me into entering a bench press competition. Surprisingly, I won easily. Within the next several months, I entered and won three additional powerlifting meets. Beginning to feel invincible, I sought out advice to prepare for my real choice of competition: bodybuilding.

Obligingly, a group of experienced competitors seemed more than happy to help me. I continued to digest bodybuilding magazines daily, and nothing that was printed escaped my voracious eyes. So when my pandering trainers' advice differed from all that was printed, I should have known better. However, I coveted victory so much that I was blinded by lust. I followed everything that my trainers told me to the letter. They had me eating pounds of steak and dozens of eggs per sitting in a single day. The next day, they ordered me to consume a pound of mozzarella cheese with either potatoes or two pounds of pasta. Some of this prescribed cuisine was alien to my family and quite expensive. That caused many obstacles and complications at home. Just as my clothes were bursting at the seams, they'd have me fast for two days. Once starvation shrunk me down again, they'd stuff me full of bloating foods. The cycle of starvation and gluttony continued until the competition. Each time I'd complain about how awful I looked, they'd jointly convince me that all would come together the day of competition. I reluctantly continued the madness. The day of the show, I still looked horrendous, but I would not quit. Each "helper" took turns adding gobs of baby oil and tanning dye on my body, particularly on my back. They explained that once I showed my back to the judges, "It was in the bag." Like artists, they appeared to be quite pleased with their masterpiece.

As I stepped on stage, one of my assistants yelled out, "He looks like a wet rat!" Another joyfully screamed, "Hey, pasta thighs!" But their true pleasure was reserved for when my back faced the audience. Howls from everywhere blared, like trumpets signaling the beginning of festivities. "Hey, pooh-pooh pants!" they bellowed out. Through hysterical laughter, I heard, "Did you crap yourself?" They had malevolently and strategically painted a brown stripe on the rear of my posing trunks. Wails of chaos echoed through the auditorium, along with the lacerating sting of the knives that had been stabbed into my back. In the center of that hideous minefield of inhumanity, I swore to myself that I would be back to have the last laugh.

The difference between wanting and needing comes down to the degree of desire.

SIX

Dedicated to You

(Expanding physically and emotionally)

Is it possible to become better because of our mistakes?

UNCLE ENRICO, OUR FAMILY'S CRAZY uncle from New York, visited us almost daily since he had moved to Florida as well. Henry, as we called him, single-handedly perpetuated my childhood memories of daily family gatherings. Henry's philosophy was exactly the opposite of everything that I had learned at church and from my mother's compassionate example. Some family members jokingly proclaimed that if someone looked up the word "obnoxious" in a dictionary, Henry's picture would be there. Henry contrived in his mind that he was our surrogate parent in lieu of my father, who was absent a lot due to his work schedule. Thus, his forceful and mostly unwanted advice was endless. My mother, who excused years of his antics with her statements—"He means well" and "Respect your elders"—allowed his tirades. He was a combination of Howard Cosell, the Godfather, and, as he would profess, Rudolph Valentino. Ironically, Henry was born on the very day that Rudolph Valentino died. Henry boastfully explained such a coincidence as "One Italian sex symbol replaced another."

Regrettably, I expressed that I was interested in a girl at school. No elaboration was required for Henry to find fault with my choice. Waves of unrelenting irrational judgments surrounded and pounded me for hours. "JoJo is too young to have a girlfriend." "If she's not Italian, tell her to get lost." "Women should be used and thrown aside." "Tell her to get on her knees and bow to the king." And finally, "She wouldn't want a fag that shaves his legs." The last statement was an obvious insult degrading the fact that I was beginning to compete in bodybuilding. Shaving one's legs in preparation for competition was a keynote of Henry's angst toward bodybuilding. He concluded that shaving my legs, having an affinity for Elton John songs, and keeping out of trouble with the law were key indicators of homosexuality.

I made every attempt to prepare Tina for her slaughtering at the hands of this sadistic old-world butcher. However, when she first came to my home, all went surprisingly well. Small talk seemed genuinely hospitable from everyone, and I believed she had escaped the wrath of our surly uncle. However, seconds after she went home, Henry blurted out, "She has no tits so get rid of her." Fortunately, once Mr. Judgment became familiar with my companion, he acquiesced.

Everyone but me realized that Tina did not initially reciprocate my pursuits. Her older sister's "He's a hottie" and "If you don't want him, I'll take him" sparked Tina's jealous streak. Once I learned that both her biological father and mother had tragically been swept from Tina's life at three and eleven years old, respectively, I became captive. While beyond my psychological grasp at the time, my attraction to her was based on my tendency to replicate my mother's nurturing traits.

Neither of us sought a carnal relationship initially. However, the daily consistency of each other's companionship brought us closer than either of us intended. Over time, temptation proved to be too much for me. Many issues and years later, I would mature enough to comprehend that our relationship revolved around an unsustainable appeal. There was an internal need, on my part, to prove that her virginity was not cavalierly taken. My professed love was, in fact, a continuous audition to assure her that our unchaste moments were justifiable. Additionally, both of us had similarly been taken advantage of in childhood, which prevented our initial ease and the appropriate perspective required for healthy sexuality. Unfortunately, I would not learn about her perpetrator until we were in counseling many years later.

While my prayers eventually rid me of the cumbersome burden that molestation at the hands of my foster cousins dealt, the same could not be said for Tina. Our shared indiscretions further reinforced her negative perspective of intimacy. She was certainly a worthy and decent person. In retrospect, we resembled a sibling relationship more than one that was headed toward marriage. Guilt permeated both of us, becoming an underlying obstacle that would formulate a key ingredient in our ultimate collapse.

The remorse of removing Tina's irreplaceable purity led to the resulting frantic phone request for confession that instigated my friendship with Father Donald O'Brien, or Padre. The shame and ever-present guilt overwhelmed me one Friday afternoon. Waiting until Saturday afternoon to attend the prescheduled confession felt like an eternity. Several frantic attempts to call neighborhood parishes paid off when an unfamiliar voice answered at the St. Stephen Catholic Church rectory. His uncanny intuition recognized the urgency of the moment. An immediate cordial invitation was extended, and within five minutes, faith met fate.

Confessions usually occur behind an opaque screen, while kneeling in a broom closet– size adjoining booth, so the priest never learns who the offending confessor is. However, that afternoon, my desired cleansing occurred face-to-face, in a well-lit room, without the cover of anonymity. Padre turned out to be disarming, creating a relaxed atmosphere of soothing comfort. Initially, small talk eased the tension. Before long, our conversation ventured into areas of interest seemingly unattached or related to my purpose. He artfully maneuvered the ebb and flow to encompass my confession tactfully, without the stigma I had fearfully anticipated.

Hours had passed, totally immersed in segments about history, sports, family, and church doctrine. Padre was incredible at utilizing analogies to simplify issues that normally appeared complex. His overriding message related to the benefits of keeping life as simplistic as possible. He went on to explain how the enchantment of childhood dissipates as life adds responsibilities and complications. He said, "I wish you could be frozen in time to always carry your innocence and outlook toward life." He offered a tactic to fight temptation. "As desires confront you, stop for a brief moment and say the Lord's Prayer. Ask for Jesus's strength to descend upon you." He expounded by contrasting the progression of good choices into beneficial habits to the patterns and repercussions of poor choices. "Drug addiction," according to Padre, "begins with a single ill-advised decision." He continued, "The first time the person experiments, he is usually apprehensive of potential problems. But with each successive usage, the hesitation dissipates as it becomes more habitual … or an addiction." His advocacy of prayer as a means to pause long enough to ponder the consequences of our impulses was well understood. I also deduced from Padre's spiel that a routine of well-thought-out choices was the key to creating success and exemplary character. This fascinating journey satiated my immediate needs while formulating the groundwork of a future fellowship.

Early the next morning, I couldn't wait to share my experience with my friend Bob. Bob and I were almost always together. We jointly worked out with weights, went to karate classes, took the same classes in school, went to church, and double-dated with our girlfriends. Within hours, Bob and I were at St. Stephen rectory, reinforcing the positive sentiments from my previous afternoon. The three of us said a rosary together and bonded.

Bob's heart was compassionate and filled with faith. Part of our friendship was built around his high levels of intelligence and morality. Our conversations were without limits due to our similar desire for cerebral stimulation. Together, we believed that we could solve all the world's issues. Our patriotism, spirituality, and shared values left no taboo subject untapped. His uncontrollable impetuousness was his weakness. He was forever backtracking to repair bridges he had impulsively damaged. Each day seemingly presented a new dilemma that kept him festering in agony and in pursuit of a new solution. He was his own worst enemy. While his internal battles raged, I never doubted his motives or goals. Our hangout sessions always involved collaborative prayers. No one escaped our pleading with God; we prayed for everyone. Bob was a good-looking guy, which caused many girls to seduce him, furthering his resulting entanglements. We verbally shared many of our shortcomings and inner ghosts, which created profound trust. Though both of us were admittedly flawed, we emboldened each other's perpetual battle against temptations and provocations.

Bob was supportive of my bodybuilding competitions. Regardless of my placing, he always found some positive aspect to fuel my drive. Off the heels of my last stage disaster, he encouraged me to compete again. I focused my sights fully on the upcoming teenage Mr. Hollywood contest. So as not to be humiliated on stage again, this time I used care and diligence in selecting the individuals who would help me.

I trained almost exclusively with Bob. We pushed and prodded each other's familiar buttons to force every possible rep out of our energized bodies. Each workout took us to new heights. I was now the one pushing leg workouts to uncharted territory. At eight weeks out from the competition, I was full, pumped, and harder than I had ever been.

We added another friend, Mitch, for our leg workouts. We had insane sessions that would last for hours. Bob's fondness for martial arts made him hesitant to continue the lunacy of our extended leg workouts. His phobia was that too much bulk on his legs would potentially hinder his leg flexibility. Therefore, Bob opted out of leg days. Conversely, Mitch had naturally colossal legs. It was my belief that if I wanted to be the best, I would need to train with the best.

We came up with twists and unconventional forms of self-torture. During one notable "leg day," we decided to focus chiefly on squats. As we encouraged each other to slowly descend and contract, a friend yelled from across the gym, "Hey, Joe, do it for me." Struggling to continue in form, I grunted, "This set is dedicated to you." I lost count of the repetitions, but I surpassed all our expectations. Dipping my profusely sweating head under the bar for set number two, I dedicated this one to another gym member, trying to outdo my last extended set. Before we were done, we'd dedicated a set of squats to everyone in the gym. We must have totaled forty-five sets by workout's end. Gym members began to huddle in anticipation of our masochism. Mitch and I made it a twice-weekly fiasco in which numerous benches were arranged like bleachers to facilitate our audience's amusement. We used a dated abacus to count our staggering number of sets. It became so absurd that we would dedicate spine-testing squats to passing pedestrians. The superintendent of the shopping plaza received several complaints, and eventually our asylum was muffled. The gym's owner forced us to close the front door during "lunatic leg days" and placed the squat rack in a narrow back room, not befitting spectators. Still, Mitch and I forged our radical routine into McDougal's folklore.

Spot-on training was coupled with piecemeal dieting. My helpful mother and grandmother's devoted deeds included preparing heaping helpings of pasta fagioli, eggplant parmigiana, and other delicious ethnic delights that were not conducive to bodybuilding competition. It became a dilemma in my home. My father felt that by choosing not to eat my mother's cooking was disrespectful toward her time and his money. He would not support the steak and eggs of my last competition. Indisputable, my mother and grandmother placed tremendous effort into our family's meals. Also as evident, my father indeed labored to provide our sustenance. My quagmire was whether to ignore their efforts selfishly, while eating what my research taught me was correct, or to sabotage my body knowingly in order to appease my family.

Incapable of disrespecting my family's perspective, I walked a tightrope between both. I decreased my portions at home and ate food that was conducive to competition, as much as possible, away from home. The results, while apparently neither conventional nor recommended, were not awful. At least the morning of the show I was not humiliated.

Bob and Mitch placed appropriate amounts of oil on me. They assured me that no mock incontinent brown marks had found their way onto my posing trunks. I looked around and realized that other competitors were superior to me. Still, I was content that the amount and quality of my muscles had improved noticeably, and I welcomed my many family members and friends in the audience.

As the judges commanded our stage movements, I felt as if I belonged. Hoping for a miracle, I prayed for God's will to be done and promised that I would graciously accept whatever decision the judges reached. Fifth place was given to someone on the opposite side of the stage, and my heart began to race with anticipation. Fourth place was awarded to the person directly next to me. Looking up toward heaven, I took a deep breath. *Could it be?* I wondered. As my name was called next over the auditorium's speakers, a simultaneous roar and rising audience members affirmed their approval of the decision. Second and first place trophies were handed to truly deserving competitors, who absolutely exceeded me in every way. Completely at ease with my third place finish, I recall being surprised that I was not devastated. I was genuinely happy for the winners, as I knew, in the back of my mind, that I would someday have my day.

Backstage, the winner was uncharacteristically cordial. He complimented me on my balanced physique and kindly advised, "Once you learn how to diet, no one will touch you."

We celebrated at a famous ice cream parlor called Jaxson's. I was moved by the amount of supporters I had. Family, Padre, friends, and many of McDougal's Gym members gorged their upbeat faces with Papa Bear–size bowls of ice cream. Mitch, who inhaled huge gulps of his banana split like a returning prisoner of war, raised his bowl and my third place trophy, toasting me by saying, "Here's to Joe's success!" As everyone repeated his kind salute, Padre leaned over to me and softly whispered, "This is just the beginning."

If perfection is one's goal, there is always room for improvement.

SEVEN

Superman in Scrubs

(A close call awakened me)

Does having fear equate to being a coward?

AN EMPTY HOUSE WAS EXTRAORDINARILY unusual. Aromatic waves of Locatelli cheese melting over freshly drained pasta would normally have me salivating like a dog in Pavlov's experiment. Bella, as we affectionately referred to my grandmother, would move about the kitchen with the instincts and flair of Ginger Rogers on a dance floor. Orchestrated movements were choreographed to the same tune that she had long ago mastered. My mother, like a prized prodigy, added the accents to the canvas in the form of perfectly placed table settings. This ritual formed the adhesive of our nightly meals. Like migrating birds from different directions, each of us would unite to share our day's woes and deeds. While the rest of society swirled by, each of us would interject our concerns and opinions to each other in an attempt to lend a hand. We knew no other way.

This night, absent were the sounds of heavy pots clanking together in such a rhythm that Ray Charles could find the kitchen. There were no orders to wash my hands as I stepped through the threshold. Henry's unmistakable criticisms of everyone did not resonate. Twenty minutes of wondering was halted by the familiar sounds of my father's work van backing into our driveway. We met each other at the front door and touched off a whirlwind of activity and terse statements that concluded as we pulled into the emergency room entrance of the local hospital. An ambulance had taken my grandfather, and he was in critical condition.

His ailing heart had failed him once again. He had gone into cardiac arrest twice before my father and I arrived. The miraculous crew at the hospital had managed to return him both times. Our vigil lasted until the late evening, and under the advice of a physician, we went home. Our fears were equaled by reality when the phone startled our already anxious home at two o'clock in the morning. We were summoned to the hospital to say good-bye to our beloved patriarch. The expectations were grim. Each of us silently engaged in our family's instinctive activity during tumultuous times: we prayed. For an hour, no one uttered a single word, yet lips could be seen moving at a nonstop pace. Regardless of the stress of this event, each of us appeared to outwardly trust in our faith. In reality, I could not help reflecting on the thought that I might not get the chance to acknowledge my grandfather's impact upon me. I wanted to be able to express to him the appreciation for his incredible journey to America, and the resulting opportunities that he afforded us. There was so much I had never said … and so much thanks to give. Up to that point, I had never expressed my gratitude to him because living together had caused me to take his contributions for granted.

Bella was a fortress. There was no mistaking her demeanor for the current touchy-feely generation. She never requested nor required, in her words, the "genteel sissy treatment that the girls of today need." Tougher than granite, she'd work harder than men half her age, without any expectations. Other than for weddings and funerals, she claimed, "Makeup is for whores." Tenderness was something she'd beat into a piece of meat, not demand for herself. Sex was not something to speak about, and it was nothing more than a necessity along the way to creating children. She had never been on a vacation in her life because they were "too busy making ends meet." Tonight, in spite of her forward-thrust chin and dry eyes, I could feel the grief radiating from her body. I grabbed her rough hand and sat close to her. For three unfiltered hours, she unleashed the saga of nearly fifty years of intrepidness. Stories she'd probably never shared before captivated my focus. The romance of interdependence that drew my grandparents together opened my mind to an era that was difficult to relate to.

Their first date was symbolic of their relationship. My grandfather picked my grandmother up in a dump truck so they could carry a discarded furnace back to my grandmother's home to keep her many siblings warm. Another memory she cherished: when my grandfather found a flattened box of chocolate-covered cherries and shared them with her instead of keeping them for himself. Such extreme hunger was commonplace during the Great Depression, while I had only read about such destitution.

Although Bella was as strong as usual, I finally saw through the leathery facade that her years of dour living had created. Once more, a heavy dose of guilt crept into me. I was again forced to recognize the relative ease into which others' ordeals and sufferings had placed me. Contrary to my blessings was the personal burden of my childhood friend, Russell Rivers. While we were both in kindergarten, Russell's parents were swept from his life because of a tragic car accident. He, unlike me, had no overseers to shield him. How had I managed to be so fortunate?

My grandmother spoke to me differently than she ever had before. Normally, the matriarchal grandmother figure would bark commands and the obedient child would scurry to obey. This long evening was a conversion. I entered as "JoJo" the child, and I emerged as Joe the young man. It was a level of respect afforded to those sitting at the adult table, which I suddenly cherished.

When a good news–bearing intern finally interrupted her, I felt as if the baton of higher regard had been dangled in front of a new generation. The smiling young physician's eyes stared beneath the vacant look on my grandmother's face. He explained that my grandfather was more stable than upon arrival. Using a notepad as his chalkboard, he drew a diagram of a heart and its "wiring," which looked more like a tree and branches. He offered the consolation that my grandfather could come home in a few days, but he made us aware that a repeat of these events would be inevitable. On his notepad, he colored dots on several branches and illustrated how the dots symbolized blocks in my grandfather's electrical system. "These electrical blockages," he said, "will eventually short-circuit without notice."

While thankful for this reprieve, the didactic side of me was stimulated by the expertise and intelligence of this mild-mannered intern. The mystifying power over life and death that enabled him and his colleagues to change the morose into the possible astounded me. I found myself asking questions that some might have thought to be inappropriate for the circumstances. I suddenly felt a spark ignite for more information and knowledge about the potential to steer mortality. I had spent so much time and effort developing such physical strength, but my muscles were useless during our family's sorrow. I had allowed

43

my mind to take a back seat to my physical being, and I felt ashamed of my present dysfunction. I was relegated to spectator. It was at that instant that I knew I needed "more than muscles" to carry me through life. Something registered in the back of my mind—something I knew I would have to explore. As the doctor walked away, I saw Superman in scrubs.

A frailer and weaker grandfather returned home. His posture had previously been straight and proud. If his face had not been so familiar to me, I would have believed he was an imposter. Even his voice had lost its demanding clarity. The devitalized and affected elder was a figment of the larger-than-life being he previously was. He began attending church without prodding. He volunteered to receive communion. His previously impeccable hygiene and clothing were replaced with relaxed and, at times, disheveled appearances. He no longer walked in front of everyone. Literally and figuratively, he lagged behind.

One afternoon, when my mother and I were walking out of the local grocery store, we witnessed a sad foreshadowing of my grandfather's future. A lost and panicked man, trapped in my grandfather's skin, maneuvered around the parking lot, attempting to find his misplaced car. Not only could he not find it, but when we pointed it out to him, he was unable to recognize it. It was a turning point in our family's dynamics.

As glum as I knew it sounded, I felt the pressure of his impending mortality. We sat and discussed events of his past. Mostly instigated by me, we would spend endless hours transferring historic events of the world into his firsthand accounts. I asked more questions than Woodward and Bernstein directed at "Deep Throat." The standard old stories were not enough. I wanted to know what he was thinking sailing across the Atlantic to a new continent. How he felt when he was without a home. Nothing slipped past my inquisition. But there was one notion that seemed extraordinarily hard for me to interpret. While I grasped why he wanted to leave Italy for the promise of freedom, I could not relate to what gave him the strength to leave his family and make the move all by himself. What followed turned out to have an impact on me that shall always give me strength. He softly explained that "fear exists in all of us." He went on: "Only a fool would not be afraid. The difference is that our responsibility to act when those around us are weak is what defines the moments that shape our lives.

These are the times that we create success or choose to fail. Those that act have a chance to succeed. Those that fail to act must live with the consequences of their cowardice. Cowards love to say they do not want trouble or do not want to make people mad," he stressed. "That is just a way of justifying being a coward. They try to make something negative sound positive. The only difference between a coward and a hero is that a hero acts in spite of his fear. If I did not come to America, no one else around me would have. I had to act." Regardless of the frail shell that expounded those profound words, I knew the same immense character remained inside. I was never so in awe of anyone in my life. To me, John Wayne had nothing on my grandfather.

My brother's wedding would be the first time that many of my New York relatives came to Florida. We always kept in touch by phone, but my desire to see relatives compounded the excitement of my brother's big day. As the best man, I was saturated with responsibilities. I did not want to look stupid in front of those I had not seen for so long. Thankfully, the ceremony went exceptionally well. Father O'Brien performed the nuptials at St. Stephen Catholic Church.

The post-ceremony wedding party would allow for relaxed and easygoing enjoyment, I hoped. Understanding that this was my brother's day to shine, I played the role of quiet assistant. Whenever I could do something to help, I jumped to serve. As I was moving a few chairs for guests, I could not help but notice my Uncle Vito using some kind of inhaler. He was the same uncle who was once our version of Jackie Gleason. He was incredibly funny and entertaining, and his inhaler saddened me by displaying his weakness. Uncle Joey's limp projected the fact that even a tough police officer and veteran of the Korean War must hang up his holster at some point. Uncle Jimmy happened to be removing his dentures when I glanced at his table. I observed him chopping up his food into bites befitting a toddler. Aunt Nancy's orthopedic shoes forced her to dance like something more robotic than human. Helping her propel her Frankenstein shoes about the dance floor was another arthritic uncle. They seemed to require each other's counterbalance to prevent a disaster.

Then my attention turned to my cousins, dancing with unabashed recklessness. Radiant smiles greeted each other as they exchanged dance partners from song to song. Running and jumping like an old PF

Flyer sneaker commercial, their enthusiasm was contagious. Those old enough to drink were draining bottles at record pace.

My head spun around the room as if I were witnessing a Ping-Pong match. Youth and energy pitted against the elderly and ailments. Fun contrasted with survival. Flexibility challenged stiffness. I became infinitely aware that the arena I watched depicted the future generation of my family nipping at the heels of its ruling powers. Those whose dominance was never questioned were suddenly threatened with a coup d'état. The reception that I had anticipated with childlike exuberance was rapidly becoming the pronouncement of change. The metamorphosis caught me off guard, but there was no denying it now. Although my grandfather's diminishing state of health was of great concern to me, he was not alone in his fragile condition. My repeated thought that lasted from that evening on was, *I guess it's really time to grow up.*

The only certainty is that our choices dictate our paths.

EIGHT

You Could Have Been Somebody

(Running never solves problems)

Why is the truth so difficult to deal with?

RENEWED ENTHUSIASM DROVE ME TO refocus my academic efforts toward loftier goals. Recent occurrences reminded me of the importance of stimulating as many talents as possible. I was forced to admit how one-dimensional I had become. I was disappointed that I had allowed that to happen. Part of my pride had come from the fact that one of my main strengths was my depth. By focusing primarily on the gym, I had become too shallow. I enjoyed mental exercise as well as the strenuous physical labor for which I had become known. Through much soul-searching, I reluctantly noticed that the intelligence I was gifted with had been neglected for my bodybuilding. No longer was that tolerable.

The mission for my final two years of high school was to absorb myself in my advanced class–laden schedule. Besides my continuation of early morning workouts, school was my sole priority. I was fortunate that once a target was established, I usually hit my mark. That is not to say that it required little pain. Quite the contrary, as few endeavors had come easy for me. Some individuals can excel the first time they engage in an undertaking. My success was a direct result of immersion and tenacity. Inspired by the humbling nature of my initial failures, I had always returned with renewed resolve and repetitiously battled for an acceptable conclusion. I would need to apply that formula once again, this time toward my studies.

Writing for the school newspaper and yearbook honed my writing skills and assisted my journalism aspirations. The task of high school photographer involved me in most important events. Participating on the baseball team was my continued desire to fulfill my childhood dream as a professional player. However, my strong fixation on working out and bodybuilding suddenly became a strain with my baseball coach. The traditional approach he advocated did not include time in the weight room. His contempt for my muscularity drove a wedge between us. There were constant and angry admonishments toward my developing physique. His tirades about fluidity versus brawn caused my eventual agreed-upon parting from the team. As a replacement, I involved myself in the Quill and Scroll, National Honor Society, and various other extracurricular activities. The workload was overwhelming at times, but it was necessary for admission to a superior university.

Each school day brought me new attention from others. One such person who noticed me was the high school yearbook instructor, Ms. B. She was young and new to the school. We were continuously around each other because both of us were unified by our bustling involvement within the English department. I was timid in her presence because she was loud and extremely confident in herself. Her youth and energy made her a favorite among students. Her affinity for men's sports placed her around many of the school's male athletes. I excused her partiality as nothing more than an inclination toward the sporting events themselves. The resulting effect was that numerous jocks enrolled in her classes. It certainly appeared to me, and many others, that they were given preferential treatment in her classes. She directed most of her questions and an abundance of her attention toward the biggest male athletes. However, her ability to delve into stimulating debates, such as Orwellian matters and Isaac Asimov's hidden meanings, was the draw that kept my interest. Her intellect helped my creative juices flow toward higher thinking. Her acknowledgment of my aptitude was flattering. I felt appreciated and noticed. When she invited me on a few yearbook-sponsored trips to compete in various essay competitions, I was honored.

Orlando hosted a national competition for the top high school journalists. Ms. B. entered me into the well-hyped main event. Not wanting to disappoint her, I reluctantly agreed. That was to be my first competition, and the dozens of other entrants were all known writers with extensive resumes. I felt like cub reporter Jimmy Olsen versus Seymour Hersh.

For the actual contest, they sent us to an isolated auditorium. We then received, with minimal details, a topic to write about. To replicate the pressure of an approaching print deadline, we were given strict time restraints. In the midst of the encounter, I engrossed myself in my improvised composition about an underdog high school basketball team that consisted of misfits. Drawing from my own personal story and dreams, the team overcame miraculous odds and won the state championship. While confident in my writing abilities, I did not disillusion myself into lofty expectations.

That evening at the awards ceremony, I was relaxed because I had no pressure or false assumptions. As the fifth through second place victors were announced, brief descriptions of their finer points were articulated to the tense and anticipatory crowd. Before first place was awarded, a drawn-out complimentary analysis of the winner's work was eulogized. The acclaim and adulation bordered on sickening. The tribute was so overboard that I recall thinking, *What an inflated ego this person's going to have. He's going to think he's God.* As the nauseating glory continued, I turned to the person next to me and mockingly said, "Enough already!"

Just as the Academy Award attitude reached the intolerable point, an improbable dark horse's surname was poorly enunciated by the emcee. The mispronounced version was remotely similar to the title on my chest tag. My ears strained to catch the second disclosure to confirm that the name just called was not a mistake. Bewildered by this distracting faux pas, I must have appeared as shocked as a lottery winner. Even though my name had never been pronounced that way, I recognized it as mine. Everyone stood and clapped with such suddenness that I was still asking for confirmation as my classmates gobbled me up in a mass of hugs and handshakes. As calmness returned, Ms. B. nonchalantly said, "I had no doubt." I was amazed that she had had such confidence in me. Later, she again reiterated her belief that my talents were "incredible."

Although I was likely not the best candidate, Ms B went on to ask me to be the editor of our high school yearbook, which afforded me tremendous responsibility and power. Other than from my family, I had never had such compliments bestowed on me. My insecure enjoyment of what I believed to be undeserving respect caused me to accept her offer. Additionally, I was working on procuring congressional appointments to the U.S. Naval and Air Force Academies. Editorship, I determined, would just about guarantee those invitations. My consent set off a series of events that haunts me to the present.

Ms. B.'s desire for absolute control over all aspects of my life became almost instantaneous. I condoned it at first, but eventually even fellow students and Tina began wondering aloud how I could tolerate such repression. On one occasion, Ms B had me excused from another class and beckoned me to her classroom. As I arrived, she demanded that I leave school to go to her house and place the clothes from her washer into her dryer. Objectionable, but I acquiesced. On one of our many school trips, we went to Tennessee to tour the yearbook facility. While I was writing Tina a postcard in my motel room, Ms. B. knocked on my door. After she entered and turned on the television, I continued writing the postcard from the prone position upon my bed. While I was in mid-sentence, the pressure, warmth, and scent of Ms. B. was suddenly conjoined and paralleling my spooked and quivering body. Her casualness toward our bodies' connection seemed much too unnerving. The instantaneous foreboding launched me like a jet from a carrier. My afterburners propelled me into the bathroom, where I remained frozen until she left my room.

Another time, she called me late one evening to tell me to come over to her house immediately. It was late enough that I had already fallen asleep. But once again, I followed her direction. However, before going to Ms. B.'s house, I stopped by Tina's house to ask her to chaperone me. Tina had previously expressed her dislike over the constant touching and uncomfortable hugging from Ms. B. The holding of hands and seemingly innocent back rubs were a daily part of life with Ms. B.

As Tina and I knocked on Ms. B.'s door, she answered in an unsuitably small white outfit. The nearly tangible discomfort accounted for the silence that ensued. An awkward hesitation momentarily prevented any words from flowing from our lips. Then Ms. B. sheepishly said, "Oh, it's fixed now. I called you to fix my stereo speaker." Tina's fuming exasperation was wholly understandable and warranted. I was so disgusted by the entire event that my quiet outrage boiled within me. The next day, Ms. B. displayed both embarrassment and anger that I'd brought Tina to her house. Pressure mounted from all directions. My personal level of frustration and indignation exceeded all levels of tolerance during the numerous times Ms. B. sat on my lap or rested her body against mine in class. Many students laughed and teased me about her lack of respect for my private space. Those and many other similarly abnormal and uncomfortable situations were too commonplace in my dealings with Ms. B.

At that time, there were no examples of inappropriate behavior in the media to raise my suspicion or cause me to question her motivation. It was a new phenomenon to me. Although uncommon, there were a few stories of male teachers whose conduct toward female students raised ire. Never, to my knowledge, had any female teachers acted in a similar way. I lacked the capacity to fully comprehend or digest what an authority figure's motive could be, other than copasetic and laudable. It was undeniable, though, that her behavior far surpassed any standard of professionalism that educators are required to sustain today. I felt smothered, violated, and trapped by the fact that she had such a position of power over my college destiny.

I believed there was nowhere to turn, so I shamefully engaged in the tactic I disdain the most: I ran. The only saving grace was that my years of academic prowess rewarded me with a slew of scholarship choices within South Florida. I applied for early admissions to a local college, and I was accepted. Fully aware that my admission to one of the prestigious military academies would be denied as a result, I'd shamefully panicked and chosen the path of least resistance. At the time, I believed that no one would believe such accusations. Worse, still, would be the perception or impression that my accounts would sound narcissistic and delusional.

With my tail between my legs, my spineless and timid response destroyed my self-esteem. The most destructive blow to my confidence was the recognition of how far removed I was from the example my grandfather had set. I was so embarrassed by my submissiveness that I could not bear to speak to my grandfather or Padre about it as it was occurring. Rather, I downplayed the entire episode to them. When confronted with fear, I chose not to act appropriately. I wanted to be Sampson, but when my back was against the wall, I was more like Delilah. In fact, I had become the coward my grandfather had warned me about, and I loathed that.

When I hinted at home about my decision for early college admission, my family was initially perplexed. They had given me credit for having much more courage than that. I'd compounded my negative worth by disappointing my loved ones. Henry took the initiative and demanded a meeting with the principal to castigate such behavior. The school's response was exactly as I expected. My motives and character were assassinated, and Ms. B.'s was vehemently defended. The vice principle actually laughed at Henry's accusations. Of course, no witnesses were allowed on my behalf, and no investigation was prompted. Adding insult to injury, Ms. B. suddenly changed my unblemished grades to project an inaccurate portrayal of me as an underachiever. At the time, I was furious that Henry chose to speak up, but I had since become aware that his outwardly unpolished and unpleasant demeanor was at times required to balance my meek inactivity. I'd neglected to act, and Henry repeated my grandfather's words from a year earlier: "I had to act." Like a slap in the face, it immediately made me realize that Henry was not the bad guy that I had childishly thought he was. In a retrospective mood, I grasped that someone must do the dirty work when others shirk or abdicate their unpleasant duties. As much as I prided myself in my muscular facade, I was clearly still not ready for weaning.

When the yearbook was finally published, it contained a statement portraying me in an extremely negative light. The implication was that I had abandoned my duties for self-serving purposes. It was an unfair one-sided narrative intended to immortalize Ms. B. and the remaining staff as victims. One more kick in the tail! Throbbing inside me was this reflective question: *Where does a man go to get his good name back?*

As I reluctantly admitted my frustration to Padre, he attempted to console my self-disgust by taking me to Disney World for a day. Padre must have sensed my objection to converse about my shame directly, for he cautiously skirted around the issue. While his intentions were to bring a smile to my face, he had no idea how many laughs "the trip" would deliver, whereas donkey calf raises would forever bedevil our recollection.

Over the years, as issues or low points had cycled through life, Henry and others unknowingly inflamed those excruciating memories. Much malaise was caused when I heard, "You could have been somebody," or "You could have graduated from the Air Force Academy." Incessant reminders were hung around my neck with the same impact as a scarlet letter. As the legend of the Phoenix rose from the ashes to renew itself through rebirth, I solemnly swore that I would re-create myself.

When we face demons, the sooner we engage them, the better.

NINE

Always a Knockout

(Some heroes never die—they live on within us)

Is greatness born or a learned attribute?

MY INVESTMENT OF HARD WORK during my Catholic school years stood as the infrastructure on which my college studies would be built. I once again collected dividends for thinking long term as a child. Just as General Sherman blazed through Atlanta, I took no prisoners en route to the completion of college. Loaded with an average of eighteen credits per semester, I studied with overkill. Each homework assignment was approached with the same tenacity as if Ms. L. had directed it. The ease of academics allowed for ventures in numerous directions. With dual majors in journalism and broadcast journalism, I began writing for the college newspaper. Along with a few other pioneers, we began a weekend radio program dedicated to the "needs and deeds" of South Florida. We produced all aspects of the show. When the local college opened a brand new campus, I was one of the inaugural newspaper writers, and I chose the name for their periodical. Bob and I donated time to a local church's youth program on various weekends. Besides my early workouts, I also worked the afternoon shift at McDougal's Gym. Bob and I were also hired with a group of bodybuilders to work on a regular basis at Temple Beth Shalom, catering for bar mitzvahs. As if my candle had yet another end I could light, Bob and I were hired as bouncers at Skip's Dance Machine.

Skip's was South Florida's premiere, and amazingly popular, weekend disco. It was the watering hole of the Serengeti. As night fell, every beast seeking his mate atomized cologne, painted on jeans, and "hustled" to the Bee Gees and KC and the Sunshine Band. Prior to the Mariel boatlift, the Cuban population was still predominantly living in Dade County. Caravans of incredibly proficient dancers would journey north into Broward County to grace Skip's with the best moves anywhere. Dance fever was contagious. The Cuban and South American influence was profound and adored. We worked hard, but we also "grooved" with the patrons. It was raw and sexy, while also delivering a form of healthy, clean fun. Pheromones dusted potential partners like Tinkerbell working overtime. Several episodes of unobstructed public copulation proved that reproductive pixie dust was more than some could handle or resist. Apparently, when hormones raged so palpably, competition for coital companions was vigorous. Alpha males postured for domain. At times, the volatile mix resulted in skirmishes that required intervention. Just as with the arrival of police officers in domestic cases, misdirected hostility was projected toward our staff.

One steamy Saturday evening in July, a nondescript fight occurred between a familiar customer and an unknown guest. In the usual fashion, we converged and separated the individuals. Once we moved the commotion outside, it appeared that the worst was over. Within thirty minutes, the unknown guest returned and attempted to slip through the front door. I noticed that he was now wearing a box cutter–style ring with a shark fin–shaped blade projecting from its base. Realizing that it was a potentially lethal weapon, I politely asked him to step back outside. Aggressively, he raised his hands into a fighting stance and positioned himself to square off with me. With the disco ball's light reflecting from the ring's blade, I gestured that I did not want trouble.

"F--k him up!" a second cohort urged my ringed menace. As my poised adversary turned his head slightly to acknowledge his friend's taunt, a wave of self-preservation that emanated from my toes tsunamied through my right hand and into his chin. Before a conscious thought came to me, his flaccid body bounced off the exit door and thumped onto the floor. It was as if George Foreman commandeered my body to repeat his Kingston knockout of Joe Frazier. As unflattering as it is to admit, my initial thought was how I relished the solid connection of my clenched knuckles and his mandible. Then, as I pounced on him, numerous onlookers yanked me away.

As moments passed, a sickening sensation replaced my initial swagger. I was puzzled by how out of character my actions were. *How could such a reaction occur without the slightest forethought?* I thought. *Was that really me?* Remorse took over, and I went to apologize to the still-dazed recipient, who was slumped on a bench outside. His ring had been removed, so he no longer posed a threat. He mumbled from his humbled mouth, "My jaw is killing me." I recall apologizing and asking, "Why did you make me do that?"

Over the next several months, fights regularly occurred. Each time, the results were the same: one of us bouncers prevailed with brawl-ending punches. Once Bob realized that his adamant fighting skills were backed by my proficiency, there was no turning back. My innocent defensive measures steamrolled into nightly lot-clearing melees. Through first-punch tactics and dumb luck, none of us were ever hurt. Skip began referring to me as "One Punch." As he delightfully proclaimed, "None of your fights ever go past the first punch. You are the nicest guy I have ever met, but if someone is dumb enough to cross you, heaven help him. It's always a knockout!" Besides the guilty feeling from leaving a host of limp bodies laid out, the compliments fed my tenuous ego. The hypocrisy of my false bravado defied my morality. As a result, a concealed crusade raged within me. Those knockouts were confidence building, but my conscience resoundingly clamored for an end to the weekend combat.

Seeking advocacy, I spoke to my grandfather about my dilemma. Direct and to the point, he gladly gave his wisdom. He seemed to tie together so many loose ends for me. "Your motivation is a great way to test if you've done the right thing," he calmly stated. Because you won those fights doesn't make you right. The first time you were justified because you protected yourself. Once you got carried away, you were on borrowed time." He went on to say, "Always check your motives before you act. Might does not make you right! Keep your ego out of important decisions. Lasting self-respect comes from being fair and firm." As usual, I was better for having had our conversation.

Still burdened by my unexplainable and ever-present guilt and shame, I was aware that internal renovations were to be evolutionary, not revolutionary. I became aware of my own frailties and consciously appraised my motivations rather than just the results. Additionally, I recalled Padre's advice to take a step backward and say the Lord's Prayer whenever temptations arose.

New members came and went frequently in McDougal's, as with most gyms. Several new huge guys coincidentally joined our gym on the same weekend. They were all impressive, and each had his own outstanding body parts. Mike was as thick as a grizzly bear and as strong as an ox. His soft-spoken style was a contradiction to his physical appearance. While aesthetically pleasing, his rugged look demanded respect. With as much raw potential as any bodybuilder I had ever met, his destiny was of his choosing.

Bob D. was high-strung, with the hardness I lacked. His pronounced veins, known as "vascularity" in bodybuilding terms, looked like blue cables barely below his lean skin. He was strong and more enthusiastic than anyone I had ever trained with.

Charlie had the looks of a gigolo and the body of a statue. Nothing ever frazzled Charlie. The phrase "cool as a cucumber" was a perfect description of him. Additionally, all his muscles were developed in perfect harmony with each other. He moved slowly, but he was consistent.

All great guys, they were more advanced than I was. I was impressed with them as people, but most of all, I was motivated to train with them. We began our assaults as a foursome. Taking turns, we propelled weights around as if we had guns to our heads. The workouts lasted hours. I picked their brains every time we trained. None of their knowledge was left untapped. As the sessions grew longer, it was obvious to all that we needed to split into two groups to accommodate work and school. Rotating partners each week enabled us to stay fresh and push each other, without the fear of stagnation. These were among the greatest gains I ever made.

While I was fond of all of them, Charlie's lifestyle seemed more interesting to me. His new career as a firefighter sounded fascinating. Between sets, I'd ask about his job, and his experiences seemed endless. Each day, new tales would tantalize my interest more. I became obsessed once I was aware of the emergency medical aspect of his occupation. It brought me back to the night in the hospital, when I was so impressed with the miracle of saving my grandfather's life. The notion that I could provide such impact upon humanity was more than inspirational. The superhuman power to return a soul from the glimpse of the "bright light" was exhilarating and provocative. All my career interests seemed to be combined into a perfect blend, as firefighting stimulated me physically and mentally. I loved the camaraderie of teamwork and the adrenaline such pressure causes. Although the stories were so casually told, I was as excited as a kid at Christmas. There was no turning back now. Charlie the firefighter had caused an inferno within me, changing my career goals dramatically.

The timing seemed perfect. I was in my last semester of college, and upon its completion, I would immediately transition into the fire academy. Exams were coming up, so I first rededicated efforts to assure myself success in my journalism degree. My room was my study sanctuary. I exiled myself with the hope of memorizing every lesson.

Finally, it was the day before my last exam. My grandfather breached my door numerous times this day, in search of one of our usual conversations. Normally, I was the instigator of such interchanges. This day, however, our roles were reversed. My self-imposed pressure had me in a less talkative mood than he was used to. Never one to hide his sentiments, it was obvious that he was frustrated by my simulated force field. For a short time, he simply stood beside my prone body as I read my notes and textbook for the twentieth neurotic time. His body language urged me to take a break, yet I stubbornly remained focused on the same paragraphs that I had retained long before. Eventually, my unyielding grip grudgingly broke his patience. As he turned to exit my vault, he forced out his prophetic and now-infamous words: "If something happens to me, please take care of Grandma."

As history has a way of sorting out facts, the next day proved how important each opportunity to express love is. What I had pretentiously construed as gibberish turned out to be my loved one's final plea.

Before I ever had an opportunity to make amends for my rude evasiveness, or appropriately thank him for all of the sacrifices he made for me, my grandfather succumbed to his heart problems. The discovery of my noble grandfather's body stopped everything in its tracks. Once the police and rescue crew declared him deceased, I remained in his room with him for over an hour. I witnessed far more than his lifeless body. As my stare remained riveted to his closed eyes, I began to drift. My mind traveled through the experiences of my grandfather, which he had shared with me so graphically. I saw a young man whose love for his family was so profound that he placed himself in inhumane circumstances with gargantuan responsibilities. All naturally occurring fear had to be swallowed because he was alert to the fact that there would be no second chance, no turning back, and absolutely no safety net. His epic valor was a cathartic study of biblical proportions. Born a common man, he excelled despite his lack of congenital moxie. With properly channeled defiance, he proved that a weakness could be turned into strength. I vicariously sensed the crunch of icy terrain beneath his frostbitten toes. His lack of suitably warm clothing on the winter docks had caused him a unique stride. Two of his toes were nearly lost from the cold's equivalent to trench foot. He never fully recovered from the condition, yet he never whimpered about it. He overcame hunger of such intensity, yet his intuition to march forward prevailed. But through it all, I understood that his only concerns while facing his antagonists were his unborn offspring. He exemplified the capacity of how one man's powerful spirit can alter the course of many lives.

At first, I was choking on heartache. But the longer I hallucinated, the more my mourning turned to resolve. It was as if the wizard behind the curtain had altered me, the Cowardly Lion. I found courage that I had sought for so long. I was the beholder of veritable greatness. The blueprint was right before my eyes. But I paused to ask myself exactly what it was that made my grandfather so outstanding. He had neither fame nor worldly riches. What he did possess in abundance were virtues such as integrity, morality, courage, and self-discipline. Not one of those ideals was inherited or assigned to him. Although somewhere along the line, he must have had role models who demonstrated such qualities, he had to earn these qualities through the trials and errors of his experiences. The truth, then, was that his greatness was not born into him but instead willed into action by his own volition. I recall thinking, *Do we all have the ability to lead or follow a righteous path? Is it simply a matter of not accepting less from ourselves?* The answers seemed quite clear. Our consciences and free will could possibly be disciplined to adhere to a higher standard. My grandfather's biography seemingly endorsed Admiral William F. Halsey's theory: "There are no great men, only great challenges that ordinary men are forced by circumstances to meet." Although the legacy of my grandfather's life greatly inspired me, the memories of our last exchange cast a spell that subverted my serenity.

**True leaders do not command, but rather exemplify
the virtues and values they espouse.**

TEN

Don't Let Anyone Write Your Epitaph

(Barriers are meant to be broken)

At what point do we allow peer pressure to win?

FIRE ACADEMY CLASSES WERE FULL for the next six months. Once my name was affixed to the waiting list, I set sail on unfinished business. Downtime was wasted time when there were so many goals to achieve. I had always been aware that new and larger accomplishments invigorated me, while idle time was the devil's workshop. Not one to purposefully tantalize a guy with a pitchfork and horns, my efforts had to be aligned with the teenage Florida Bodybuilding Championship. It was one of the few state titles universally respected by all national competitors, and at nineteen years old, I did not want to miss my last opportunity to compete as a teenager. Additionally, such intense training would prepare me for the rigorous routine of the fire academy. With such an advanced trio of training partners, what could go wrong?

Each morning's before workout internal psych up revolved around two themes. Primarily, I was motivated to pay tribute to my grandfather's life. His Harriet Tubman initiative and daring had opened doors to possibilities that I refused to squander. The lingering ache of his frostbite surely surpassed my temporary burn from lactic acid. Toughing out high rep sets of hack squats was comparatively a breeze. The second thematic inspiration was not to set limits. I refused to allow my previous personal records to derive my new psychological ceilings. I planned to shatter my old high-water marks, which I'd only established as starting points.

The point of my competitors' fatigue became my opportunity to flourish. I craved others hitting the wall, as it marked my moment of acceleration. There were days when I finished my workouts in solitude because others had dried up their wells. At times, I felt like Chuck Yeager in an X-15, soaring where others hadn't dared. His brilliant quote "Rules are made for people who aren't willing to make up their own" seemed a direct reference to my mental state. We performed sets of "21s" (a high-intensity technique in which seven reps are performed through the bottom half of the range of motion of a given exercise, an additional uninterrupted seven reps are performed through the upper half of the range of motion of that same exercise, and then seven ungodly and burning reps of that same exercise are performed through the entire range of motion—thus the term "21s") for every body part. Drop sets were a standard practice. As soon as the last possible rep at a designated weight was accomplished, just enough weight was removed to continue contractions. There were days when leg press sets would have four or five consecutive plate removals to force one prolonged and agonizing set. During these times, I came to understand that one could achieve a point where all sensation of pain is lost and a surreal out-of-body escapade begins. Crashing through the pain threshold tests every instinct of one's being, but the results are prodigious. Two and three exercise supersets (the bodybuilding term for successive exercises performed one immediately after the other without rest) were added. Partial reps, negatives, and forced reps rounded out the repertoire.

Just as I hit my stride, a wrinkle was added. I received notice that one unexpected opening in the fire academy became available, and they were offering it to me. The catch was that training for the Mr. Florida Championship would need to take place while I was in the heart of the fire academy. Never one to paddle with the stream, I decided that I'd face the waves head-on.

Nature has a way of reminding us who is boss. While enthusiasm can temporarily overcome many obstacles, eventually every flight must land. I never considered quitting either venture. Bodybuilding was sacred, and my career in the fire service was essential. Rappelling down the side of a smoke tower with my knotted biceps elevated a reasonable action to a precarious one. Climbing that seven-story smoke tower multiple times on cramped quadriceps made every stair meaningful. Holding ladders overhead following deltoid supersets of military press and upright rows burned that much more. Still, my uncompromising drive compelled me to continue.

While not unprecedented, finishing number one academically in my class was unforeseen. My study habits were tuned like a Ferrari, but my winding road was bumpier than most. The completion and certification of the academy made me proud, but it left me drawn and overtrained. With barely two weeks before my competition, little time remained to simultaneously harden up and replace emaciated muscle. Once again, with my back against the wall, I dragged my skeletal remains for their predawn torture.

Arriving at the auditorium seemed anticlimactic. While I was harder than I had ever been before, the fullness required for first place was lacking. My heart and drive were second to none, but my honest self-assessment recognized the stacked odds. It was apparent that I'd require alternative tactics to pull off a victory. Emphasizing flowing and artistic posing maneuvers, I did my best to draw attention away from the larger, more deserving competitors.

Immediately before taking center stage for the final results, I walked by a small group of backstage assistants frantically oiling and tanning their prized lightweight. I paused to notice that the same saboteurs whose Rembrandt rendition defaced my initial foray were in the midst of another ambush. The three infamous poop pranksters were about to devastate another beginner. They were prepping the victim's posing trunks with the same strategic brown streak that I ignorantly wore. Before I could come to my co-competitor's aid, we were ushered to our marks on stage. I realized that the poor rookie's uncultured debut was about to elicit the same shame I'd cut my teeth on. I recalled my desire to disappear, knowing how bad he would surely feel when he found out.

While my second place finish was short of the Promised Land, it was a fair and proper decision. Though disappointed and relieved at the same time, there were more important tasks at hand. The devastated rookie dejectedly led his copper racing stripe to the hidden bowels behind the curtains. After a few obligatory photos, I rushed to find his fuming tirade of garbage can tossing. I hugged him with genuine empathy and explained our similar introductions to the sport. He paused and said, "I just want to run away and hide." After a few calming moments, I just shared, "Don't let anyone write your epitaph. You decide how your story ends."

Returning to McDougal's seemed pointless. My three training

partners and I had reached the point where we'd outgrown the gym. While I loved the environment and the gamut of personalities, its minuscule dimensions and restricted amount of weights and machines were no longer adequate. A new massive facility had created quite a stir among bodybuilders, and it fit our expanding aspirations perfectly. Apollo Gym was more than ten times larger than McDougal's, with a multitude of machines and equipment. We were warmly received by a virtual who's who of Florida competitors. Training, which had always been good, reached mythic levels of intensity. The synergistic energy could have lit up Times Square on New Year's Eve. An added bonus was the over-the-top cluster of courteous and attractive people. While McDougal's had a youthful hooligan-type clientele, Apollo reflected the best of many congregations. Lawyers and doctors rubbed elbows with students and models. Many close friendships were rapidly formed.

The owner, Bert, was quiet but cordial. His training partner, Gil, was also a Dade County police officer. Several years earlier, Bob and I had studied Kenpo Karate under Gil's tutelage. Gil had an Incredible Hulk tattoo on his arm, which would come to personify him perfectly. Bert immediately offered me a part-time job working weekends and evenings. While the training environment was hard-core, benign and genial ribbing was abundant. As time passed, a level of endearment and trust developed between many of the members and myself. One attentive couple, John and Reve' Walsh, entrusted their son to my care while they worked out. During these brief periods, little Adam Walsh would color and draw pictures in the office with me, just steps from his mother's workouts. With my workout facility on par with my needs, it was time to focus on my career.

I submitted applications to numerous South Florida fire departments. The economy was spiraling downward in the late 1970s, and fewer openings were posted than usual. However, my high academy ranking, top test scores, and unblemished background gave me high hopes and increased odds. Several departments expressed interest and set up interviews. One such department was Port Everglades Fire Department. One of my academy classmates already worked for Port Everglades. We had teamed up for several challenges during class and developed a good rapport. Hearing of my interest for employment, he kindly offered to have his father put in a good word for me. Their personnel division moved up their interview date and removed some of the customary red tape. The interview and follow-up hiring procedures went well, and I was hired rapidly.

Port Everglades Fire Department was different from most departments. The majority of agencies had a multi-tier organization that delivered both fire suppression (firefighting) and the newly developed emergency medical services (EMS). In addition to fire suppression, Port Everglades personnel were cross-trained as a police agency instead of EMS. Also, Port Everglades' work schedule utilized rotating twelve-hour shifts as opposed to the standard twenty-four-hour tours of duty.

Seeing my newly altered uniform made my widowed grandmother emotional. Her once-mighty chin quivered as she said, "Too bad your grandfather isn't here to see you. He would be so proud." While walking out of our door for the first day of my career, I turned to her and said, "He sees me because he is always with me."

Reality rarely surpasses fantasy, but my work was the exception rather than the rule. I loved my job beyond words. Every alarm and task was as exciting as the invention of the wheel. Unlike most civilian jobs, there were no dull or boring shifts. The low-ranking employees patrolled the port and surrounding neighborhoods. When an alarm sounded, firefighters at the station boarded the engines, and the patrolling personnel met at the location of the incident. Turnout gear, or bunker gear, was donned in order to mitigate the emergency. Auto accidents involving tractor-trailers carrying hazardous materials, shipboard incidents, cruise and naval ship assignments, and injuries were all routine runs.

One evening, a vicious lightning storm besieged South Florida. Dusk had just passed. The alarm sounded just as I was returning to the station from an assignment. I was ordered to leave the patrol car and jump onto the engine with the rest of the crew. As soon as we turned out of the firehouse, a glow extended above a massive land fuel tank to our west. It was apparent that this would be no standard fire. The raging flames pasted blistering waves of radiant hell on any exposed skin. Each step up the external stairway brought us closer to a ringside seat at Gehenna. The inferno swayed and seduced us like a devilish invitation. With the nozzle strategically shielding our vulnerable faces, we advanced until our bounding pulses warned us against further ascension. After fifteen minutes of battling gusting winds, epic heat, and common sense, our labor was rewarded by the fire's retreat. We were greeted as conquerors as we returned to terra firma. In our post-incident assessment, it was brought to our attention how fortunate we were that the floating lid did not tip with the weight of water or our knees. The port commissioners acknowledged our efforts with individual awards for bravery and valor.

The many facets of my life synchronized in such harmony that I felt very secure. A vision of the future lacked only one aspect: marriage. In order to achieve my characteristic desire for balance, I asked for Tina's hand in marriage. Upon her acceptance, the standard steps and measures were set into motion to facilitate our wedding.

Padre performed our ceremony at St. Bartholomew Catholic Church. Our ceremony was conventional and well attended. Although it was pleasant and fun, a few underlying issues prevented the typical fantasy type of setting. My grandfather's absence loomed the heaviest. On such an occasion where delight and exaltation should reign, my heart felt hollow. The other significant concern was that I realized that I loved Tina in the wrong way. I respected her and cared dearly for her, but I was not romantically "in love" with her. Neither mature enough to totally comprehend that concept nor intellectually astute enough to turn back, the show went on.

Returning to work from a short honeymoon, things began to change. My co-worker and former classmate, whose father put in a good word for me, began demanding favors in the form of a quid pro quo. Initially, because of his seniority on the job, he delegated many of his responsibilities to me. This began as simple chores, such as locking gates or retrieving a cup of coffee for him, and then it stepped up to the point where he'd sleep during his turn to patrol and expect me not to report him. Before long, he had me acting as a personal valet to sooth his every whim or desire. Eventually, it metastasized to off-duty demands also. His father desired a case of Chivas Regal scotch whiskey and felt that it would be appropriate for me to purchase it for him. Once I gave him the first case, he requested a second case.

His father was a high-ranking and "connected" delegate for the Democratic Party, and my co-worker demanded that I change my voter registration status from Independent to Democrat. Also, he pressured my father and me into going to Democratic fundraisers and donating cash. He even commanded me to vote for all Democrats and insisted upon seeing my ballot in an upcoming election. His bullying to drive me to the polling place was his reassurance that I'd adhere to his vote tampering. I became his Dred Scott.

On the few occasions that I offered resistance to his stipulations, he actually asked, "How much do you like your job?" It was his way of insinuating that because he helped me get my job, he had the power to take it away. Originally, I bought into the notion that even if his father's "words" only helped a small percentage, the respectful counter-response would be to show appreciation. It finally reached the point where it became clear that no acknowledgment, retort, or "kickback" would ever satisfy him. An explanation of my sentiments was shrugged off with more threats for my job. Several more attempts at mature dialogue were ignored. His next endeavor was to recruit a union crony to criticize and lambaste my every move.

Another union member confided that the union controlled the fire department, and the Democratic Party owned the union. This conjured up childhood memories of my grandfather's conflicts with Mount Vernon's political machine and his earlier exodus from fascism. After much internal debate and chaos, I refused to consent to such duress or servitude. My grandfather had made many sacrifices over a half century earlier to prevent such political tyranny from extorting my freedom. No sum of money or job was worth disrespecting or renouncing those deeds and memories. The part that I do regret is how I mishandled my resignation. The fire chief was always kind to me, and I should have been more honest with him about the reason for my parting. Instead, I simply told him I wanted to pursue another career.

It was possible that Ms. B.'s vengeance and enduring yearbook mischaracterization of me had a subconscious influence. Even though my rationale contained elements of honor, my execution was less than stellar. In fact, it bordered on gutless.

Drive yourself to your own destiny and you'll take control over your life; if you allow yourself to be a passenger, you shouldn't complain.

ELEVEN

Twilight Zone

(Some things just don't make sense)

**How is it that some things we don't understand
still have a profound impact upon us?**

ONCE AGAIN, APPLICATIONS WERE DISPERSED throughout many South Florida fire departments. Full-time employment at Apollo Gym was intended to bridge the gap between the present and the future. The more time I spent at the gym, the more the complete world of hard-core bodybuilding came into light. There were several occasions when used syringes were found in the trash. Sympathetically, I pitied the "poor diabetic" who required such medical necessities. I had been blessed with excellent health, and it was sad for others to be so unfortunate. Eventually, though, reality replaced my compassion.

One afternoon, Bert requested my assistance in replacing acoustic ceiling tiles in the men's room, following a roof leak. As we were nearing completion, one tile seemed more burdensome to remove than the others. It was much heavier and required two people's efforts. Suddenly, the center of the tile collapsed under the oppressive mass of hundreds of used syringes, ampoules, and vials. They precipitated like daggers to the ground. The locker room floor looked like Dr. Frankenstein's laboratory. Absolutely astounded, blood drained to my feet as the magnitude of our discovery set in. Contrary to my reaction, Bert calmly put all the contraband into a garbage bag and placed it in the trunk of his car. I doubtlessly rationalized to myself that Bert would later dispose of the items discreetly and then search for the culprits.

Late one evening, while preparing to close the gym, I made my last rounds to assure myself that I had completed all my duties. Stepping into the locker room was like walking into Rod Serling's *Twilight Zone*. Totally unfazed by my clumsy entrance, two gym members carried out their deliriously idiotic exploit. Frozen with jaw agape and eyelids expanded, I watched in amazement. Mark was bent over the filthy toilet, leaning on its back tank, with his navy blue warm-up pants at his ankles. Kevin plunged a syringe deep into Mark's right buttock, which was covered with the telltale acne associated with testosterone usage. As soon as Kevin finished inserting the potion into Mark, they promptly changed positions. Using the same contaminated hypodermic needle, Mark lined up his target. As Mark's hand thrust forward, the loosely held needle bounced off Kevin's flexed and equally blemished cheek before falling into the toilet. Mark reached into the nasty water and retrieved the dripping vessel. He simply shook it off and successfully delivered Kevin's dose of pharmaceuticals. Incapable of silence any longer, I burst out with, "Are you guys freaking crazy?" They unapologetically laughed and strolled out of Apollo.

A few mornings later, I received an important phone call at Apollo Gym. A deep voice from California was inquiring about me and a few other competitors. The professional yet friendly gentleman's attention focused on my goals and accomplishments. Representing *Muscle Digest* magazine, Louis requested a resume from me for possible employment. His embellishing statements were flattering. Excitedly, I expressed him an overnight package containing my resume, samples of my writing, and competition photos. Before I could blink, I was offered the opportunity to take over the editor in chief position for one of bodybuilding's famous magazines. I was ecstatic. A whirlwind of activity went into our relocation to Los Angeles.

One day before our move, a frantic Reve' and John Walsh notified us at the gym that their adorable son Adam was missing. He was last seen in the Sears department store at the Hollywood Mall. They requested as many gym members as possible to form a search party for little Adam. Missing children cases were not heavily publicized at the time, so there was a natural propensity to expect a positive conclusion. The only story of a kidnapping that I recalled was the 1932 Charles Lindbergh Jr. nightmare that I had read about, and that seemed far too horrific to occur to friends of mine. So, of course, I believed that the beloved child of friends, who innocently drew pictures while sitting on my lap, would turn up fine. Our flight left on the morning of the scheduled search. Hence, I was not able to participate, and I left in a preoccupied and somber mood. Upon arrival in Los Angeles, I immediately called home, expecting that Adam had been found, and that there was a straightforward explanation. Although concerned, I hoped that my prayers for his safe return would be answered.

Muscle Digest had a reputation for turning out authoritarian articles intended for devout followers of my beloved sport. I anticipated meeting the publisher. Louis was nice and helpful, and I was sure that his immaterial phrase about Mr. W's eccentric behavior was exaggerated. Two seconds into our initial meeting proved Mr. W to be an amplified caricature far beyond Louis's description. We were called into a squalid storage room with folding chairs that had cat feces on them. Numerous feral cats, with the accompanying pungency one would expect from an unkempt litter box, dodged our hesitant steps. Tina and I paused beside two seats, grappling with the most appropriate way to perch alongside stool samples without offending our host. Mr. W nonchalantly brushed our speed bumps off the chairs with his bare hands, saying, "Oh, that's no big deal." Before the hardened remnants hit the floor, we went blank. At that point, he could have either read excerpts from *Gone with the Wind* or explained Einstein's Theory of Relativity, and we would not have heard a word. Tina and I had matching vacancies from our chins to our hairlines. We were miles away … but of the same uneasy viewpoint. We were disgusted and instantaneously recognized that my foot would not fit into Mr. W's glass slipper. A short while later, as his parting handshake awakened me from my stupor, he mumbled a sentence about a pending bankruptcy.

Later, Louis clarified that *Muscle Digest* had, in fact, filed for bankruptcy. I had just dragged my wife three thousand miles across the country to discover that our California gold was actually litter lumps. From the second that Mr. W's hand connected with the cat droppings, Tina wanted to return to Florida. I was not about to give up so easily.

My workouts had become my refuge from the antagonists of the world. Surely, I believed, solace awaited me in the famous gyms of Southern California. Upon stumbling upon Arnold Schwarzenegger and Franco Columbu at World's Gym, I was convinced that all would be fine. Until, that was, I made the mistake to ask the Austrian Oak a question about training. I truly anticipated that one of my heroes would give me a friendly and helpful response. That's why the belittling tirade that his massively developed frame dished at me caught me completely off guard. He castigated everything from my height to my haircut. By the time the last maligning words were absorbed by my meek ears, I wanted to crawl under a dumbbell. To me, his conduct was shameful. He should have realized that recognizable public figures are the face of every sport, and such egotistically driven mortification of a novice was unjustifiable. I vowed never to treat any human being as my inferior, regardless of my achievements. Arnold's overbearing and totally uncalled for territorial triumph convinced me that Santa Monica might not be the paradise I'd thought it was. To avoid any further contact with my once-idolized bodybuilding superstar, we decided to settle in Orange County.

We both immediately sought forms of income. Tina quickly gained employment at a child care facility. My nutritional experience landed me a position at a vitamin and supplement store next to El Toro Marine Air Base in Irvine. The economy was in a recession, and employment was more difficult than usual to secure. While Tina constantly verbalized her wishes to move back to Florida, I was resolute about making our move result in a positive conclusion. I also began volunteering for the Los Alamitos Naval Station Fire Department. It was my foot in the door for eventual full-time employment. My days were full. Early morning training at Dan Howard's Gym in Fountain Valley took place before every sunrise. This time, I was quite careful not to ask training questions of anyone resembling a competitive bodybuilder. Employment at the health food store or volunteering at the naval base saturated the vast part of my day. My spare time was filled with writing tons of song lyrics, which always increased when I was depressed. Whenever possible, I called home for updates about Adam Walsh.

Certain events in life impact us so abruptly that the metamorphosis leaves us transformed forever. Such was the horrific phone call about beautiful Adam's fate. When my father explained the previous day's gruesome discovery, my purity was also decapitated forever. I recall looking upward and screaming, "My God, how could you let that happen?" I became bitterly enraged and livid at God. All the glow and effervescence of my childhood was ripped, like an unanesthetized surgical procedure, from my foundation. The raw wound festered like a daily dose of acid. Each day, I awoke to recall that yesterday's nightmare was today's poison. I thought back to Adam's soft angelic voice, and how his face would light up when Reve' smiled at him. How the bounce in his fledgling walk gleefully carried him to the safety of John's arms. *How could such cruelty be directed at such a clean slate? I* agonized. *Monsters were supposed to be in science fiction, not real life. And what must John and Reve' be going through?*

I wanted to kill whoever could have looked at Adam with vile thoughts; imagine what John must have been feeling. Then the sensationalizing tabloids began transforming John and Reve' into negligent parents. They were wonderful people who had their hearts gnawed on by hungry jackals. I recalled helping Reve' prepare for a figure competition, which she won. It was her special moment, when her insecurities absconded just enough for shy smiles to radiate elation. The pride on John's face was so obvious when his beautiful bride was announced as the winner. Life was so unfair! My faith was tested more than during any other time in my existence. I could not pray without scolding God anymore. I must have asked the same question a thousand times: *Why?*

Then one day, while attempting to traverse the fissure with my Maker, a long-forgotten image of a whiskered vagrant emerged from my memory. The suddenness of the flashback frightened me. When the imprints were first engraved into my gray matter, they were quite humorous. But on this day, all facetiousness was absent. My recollection of a laughable childlike man with a prominent chin singing to my cousin Charlie, my brother, and me outside of Sears suddenly became ominous. About eight years earlier, by the west entrance to Sears at the Hollywood Mall, a disheveled stranger approached us on two separate occasions. Our naive perspective of the world caused his songs and idiotic chatter to be little more than fodder for our immature wisecracks. The peculiar part, though, was that one of his songs stuck somewhere in my subconscious as he crooned, "Hippie dippy, pumpkin pie, kissed the girls and made them cry." His sidewalk solo was the focus of our amusement, along with his oversized clownlike shoes. Somehow ignored at the time, but now so daunting, were his intimate questions and attempts to solicit personal information. The long ago summer of "Tie a Yellow Ribbon 'Round the Old Oak Tree" and "Bad, Bad Leroy Brown" abruptly took on a significance that I needed to share. I asked myself, *Could this be the clue the police might need to find Adam's murderer?* I could not be sure, so I immediately called long distance to the Hollywood Police Department.

The detective who took my call made me feel like I was a wacko. His repetitive stressing of the eight-year gap between our drifter's ballads and Adam's abduction drove home his belief that I was wasting his time. Unsatisfied with the results of my first tip, I made a second attempt. This time, I insisted that the second detective allow me to finish speaking. But he was also doubtful and contentious. Lacking the confidence to compel or insist upon an investigation, I regretfully deserted my duty to pursue any further action.

Years later, after Ottis Toole died of liver failure in a Florida prison, he was named as the likely suspect in Adam's brutal murder. As his somberly familiar photos surfaced in the news media as the deceased perpetrator, my regrets blossomed into abject guilt. We had actually encountered a man that seemed to be the alleged murderer whose own grandmother pridefully dubbed him "the devil's child."

The phone calls home grew longer and more passionate. Each "I love you" was professed with more emphasis. I yearned even more for the Sunday family dinners. But I had business to take care of. Tina's relentless homesickness had to take a backseat.

Our menial jobs paid significantly less than our Florida employment had. Also, California's taxes and cost of living far exceeded what we were accustomed to. Each week that passed, we fell deeper into a financial hole. We were traveling one step forward and two steps back. We had an efficiency apartment with a fold-up Murphy bed directly adjacent to the kitchen. One could truly have fallen out of bed for breakfast. Our only furniture was an army-style trunk that served as a sofa, chair, and table. Our only source of light in the evening was a caged automobile drop light.

As time went on, meals became scarce. We barely had enough to sustain us through each day. Waking up with hunger pangs served as our barnyard rooster. Then we shamefully discovered our answer for dinner. We walked to a local grocery store. Grabbing a shopping cart, we'd blend in by placing numerous items in the cart before beelining to the bulk food canisters. Both of us selected our evening's delicacies with the vivacity of a Vegas buffet line. We meandered through the aisles until our guilt was temporarily superseded by gastric satisfaction. As self-incriminating as it is to admit, that routine went on for almost a week.

I justified my disgraceful behavior and remorse by blaming and taunting God with blasphemy over the loss of Adam. While dishonoring myself, I couldn't erase the thought of my grandfather eating rotten bananas to avoid lowering himself to the depth that I had plunged. I wondered how many nights, if any, he lay under the midnight sky and chastised God for Satan's stunts. As lonely as he was, he couldn't hear the reassuring voice of a loved one on the other end of a phone. As many times as he was called "wop" and "Guinea," how did he not get bitter? As his kidney began to fail, I could not imagine what kind of fortitude he must have had never to cry out, "I've had enough." Like a slap in my face, I stood up and proclaimed to myself, *Enough!*

I immediately sat Tina down and explained how sickened I was by my actions, and I told her that my excuses for continuing such shameful behavior were over. I immediately called Padre for a long-distance version of confession. He reminded me to pause and say a quick prayer each time I felt temptation's alluring tug. I prayed that evening with much more humbleness and contriteness. While praying, I thought of how Moses was allowed to have endured so much strife and hardship to prepare him for God's plan. I saw the similarity to my grandfather's adversity. Then there was a sudden and uncomfortable ugliness when the dissimilarities of my circumstances were discerned. I had deceived myself with an internal shell game by falsely viewing my motivations as gallant and virtuous. The barren deserts they overcame were in the service of others. My trivial blips from pleasure were self-serving. I was nowhere near the man whose genes I carried. Any other conclusion was delusional and a charade.

The next morning, my mother called and told us that my sister-in-law, Valerie, was pregnant. Tina wept with happiness. Then she paused and said, "But we won't be there." She hugged me and begged, "Please take me home. I want to be a family again."

My mother, still on the phone, echoed Tina's request to reunite our family. She said, "We need you."

In a peculiar and unexpected way, we had discovered our journey's purpose, and I understood my lesson.

We are molded by, and thus the products of, our experiences, regardless of their darkness or complexities.

TWELVE

No One Has It Easy

(Returning to my new reality)

Can we go home again?

THE CONSISTENTLY GENEROUS BERT IMMEDIATELY rehired me at Apollo Gym. Respectful of his business, I made him fully aware that my career as a firefighter would soon take precedence. I once again supplemented training with adequate nutrition, and quick weight gain ensued. In so many ways, it was as if we had not skipped a beat. However, several months away from my parents brought my attention to some changes. The once invincible look of my father was replaced with a more vulnerable appearance. His Elvis Presley coiffure was becoming overrun with streaks of silver interspersed with glances of bare scalp. His stern look made way for a more passive presence. But his example of unselfish labor remained unaltered. My mother, once the showpiece of perpetual motion, had lost a half step. The daily grind's friction had modified her movements. Bella, still adjusting to the loss of her mate, lacked some clarity of thought. Each response required an extra second as she searched for an answer. I was witnessing the onset of the waning process.

Testing procedures placed me near the top of Pembroke Pines Fire Department's hiring list. Within a few months, I lost my civilian status for the second time. This time, my desire to become a paramedic fueled my excitement. The first step was the completion of what is referred to as "death camp." It was the department's version of boot camp, and it served as an ego boost for the aging officers who needed to assert authority. The Napoleonic complex was clearly alive and well within a few of those chieftains. Physical challenges were one of my strengths, so I faced it without anxiety. Some probationary firefighters had never experienced the restrictive rules and rigors of the profession, so trepidation was everywhere. I had a definitive advantage, both physically and mentally. I breezed through every phase with nary a missed step. Other than a minor case of shin splints in both lower legs, I was unscathed. Within a few weeks, a distinct line of demarcation separated those who were "on the bubble" from those whose pre-class preparation was evident. Due to difficulties involving their low levels of physical fitness, a few individuals faced the possibility of expulsion daily.

Unofficially, I quickly assumed the role of class leader. Each time my classmates were faced with extra punishment, such as running or push-ups, I chose to perform their sanctioned tasks alongside them. My initiative and constant pep talks squeaked two classmates through to graduation. I derived tremendous satisfaction from the knowledge that my efforts helped them benefit.

Shift duty was once again fantastic. There was an immediate bond with several other rookies, who remain close friends to this day. While work was tough, it was like a fraternity. There is no other endeavor where one moment the loss of human life from horrific circumstances must be handled, followed by practical jokes and belly laughs the next. The awareness that our lives were dependent on each other's knowledge and daily unsung heroics drew us closer. Someone else's mistake or poor judgment could have potentially resulted in another's injury or funeral. The escalation of trust came as a direct benefit of not wanting to let other crew members down. We shared and discovered intricate personal details about each other by living within such close proximity. Nothing became off limits. Sarcastic comments about each other's unique or embarrassing body parts were commonplace. Some guys even shared their wives' or lovers' bedroom preferences, turn-ons, and hang-ups.

One morning, after transporting a patient to a local emergency room, a conversation began about the ethical, righteous, and virginal women that one would choose to marry. We contrasted them with the vampy type or seductive women. Mike, an upright and respectable paramedic, claimed that his new girlfriend would never check guys out or gawk at men. He explained that her noble innocence would prevent any acts that could be construed as "whorish."

I interjected that I did not believe that simply looking at a person of the opposite sex was a testament against a person's purity. Jim, one of my favorite workmates, agreed strongly with me. I expressed to Mike that I was sure his girlfriend was a wonderful and admirable girl, but I was equally positive that she instinctively glanced at men she believed to be attractive. I continued that while she likely would not ogle another man, riveting her eyes on him, I was sure she was not oblivious to her surroundings. Mike vehemently opposed our perspective and assured us that any girl who would stoop that low should be shunned and disregarded as a tramp. Jim and I scoffed at Mike's double standard and expressed that we both looked at women while retaining our principles; we did not lust or covet. We felt that women should be allotted the same criteria. Mike's orthodox and pious upbringing provided him with a more straightforward view.

After twenty minutes of contentious back-and-forth agitation and typical debate, we agreed on a tactic to resolve our disagreement. I came up with the warped idea that I would place an enormous Ace bandage strategically in my pants to give the illusion that I was an incognito porn star. Then we would test my theory by finding an agreed-upon "sweet and innocent" girl. Jim, always one to instigate firehouse pranks, suggested that Mike's charming girlfriend should be our laboratory rat. I quickly jumped in and disagreed because I did not want our tongue-in-cheek experiment to potentially devastate Mike's relationship. Upon hearing my caution, Mike insisted that his chaste mate absolutely would prove Jim and me wrong. Reluctantly, I agreed to test our hypothesis.

Coincidentally, Mike's prudish partner just so happened to be working around the corner from our location. In preparation for proving my supposition, I reached for the largest Ace bandage on our truck. It would have made John Holmes envious. With the diligence of Michelangelo perfecting a cartoonish version of his *David*, I placed my extra appendage in the exact protruding position to illicit the maximum affect. The front panel of my trousers was screaming for mercy, much as a training bra would appear on the French dancer and actress Lolo Ferrari. With our preparations complete and our contradictory conjectures established, we sadly divulged Mike's error in philosophy.

As Mike led us into his darling's office, her unsuspecting pristine reputation was about to be pulverized before Mike's judgmental eyes. As their unimpeachable glances met, it was obvious that mutual respect and admiration existed. Their puppy love was clearly childlike and wholesome. My firsthand view of this display of incorruptibility made me vacillate as far as our unfair test. My shame for what I knew would occur twisted my guts, but my embarrassment about backing out kept me from retreating.

As Mike introduced me, I sheepishly stepped from behind the door to unveil a dose of reality to Mike and his girlfriend. As she instantly focused on the humongous alien object attempting to escape from below my belt, the rest of her surroundings seemed to vanish. As hard as she tried to break the curse, her eyes were incapable of pulling away from the monstrosity before her. As she sat at her desk, my slowly swaying hips apparently hypnotized her, as the rotating giant was practically at face level. Still staring, she knocked a pencil holder and book to the floor as her flailing hands reached for objects without the aid of her preoccupied eyeballs. As she stepped from behind the desk to pick up the book from the ground, her agape-jawed expression came within inches of the protruding menace. Still, she remained fixated and under its spell.

Slowly standing up and totally incognizant of Mike's presence, she blurted out to me, "I'll bet you're a real lady killer!" Just then, from the hallway and out of sight, Jim hysterically chided, "She's saying she likes pain!" Totally disconnected from Jim's giddiness, she added, "Has anyone ever told you that you have the most beautiful blue eyes?" It must be noted that I have greenish hazel eyes, not blue. Jim then roared out, "She means you have beautiful blue pants!"

With that awakening, Mike lashed out at all three of us in the room. He stomped down the echoing hallway while shouting that Jim and I were "a--holes!" Even as Mike exited in enraged and loud fashion, Miss Saintly never acknowledged her man's departure. His stormy farewell signaled the conclusion to his high-minded dreams, and I immediately recognized the pain and disgusting impact that I'd caused. With my head down, I slithered away like a seductive serpent. While the scales on my cold-blooded belly attempted to catch up to Mike, Jim was doubled over in laughter. Our innocent victim was still pleading with me to return to her office, presumably for one last glimpse of the python-like bait. It was clear she had fallen for the false advertisement.

As superficially funny as that was, I was disappointed in myself for callously utilizing other people's heartache for my entertainment.

The guilt made it difficult to comfortably converse with Mike for quite some time.

Still, though, we shared family birthdays, home improvements, and vacations off duty. During the pre-9/11 days, the public was indifferent about our job's inherent risks. Fortunately, the esprit de corps within the ranks always created pride.

My chosen career path was emergency medical services, but that required much additional college time. So over the next three years, I once again torched my entire candle. I worked twenty-four-hour shifts while attending college. As tough as it was, the subject matter was fascinating and rewarding. At the time, very few firefighters were paramedics, so the intricate knowledge of human anatomy, physiology, and emergency medicine placed one among the elite. While always the focal point of well-intended teasing, those who performed advanced life support were given a higher level of respect. Life was going almost too well. It was just a matter of time before something had to give.

One Saturday evening, my wife and I were out for dinner with Bob and his wife, Maria. A familiar officer from another fire department approached our table. He informed me that he'd just returned from a local hospital, where my father had been admitted into the emergency room. We rushed to find out that the remaining male leader of our family had a myocardial infarction (heart attack). Suddenly, our path was unsure again. Although my father's heart damage was minor, it was clear that the external changes I had observed had a matching internal component. My mother relied on my interpretation of the medical jargon. Her emotions swayed with each of my assessments of the test results. Having my expertise soothed her and brought calm to an otherwise worrisome condition. Recognizing that we'd dodged a bullet, I had an added incentive to master my profession.

My father's rehab was brief and incomplete because he knew my mother and grandmother were dependent upon his income. He barely hesitated in his long-established routine to allow his intravenous site to coagulate, and then he was climbing behind, lifting, and diagnosing appliances again.

A few days later, during my early workout, I shared our family's woes with Gil. It appeared that he too was dealing with problems of his own. His pirate-like eye patch, and obviously morose mood, led me to believe it was time to talk and empathize. He started the conversation by explaining that his resemblance to Long John Silver resulted from a flying lead shaving landing in his eye while he clanked dumbbells together. During our brief talk, he expressed how unhappy he had been with his police career and said that he was quitting law enforcement to buy into Apollo Gym. I frivolously uttered, "You must have robbed a bank to get that kind of money." He seemed to pay no attention to my flippant statement. I had mixed emotions, though, because I remembered my hardship when I quit my first fire service job, and I did not want Gil to suffer. Yet I selfishly looked forward to seeing him more often.

Following my shower, as I was about to leave the gym, a familiar member hugged me with tears squeezing from both eyes. She explained that her brother and two friends were murdered in a remote fishing campground in the Everglades. Our hearts, separated by inches and flesh, commiserated together. After some sincere condolences and words of encouragement, I thought, *I guess no one has it easy.*

Months later, my brother and sister-in-law added eight pounds of love to our family. As wonderful as Anthony's birth was, there was also relief because of the miscarriage of Valerie's first pregnancy, which had instigated our return from California. We all fought for time with our gift from God. My nephew Anthony was the perfect balance for the world's heartaches. In referencing his birth, Bella said, "For everyone God takes, he replaces with another." While she was making it clear that our family gained Anthony to replace my grandfather, I also thought of little Adam Walsh. In addition to Anthony's presence, Gil's excited phone call elevated our blessings. Gil's cheer was a pleasant alternative to his recent pensive demeanor. He shared that he and his wife, Nelli, were expecting their first child. His contentment allowed me to share in his jubilation.

A separate phone call interrupted my busy schedule one day. Friends from high school called me with an awful account of how a mutual classmate, who was also a gym member, had been killed. Their newsflash floored me. He was such a well-liked and friendly person. "What is this world coming to?" I expressed.

Weeks later, during a chest workout, I overheard a loud wail from across the gym. It came from two members sharing a shocking account of a different gym mate who was found dead. Gil and I sat for a while and discussed the peculiar and freakish coincidences of the ostensibly unrelated deaths. A macabre mood rolled into Apollo like San Francisco fog.

Still digesting the bizarre disjointed murders, I decided it was time for good news. I reciprocated a call to Gil and Nelli to advise them that Tina was pregnant as well. We were walking on cloud nine. The amount of love that Anthony brought to our family would now be compounded. So much promise and fulfillment was being bestowed upon us. Still, the thought that my grandfather would never hold Anthony or my child was sad.

Both Tina's and Nelli's stomachs began showing their pregnancies right away. Both were frequent gym users, and their two blossoming middles were the perfect antidote for the confusion surrounding our slain members. Plus, it certainly gave me reason to pay closer attention during obstetrical clinics at school.

Late one evening, my home phone awoke us. I had heard my name pronounced and emphasized many ways over the years. But this short-of-breath and relieved-to-hear-my-voice version made the hair stand up on the back of my neck. The urgency in my mother's voice alerted every emergency measure within me, informing me that what was to follow was serious. Her adrenal glands contorted her tongue into a stumbling and twisting spasm that would not cooperate with her desire to deliver her thoughts. Her stuttering utterances finally spit out, "Dad had a heart attack—hurry to the hospital!" Without another word, I was at the hospital. This time, the temperament of the physicians was different. Their phrases were spoken faster and with more emphasis. They called us into a quiet half-lit room and told of my father's status. His electrocardiogram showed signs of severe ischemia (lack of oxygen), and they needed to rush him to the catheterization laboratory. We signed a stack of unexplained and unread documents, kissed my father's ashen face, and watched him disappear down a long hallway. For only the second time in my life, I noted the presentation of my father's emotions in the form of a teardrop.

Within an hour, we were advised that surgeons were preparing my father for cardiac bypass surgery. Our hustle and bustle slowed to a snail's pace for an all-night vigil. Each tick of the audible second hand seemed to pause as if to remind each of us how precious time together was. Our imploring prayers reminded me of when my grandfather's life was restored. Distress was not kind to my mother's features. She looked drawn and spent. It was obvious that her thoughts had explored many unpleasant possibilities. But with each hour, she moved closer to me, until we were leaning on each other. I also sensed that our connection did not stop at a superficial level. She was deriving her strength from my assurances and confidence. By morning, there was an implied understanding that all decisions and answers would pass through me.

As the doctor finally approached, after eight hours, my mother looked toward me first, as if to impress upon the surgeon who was in charge. Noticing her body language, the physician explained to me that my father had had quadruple bypasses and made it through the surgery.

Entering the cardiac intensive care unit was sobering for all of us. My mother approached the man she had always considered "her rock" with the same pampering gentleness with which she tended to little Anthony. Her maternal instincts had immobilized her marital status, and she was now the mommy. She stroked his arm and spoke to his comatose ear with the sweet affection they hadn't exchanged since courting. He no longer looked like the invincible daddy I'd hid behind as a child when I was scared. Neither did he display the vitality of the pretend pony upon whose back I galloped. Hidden was the aggressiveness that challenged and conquered many who had dared to disregard his machismo.

Walking into that room containing a grand assortment of lifesaving devices, I figuratively looked up with awe to my father's enduring grip on us. A realignment of the galaxy repositioned our orbits so that my revolutions migrated closer to the center of the family's universe. Unlike the greed and cunning of Genghis Khan, this seizure of power was one of necessity. When I kissed my father's hand, my ascension to the position of eminence was all but complete.

We must be flexible because life is forever changing.

THIRTEEN

The New King

(The birth of a new dynasty)

Will ecstasy and sorrow balance out?

MY FATHER APPEARED TO BE recovering well from his quadruple cardiac artery bypass surgery and the following complication of a pulmonary embolism. Frugal living relieved any excess financial pressure that could have compounded our emotions. Out of every situation, I discovered, a lesson can be gathered. While never falling into the "keep up with the Jones'" trap kept my family from living the high life, it certainly aided during times of tumult. They never had collection agencies requesting overdue payments, and they never faced the threat of foreclosure. By living within their means, they not only survived economically, but their example formed a deterrent against foolish spending habits for me.

The whirlwind of life's conflicts dealt out sadness at times and satisfaction at others. As the pendulum returned from the depression of my father's surgeries, it swung toward elation. The protruding midsection that Nelli had sported for forty weeks vanished with the introduction of a healthy son. Ironically, Uncle Henry's second marriage produced a baby at the same time Gil and Nelli's child was born. Visiting the hospital brought double the pleasure. Henry's daughter was also wondrously healthy and perfectly normal. Henry's diminutive addition had the instant mellowing effect that nearly sixty years of hard knocks could not. The sudden tenderness he displayed when he coddled his daughter was no less shocking than it would be to watch Madonna have an overnight conversion into Mother Teresa. An area within Henry that had been untapped was now a burgeoning garden of sensitivity. The tears irrigating his cheeks with happiness seemed so out of place on the man who'd derided male emotions just a few scant months earlier. Appraising the magical affects of childbirth had me pondering what its effect would have on me.

Graduating from school as the valedictorian of my class was fulfilling. It is always satisfying to be recognized by one's peers for exceptional efforts. It was particularly gratifying because I had a passion for my career. The subject matter fascinated me, and it was applicable to everyday living. Pembroke Pines Fire Department rewarded my achievement by placing me in command of a rescue squad. I was so lucky to have had extraordinary personnel assigned with me. Two of my favorites, Roger and Jim, were hired as part of the same probationary class I was. We developed an unequaled working relationship. As my grandfather always said, "Each finger has a purpose," and the three of us worked like different fingers on one hand. During the most difficult of calls, we coordinated well and performed our duties with expertise. I rarely needed to give out orders, as our unity and symbiotic coactions meshed perfectly. As much as we blended during times of critical need, we developed a strong diversionary comedic side. When not on emergency runs or training, we constantly carried on like fools. It was the best of both worlds.

Less than two months after graduating, the powers of a love beyond my comprehension elevated me to a heavenly state. I had never lacked the feelings of commitment and appreciation that were essential for relationships, but this burst of adulation and devotion was like the impact of a freight train. All that I had held dear was suddenly thrust aside for the entrance of Matthew, my little man. I felt as if I were floating above all the insignificant issues that seemed to encapsulate mankind. The wasted grievances and contrived worries that we humans grapple with were rendered meaningless. It was as if a new king of my empire was born, and I volunteered as his servant. As days passed, I had an awakened perspective of my parents' sacrifices for me. I suddenly comprehended the magnitude of their selfless existence.

Holding Matt seemed quite natural. There was no doubt that he was as much a part of me as my own flesh and blood. Feeding him was exciting, as he peered at me with undeveloped vision. Small involuntary movements that expressed his contentment as I fed him formula bridged our communication gap. Even changing diapers was one more way to bond and exchange contact. The day my leave ended, my tears symbolized the agony of disrupting the routine I had come to revere.

At shift lineup, I proudly brandished Matt's photos like a schoolboy playing show-and- tell. I was aware that others did not share the intensity of emotions I had for my newborn, but I used any excuse to look at Matt's pictures or talk about him. Jim and Roger sensed my giddiness and exploited my mood into an excuse to cut loose even more than usual. My first day back on duty came to be known by Jim, Roger, and myself as the "day from hell." Over the years, each time we reminisced about it, hearty laughter made it difficult to contain ourselves.

Our first run, early into the shift, necessitated transporting a patient to a hospital far outside our city's boundaries. Upon proper transfer of the patient to the receiving hospital, our blissful mood reached an even higher level. Jim, a well-known slave to the King's and the Golden Arch's fast food, decided to order breakfast at a Burger King drive-through. While I was aware that fire department rules strictly prohibited drive-through use, my joyous feeling could have been coaxed into doing nearly anything. Once Jim's breakfast order was placed, our rescue truck's clanking diesel engine went into cardiac arrest.

After several frenetic minutes of unsuccessful attempts to restart the engine, it became apparent that we needed mechanical assistance. Jim notified our dispatch center that we had vehicle problems, but he craftily gave them a different location so as not to get us into trouble. He believed that it would take about an hour for help to arrive, leaving us plenty of time to push our vehicle several blocks to the location he'd given. A chief who happened to be out of our city on a special detail overheard our radio transmission and advised us that he was "around the corner" from the false location Jim had given. Panicking to reach our erroneous address before the cavalry's arrival, two of us ran to the rear of our heavy rig and began pushing it like an insane exercise technique. We were saturated with perspiration from the July humidity and lunacy of our mischievous exertion. Just as we cleared the Burger King parking lot, thinking we were home free, we were startled by the yelp of our astute chief's siren. He was directly behind us and had caught us red-handed. Aware of Jim's insatiable appetite for the crowned one's junk food, the chief laughed it off and teased us about it for years.

After switching rescue vehicles, we were quickly back in service.

Still chuckling about our chaotic caper, we received our second alarm of the day. Roger strategically parked our vehicle in front of the ill person's home, and we all retrieved our designated equipment. As the three of us advanced to the patient's front door, we noticed that our rescue truck had abandoned us and was rolling down the street. Roger had forgotten to place the transmission into park, thus resulting in a runaway vehicle. The "Three Stooges" dropped the equipment and dashed behind the truck in an attempt to catch it before it crashed. Just as Jim and I were about one foot from the rear bumper, the vehicle abruptly stopped, causing us to implant ourselves into the rear of it. Fleet-footed Roger had beaten us to the cab and applied the brakes. Fortunately, Roger prevented an accident. Unfortunately, both Jim and I lacerated our knees and suffered numerous abrasions to our pulverized faces.

We handled the emergency without incident once at the patient's side, although we required much more treatment than the patient did. Our once-pristine uniforms were torn and drenched, we had road rash, and we were bleeding from numerous areas.

A short time later, we were sent to a shopping center to pick up some items for our captain. The outdated replacement vehicle that we were now in did not have a functioning lock on the medicine compartment door. Always clever and cagey, Jim had noticed that each time we returned to our vehicle, I fanatically kept checking that none of the medications had been stolen. As I approached our vehicle with the captain's goods, I habitually and predictably opened the medical compartment again. As I opened the heavy door to the massive compartment, a gruesome face with an associated bloodcurdling scream followed the path of the opening door. Before I was able to formulate a thought, my petrified reaction was to slam the heavy diamond plate door shut as I jumped backward. Within a second, I realized that the gruesome face was familiar. It was Jim's contorted Quasimodo impression in an attempt to scare me. Without my knowledge, Jim had crawled into the medical compartment to hide. Realizing the creature was actually my partner, I sheepishly reopened the squeaky door. Lying there unconscious and bloodied, with diamond-plated impressions imbedded on his face, was Jim. Roger was hysterical as I helped our battered and hapless co-worker.

Thank goodness our *Creature Feature* actor quickly awoke, and he'd suffered no serious injuries. However, by the time our tour of duty ended the next morning, we looked as if we'd returned from Gettysburg rather than Pembroke Pines. Thus, over the years, many fire personnel embellished our legendary day from hell into a saga on par with *The Adventures of Huckleberry Finn* and *Tom Sawyer*.

Off duty, my attention was divided between my father's rehabilitation for his inevitable return to work and our family's additions. The added responsibilities allowed for no rest, but I still never missed a single workout. I immersed myself into the father role. Each time my son required diaper changes or feeding, I jumped at the chance. Sleep deprivation became as common to me as to inmates of the Hanoi Hilton. It was a rarity to have a quiet night shift while assigned to a rescue squad. And it was certain that my son required an average of two nightly feedings and the corresponding diaper changes. Our fire department had a shortage of paramedics, which meant overtime shifts were much too abundant.

The western region of our city had a drag strip and one of South Florida's only concert venues: the Hollywood Sportatorium. All premiere bands and musical artists included this arena on their tour schedules. Several paramedics were required at all concerts. Each weekend, consequently, I ended up working overtime on a detail at the drag strip, a concert at the Sportatorium, or both. Many famous musicians requested oxygen or some other form of first aid, which allowed us to meet them backstage.

One weekend, Elton John was scheduled to perform on both Friday and Saturday evenings. On Friday, I was assigned to work at Elton's concert. Having grown up as a true fanatic of his brought me an added sense of excitement. Once at the concert, I noticed that Elton's bodyguard was a gentleman I had trained with while living in California. I expressed to him my lifelong affinity for Elton's music. Unbelievably, he arranged for a private meeting the following night. As a gift, I bought a Miami Dolphins hat for Elton. We discussed music collaborations, and for his review, I gave him some lyrics that I had written. During our brief meeting, he showed tremendous interest in my fire department jumpsuit and my badge. In a moment of weakened confusion, I gave Elton both the jumpsuit and the badge. Although inspired by the opportunity to meet him, some of the luster was removed and I was saddened to realize that one of my true idols appeared to be high and jittery to the point of being uncomfortable in his own skin.

While he will always retain a special spot in my heart, I actually pitied him that evening, seeing him as a vulnerable and insecure individual rather than the superstar his talent represented. My disappointment triggered me to vow that if I was ever in a powerful and influential position to be such a role model, I would remember how much my conduct and behavior could impact others.

A few days later, a picture of Elton wearing my jumpsuit and shining badge while frolicking at a Florida amusement park appeared in the local paper. As the photo was circulated around the fire department, one of our administrators caught wind of Elton's use of "official fire department property." I was called on the carpet to answer for my choice of gifts to give him. I volunteered to pay for the items, and this poorly thought out episode of my charity quietly went away.

Meanwhile, my father's rehab was successful enough to allow him to return to work. The same brazen attitude toward others eventually returned. But his physical status never matched its previous level. Never one to complain, his valiance inspired me. Noticing his debilitated capacity, though, was difficult to ignore. His movements were guarded, as if he was questioning when the next infarct may occur. The sureness that once allowed for unmeasured activity gave way to calculated concern. He didn't offer his dexterous skills so freely. It was evident that he would not become the nimble fellow he had been. Though his convalescing was over, we all placed less burden and dependence upon him. We all had to chip in a little more. He had always delivered our necessities, and we would now need to supplement his. My mother, who suffered from severe glaucoma, had to find employment to replace the side jobs that my father had always performed. Once she began to work, the nightly family gatherings were not as regular or as enthusiastic.

It is impossible to appreciate the height of the mountains without having experienced the depths of the valleys.

FOURTEEN

Not the Person You Think

(Okay, so maybe I am stupid)

Is blind loyalty a good thing?

THE GREATEST FORM OF RESPECT I could have received was to honor those who were dear to me. An amazing outpouring of kindness and affection overwhelmed my son's arrival into my inner circle. The fact that Memorial Hospital provided separate rooms for the overwhelming numbers of well-wishers, co-workers, family, and friends to hail my son's birth was remarkable. But the continuous onslaught of floral deliveries, stuffed animals, and visitors to our home in his first few months was staggering. It was emotionally moving to have such tangible evidence of my personal affirmation transferred to Matthew. I was forced to concede that somehow we had gained a significant amount of favor and regard.

One unforeseen connection that followed childbirth was the instantaneous network with other new parents, who related with their counterparts by virtue of their priorities and experiences. Before long, we were doing the christening and child party circuit, which was actually very pleasurable. We truly enjoyed the company of Bernie, a police officer, and his wife, Peggy. They had a daughter who was a few months older than Matt was. They had exceptional morals and kindness. As soon as both children were old enough, we planned the much-desired Disney World vacation with them. We arranged the trip many months in advance, and the anticipation was exciting.

We continued our already established relationship with Gil, Nelli, and their son. Gil worked at Apollo ever since quitting the police department, so we were in constant communication. One day, a new friend of Gil's visited from New York. He worked out at Apollo with Gil. The camaraderie at the gym prompted an infusion of friendly teasing and aggravation from me. Through my time in my fire service career and years in various gyms, I'd developed quite a degree of instigative "skills." Within the firehouse, those you liked received the most taunting, and those you disliked were ignored. Thus, my way of acknowledging and welcoming Gil's friend was to agitate him relentlessly. Some of the zingers I unleashed were vintage firehouse; from my perspective, that was akin to rolling out the red carpet for him. Unfortunately, he was testy and sullen, failing to receive my overtures as they were intended. My ignorance and discomfort over my rejection caused me to pour the needling on even more. I knew I had struck an unintended nerve when Gil's friend gave me a look reminiscent of the kind my parents gave me growing up when I crossed the line. With that, he whispered something in Gil's ear and stormed out of Apollo. I apologized to Gil immediately, and Gil just shrugged it off.

Several days later at the fire department, we received an alarm for a double homicide. Upon our arrival, we noted that the police had already entered the home. They said that our rescue crew was not needed. They advised us that the individuals were obviously deceased, and our entrance into the residence could potentially compromise the gruesome crime scene investigation. That was not unique in my experience, so the call was cleared, and nothing unusual was thought about it. Hours later, I received a phone call advising me that an old gym buddy and Gil's new friend from New York were found murdered in my district. It was quickly confirmed that it was the double homicide I'd gone to earlier. I instantly remembered the unwelcome ribbing I had given Gil's friend, and I felt a tremendous amount of guilt. I decided to call Gil to express my remorse, but I was unable to contact him. *Gil's poor, innocent friend was brutally murdered just days after my insensitivity.* I brooded. I had difficulty ridding myself of how my stupidity aggrieved a quiet man so close to his untimely and barbarous demise.

When I saw Gil a few days later, he was obviously still distraught over his shocking loss. Respecting his decision not to discuss it, I simply offered my condolences. It took Gil a while to get over his profound pain, and he withdrew for several months, becoming much less jovial and talkative.

Corresponding with Matt's second birthday, the time for our well-planned Disney World adventure arrived. It could not have come at a better time because the tension at Apollo was as thick as Cheyenne Mountain's impenetrable door. Tina and I followed Bernie and Peggy convoy style. The rearview mirror held continual and untimely deaths, while the windshield promised the lure of children's fantasies and innocence. The weather was flawless, and the crowds were not too suffocating. It was as perfect as I'd hoped. The look in Matt's eyes was that of cartoon-like ecstasy. His perception was that Cinderella Castle was scratching the puffy cumulus cotton balls as they marched in formation overhead. He heard the echoes of the Lilly Belle chugging circles around the Magic Kingdom, and it rallied his love of trains. He tried reaching up to touch the monorail's belly as the tracks intersected above his outstretched fingers like spider webs. Overstuffed characters stepped out of the pages of his books, creating three-dimensional wonder. Parades of color and lights surely introduced snapshots of pageantry to his virginal brain. It was great to forget about the bite of reality. We needed the cleansing.

After breakfast with the Disney characters, Bernie asked me to get ice with him. Even though I had already filled our room's bucket earlier, I obliged. As he emerged from his room, I reminded Bernie that he had forgotten his ice bucket. Without a word, he continued his stride while looking in all directions in an apparent attempt to confirm our solitude. Sensing the ice bucket was a ruse, I kept pace. He continued to an outside parking lot, where unwanted observers would be absent. I wasn't sure if he was about to advise me that my zipper had been down the day before, or that he'd forgotten his wallet back home and needed a loan, but the tension certainly unnerved me. Bernie began by stating that he was aware of my fondness for Gil, saying that he would never tell me whom to like. Then, in a confused state, I listened as he cast nonspecific descriptions of a Gil with whom I was unacquainted. He warned me that being in Gil's company could be detrimental to me, and that I should rethink my association with him. He finalized our ice errand with this guidance: "I can't elaborate, except that Gil is not the person you think he is. The so-called friend that you were teasing at Apollo—who was found dead, in fact—was a hit man brought down here to carry out a contract murder. Don't ask questions. Just be careful!" With that terse admonishment, Bernie solemnly retraced his steps back to our rooms.

The rest of the trip, while great for Tina and Matt, was spent deciphering Bernie's intelligence briefing. Two plus two, somehow, did not equal four. He was certainly as imposing as the Incredible Hulk, but the Gil I knew was a devoted husband and father. Also, Gil was capable of reciting Bible verses with the precision of a Shakespearean actor. Bernie must have mistaken my friend "Bruce Banner" for the intimidating character tattooed on his arm. Or had I successfully incorporated denial to negate any connection between Gil and the subconscious questions my intellectual side posed? Why hadn't I asked questions about the cascading drug paraphernalia that rained from Apollo's ceiling panels? Was I ignoring the obvious? Were Gil and Bert involved in something bad?

As time passed, Apollo's grumblings reached a fevered pitch. Multiple stories and speculation circulated like debris in a twister. Even if one was capable of dodging the rubbish, it was impossible to avoid the dust and grime. Just as it appeared the inclement conditions were beginning to fade, the unbelievable news of another loss to our gym family was announced. This time it was Tommy, a well-known gym member and bodybuilder. Gil and Tommy were close friends. The word circulating around the gym was that he was gunned down while driving near his home. From that point on, it was as if all who survived performed a silent head count each day. The relief of seeing familiar faces alive was surpassed only by the fear of whose funeral would be next. There were no regular days anymore. The uncertainty of Russian roulette plagued our workouts. While Apollo still possessed the best equipment in South Florida, members scrambled to other gyms as if someone had screamed "fire" in a movie theater. The exodus was constant and undeniable.

As I drove into the parking lot one day for my afternoon shift, a longtime friend who worked for the local sheriff's department shook my hand to say good-bye. He said he was joining another gym and advised that I consider the same relocation. He explained that he trusted and respected me, so his recommendation should remain between us. For the second time, an officer of the law had tipped me off to a Gil much different than the friend I knew. This alert, however, detailed that Gil was being investigated for the initial three murders in the Everglades fishing campground. Additionally, the subsequent killings were believed to be the silencing of witnesses. He clarified that Gil's hit man "friend" was summoned to Florida from New York for that very reason.

Supposedly, after whacking potential whistle-blowers, Gil assassinated his New York friend as an additional cover to protect himself and Bert. This specific information literally made me nauseated. When I walked into the gym, I felt like a zombie. I did not want to believe such a heinous scoop. As chance would have it, Gil greeted me as I entered the office. He looked at me and said, "You look sick." Thinking I was slick and clever, I deceitfully tested Gil by saying I had been thinking about the double murder I witnessed on duty a while back, and it disgusted me. Gil asked me what I saw. I had not actually observed the inside of the crime scene, so I made up a story to check Gil's reaction. Officers on the scene had advised me that both victims had died from point-blank gunshots to the rear of their skulls by two different handguns. However, I erroneously stated to Gil that both victims had their throats slashed, telling him the scene was repulsive. Gil reacted exactly how I would expect an innocent man to react. Never losing eye contact, he consoled me and said, "I understand why that upset you." He expressed himself with compassion. As far as I was concerned, Gil passed my scrutiny, and the widespread speculation was wrong.

At home that evening, I mentioned the day's events to Tina. She had been hearing much of the same rumors about the possible suspects also, and she had a much different opinion than mine. She informed me that Bernie and Peggy were moving to North Carolina for their own safety. Peggy had explained that Bernie felt that Gil was a threat to anyone who knew any information about the murders. Tina and I had never witnessed any criminal activity, let alone murder. Thus, I felt that Bernie, Peggy, and Tina were overreacting. Tina went on to state that she believed my naïveté and loyalty were blinding me. She felt I was the last person in Florida capable of seeing the truth. "Don't you see? You antagonized a *hit man*, for God's sake!" she barked. Her discussion with friends enlightened her that at least seven acquaintances of ours had been murdered in the last several years, and all had some connection with Gil.

I offered a different rationale—that many of us who had been long-term members of Apollo had indirect contact with the seven murder victims ourselves. Therefore, any of us could have been suspects and accused of guilt by association. The disagreement grew heated as her apprehension and fright clearly drove her emotions. My defensive measures deduced that Gil was suffering as much as anyone else, and unfounded accusations were unjust, triggered by jealousy of Gil's widespread appeal to women and cowardice from men. I concluded my argument by stating, "Even if most of the stories were true, all of those murdered had purported drug dealings, which had nothing to do with us. We've never touched a drug in our lives." By the time we ended our conversation, we could not agree on any of the widespread speculation.

Within a week, a detective called me at home as part of the ongoing murder investigation. We arranged for an evening meeting at my home. During the questioning, Broward Sheriff's Office Detective Damiano grew frustrated with my inability to provide the answers he sought. He admonished my skepticism of his conclusions. His strong opinion was that both Gil and Bert were mafioso-connected murderers who had talked on too many occasions in my presence for me to profess such ignorance of their undertakings. As I expressed to this investigator, I sincerely would not want Al Capone–types of guys, as he had portrayed them, walking the streets. But contrary to his assessment that my "stupidity" was a contrived cover for friends, I was placed in the unenviable position of having to convince him that my stupidity was real.

We tend to judge others by our own lifestyles and levels of morality.

FIFTEEN

A Caged Animal

(Dear friends and dear dreams)

Can we dip our toes in the water without wanting to submerge ourselves?

IT WAS AS IF A massive iceberg had torn a gaping hole in the side of our Titanic and the water was rising. I continued my workouts, just as the band continued to play, oblivious to the inevitable. Firefighters and police officers were offered significantly discounted memberships, so we waded in the ankle-deep undercurrent. We were among the gym's last bastion of supporters. Through regular reports about the gym's apparent connection with the string of unsolved murders, the news media had been assisting with Apollo's demise. No land was in sight, and it appeared that things could not get worse.

Within the hard-core bodybuilding world, Apollo Gym became known as the mecca of anabolic steroids. Bodybuilders who used such drugs knew where their bread was buttered. The locker room's alter ego as a pharmacy was thought to be an inside secret among many of South Florida's competitive bodybuilders. Apparently, many of the drug abusers felt such acceptance with their habits that they freely stashed their pharmaceuticals around the locker room. Because of my nonuse, there seemed to be an injunction, though, to forbid the discussion of steroids in front of me. While I never questioned anything, the numerous times that conversations abruptly ended as I approached should have tipped me off that Bert and Gil kept me out of the loop. However, television news crews, ever circling like sharks, eventually caught wind of the illicit drug usage within Apollo's stained walls. In addition to the homicide task force, a new investigation was promptly begun. Many gym members who were police officers were ordered to double as undercover narcotic investigators. Since a handful of the officers were not strangers to syringe-tainted muscularity themselves, they naturally warned their suppliers of the probe. Although no arrests came from this drug reconnaissance, most of the drug users fled to less-scrutinized gyms.

As the silence of empty equipment became deafening, talk of closing the doors became the next motive for gossip. At that point, I had to contemplate the move I had resisted for so long. Although the familiarity of the equipment and my desire for stability kept me stationary, the writing on the wall became florescent. While discussing potential alternative gyms one afternoon, two longtime friends confided in me their plans to open a local bodybuilding gymnasium. They urged my patience because factors would prevent their facility from opening for another six months. Jim and Jamie were fantastic people, so I agreed that I would join their facility as a member and possibly an employee when it opened.

Somehow, Bert and Gil found a buyer for Apollo Gym. A wonderful guy named Dan purchased it with the notion of cleaning up Apollo's reputation and restoring it to its once-lofty status. He immediately spent tremendous time and money attempting to appeal to a cross section of potential members. For a while, there actually appeared to be an increase in the number of clients signing up. I enjoyed working for Dan, but the momentum of Apollo's accumulated body shots had tremendously weakened its knees. It was no longer a matter of if, but *when* its historic final chapter would be written.

At the same time as my contemplated workout facility transition, there seemed to be an increasing distance in my marriage. We had been together for a total of ten years, but we had never developed the romantic qualities required to sustain such a relationship. There was no doubt that Tina was a good person, who deserved love as much as anyone did. However, our sibling-like accord prevented either of us from finding complete fulfillment. Our association focused solely on our bond through Matt. Such infrequent and uneasy physical contact caused us both to yearn for substantive personal gratification. The normal bickering that most marriages endure did not have the balancing mechanism of "making up" in ours. Each small disagreement separated our distance, with no method of bridging the growing gap. Still, we chose to endure for Matt, and the hope that there would be a miraculous spark.

The grand opening of Master's Gym symbolized a new beginning for many aspects of my life. The change of workout locations was a major change that was quite necessary. Jim and Jamie were knowledgeable and therefore chose excellent equipment and provided a good ambiance. Our long-standing relationship allayed any discomfort associated with the move. A mutual respect caused all of us to agree upon my part-time employment with them. Master's was much closer to my home than Apollo, so early workouts were much less hectic. Sadly, though, since my beloved sport became infested with skyrocketing anabolic steroid usage, my aspirations of competitive grandeur had to be postponed. It had become clear to even a self-delusional dreamer like myself that I was no match for the popped-out vein and ripped look of drugged-up bodybuilders. Although my training was still excellent, it had taken on an entirely different perspective. I reluctantly saw it as a means for long-term health and as an adjunct to my fire science career. I also incorporated a modified vegan diet to maintain optimum cardiovascular health. The alterations in nutrition resulted in significant weight loss. While thinner and less strong, I found solace in my new gym. Jamie and Jim could not have been nicer or more accommodating.

One afternoon, I returned home to find the phone ringing. Padre was having a heart attack and needed my help. Naturally, I immediately went to his aid. For the next several days, I spent every moment catering to his needs. His colorless expression was all too familiar from my father's ordeals. Padre seemed lost. The emotional impact rocked him much differently than I had witnessed with family members. The ornery contrarian within my father was never curtailed by the fear of the Grim Reaper's potential arrival. Padre, on the other hand, projected a childlike temperament. Tucked beneath the hospital sheets like a scolded toddler, he followed every command as if dreadful of a reprimand, or worse. Every time a nurse entered his room, he appeared to be anticipating an ordered march to the gallows. He had accepted that the hangman was coming and no stay of execution could reverse his destiny. I insisted that none of the medical charts or test results (into which I inquisitively snooped) depicted the gloom and doom that his Nostradamus beliefs foretold. Three days of reassurances and pep talks seemed to relieve most of his ominous foreboding.

As he gained confidence, we eventually morphed into our standard dialogue. His natural propensity toward unselfishness once again awoke. He noticed that I wasn't projecting my normal radiance of happiness that caused him to dub me "Sunshine" some years earlier. His questioning brought out my despondency with my marriage. He said, "Marriage is a lifelong commitment that most people enter into without the understanding required to make such a pledge." After his official dogma was proclaimed, he went on to say, "You married at such a young age that there is no doubt that you and Tina weren't even aware of who you guys would become in the future." Without any judgment, he advised me, "It's perfectly fine to make yourself happy too, Sunshine. You are so good at taking care of everyone else's needs. You deserve happiness too."

Master's Gym differed from Apollo in many ways. One such difference was the lack of heavy crowds or mad rushes. It was a laid-back job, allowing me to converse with many of the patrons at greater length and in greater detail. I had always savored good conversation, and I commenced many friendships during that time. One of my most enduring and devoted friendships began during my tenure at Master's Gym. What began as cordial greetings and daily discourse led me to become close to Criss, who was my father's age. He was always willing to engage my gabbiness. His mature and stoic viewpoints quickly gained my admiration. Sharp wit and intelligence separated him from the pack. He had an almost clairvoyant depth that projected an inner peace. His daily entrance was reminiscent of royalty blessing the premises with an aura of superiority. In no way was he haughty or pretentious, but his masculine grace, ease, and quiet confidence demanded a high level of respect. He was a combination of Muhammad Ali and Teddy Roosevelt.

Over time, we grew closer and confided in each other about our daily issues. Criss told me that he and his wife did not have much family in South Florida, so I offered an invitation for them to spend Christmas with my family. Meeting his wife, Vivian, was the cherry on top. Her soft, angelic voice was as sweet as her personality. Each sentence she spoke reassured us that she was as genuine as Criss. They were the perfect match. Their virtues and internal beauty captivated my entire family. By the time they left that evening, we knew that our family had grown to include them. Over time, they have proven to be beyond what anyone could hope for in friends, mentors, and family members.

I offered my spare time at Master's to many of the interested patrons, offering them free training advice and personal training sessions. While personal training could be a quite lucrative profession, I felt that too many unqualified instructors were causing more harm than good to their clients. I had watched in horror as unscrupulous entrepreneurs contorted some paying clients into unsafe positions. It was my way of "taking back" the sport that greed had bastardized. Once my complimentary training sessions became known, many gym members requested specific times and assistance.

The time engaged in one-on-one training triggers a sense of trust and attachment. One female trainee's initial attraction to my gratuitous service was her desire to compete someday. I understood the psychology and preparation required for competition, so it seemed like a perfect fit. I knew that her genetic potential was limited, but I was equally aware that desire had overcome greater obstacles. With the implementation of sound nutrition, SC made an impressive transformation in a remarkably brief time. She began getting compliments, when she previously might have been overlooked. Her short, buxom appearance suddenly presented as shapely and petite. Her husband remarked how incredible she began to look. Her self-esteem improved to the point where she actually moved her timetable forward as far as competing.

We raised the intensity of her training significantly beyond her previous levels. Her muscularity and symmetry quickly outweighed her perceived flaws. SC had a flair and aptitude for showmanship that allowed her to project confidence beyond her body's development. Her piercing eyes emitted a flirtatious attitude that demanded attention. During every training session, I encouraged her to improve all aspects of herself. Much as has become my style over the years, my concern for my clients did not end at the gym. She shared many of her personal issues with me, and I was willing to offer my advice. I had been fortunate enough to receive similar advice from my mentors, and I was only passing it along.

Much debate went into choosing the proper low-level competition for her inaugural foray, so as not to overwhelm and discourage her. The only negative about the venue of her chosen contest was its distance from South Florida. Otherwise, it perfectly adhered to her desired schedule.

With each week's sessions, SC markedly improved. The day before she and her husband left, she professed exceptional gratitude for my advice, comfort, and support. Once at the competition's location, she began a series of phone calls generally not associated with pre-contest issues. We spoke for hours about the intrinsic qualities of winners, and I offered suggestions to inspire her. We touched on all aspects of life. She seemed to be having internal struggles, and each time her words hinted toward a rakish tone, she would quickly about-face and become timid. I blew the erratic fluctuations off as pre-contest jitters. However, the endless hour-long conversations caused much bitterness and criticism from Tina.

The next afternoon, her husband called with fantastic news. SC had won her weight class at the competition. When she spoke to me, she was choking back a victor's emotions. She and her husband both expressed the highest praise for my contributions to her special night. I was happy for her victory, but I honestly had not expected her to win first place. She certainly had improved, but not to the point where she should have been competitive at that high-level competition. I was confused. How had SC managed to pull off a victory without the use of performance-enhancement drugs in this era? The next day, one of my many associates within Florida's bodybuilding hierarchy answered all my questions. He informed me that SC was the sole competitor in her weight class. He complimented me on the job I had done with SC but stressed that she was not quite ready for higher competition.

My voracious appetite to compete had been dormant, but my passion and desires were titillated by my involvement in SC's preparation. But I felt like a caged animal because of my awareness of the drugs within the sport. I felt trapped between my extreme desire to excel in bodybuilding and the reality that I refused to acquire the competitive edge of steroids. I wanted to compete so much, but I knew I would not have a chance. I had purposely avoided magazines and refused to attend competitions for fear that my ravenous competitive libido would be stimulated. The personal dreams that raged within me would have to be controlled for a while, but I postulated that one day I would get to make that special victor's phone call myself.

**All the potential in the world is meaningless
without sustained effort.**

SIXTEEN

Something Was Missing

(Stoking the fires within)

Can we restrain our passions forever?

HOT OFF THE HEELS OF her successful bodybuilding exposure, my champion trainee sought to compete at a higher level. Cautiously, I explained to her that I felt it would be appropriate to remain at the same beginning level until she actually defeated similar-level competitors. Her strong will and pride overrode my unhurried approach and accelerated her aim at an intermediate level trophy. Although I feared for her emotional devastation, I agreed to help.

However, I also had several other clients to which I had made commitments. One such individual was unique. Lonnie, an affluent middle-aged redhead, had the modest goal of remaining attractive. Her husband was financially successful, so she did not need to work. The gym replaced the time she would have spent at a job. She was warm and affectionate to all members and requested some sessions from me. She was such a pleasure to be around, so of course I complied, and most of her goals were realistic. She did have a popular quirk, however. In the midst of each set, her breathing and modulating groans stopped everyone within shouting distance in their tracks. Regardless of a member's concentration, her rhythmic moans were enough to cause fantasies of lewd and salacious activity. New members would stare with jaws dropped to their sternums as Lonnie "climaxed" through each repetition. Some female members found her orgasmic reenactments so offensive that they either walked out or complained to the owners. Conversely, some male members found themselves reaching for a postcoital cigarette as Lonnie completed her performance. She became somewhat of a celebrity. When questioned, she always gave the same lighthearted response: "It's not that bad. You're exaggerating."

Attempting to convince Lonnie that I was not exaggerating, I decided to record her explicit pornographic spectacle during one of her training sessions. As Lonnie climbed into a supine position for bench presses, I clandestinely slipped a mini tape recorder beneath her bench. What followed would have transformed the worst case of impotence into an engorged case of vasocongestion of the prostate (also unaffectionately referred to by men as blue or indigo frustration). It was as if she were auditioning for her triple-X debut. That tape became popular for quite a while in Master's Gym, with Lonnie actually enjoying the attention that her soundtrack created. Eventually, it was such a daily routine to play it for members' enjoyment that it became stale, and the recorder and tape were relegated to my junk drawer at home. Until, of course, my father-in-law decided to record a union meeting at his job. Tina, unaware of the recorder's contents, loaned her father our pocket-size machine.

When he brought the recorder back several days later, he was acting peculiar. Usually not at a loss for words, his discomfort was flagrant. I finally probed and prodded him into confessing what had him dismayed. As he sheepishly tried to explain his bewilderment over the tape's contents, I burst into uncontrollable laughter. Lonnie's lullabies had once again provoked strong sentiments, as Tina initially felt betrayed, and her father believed that the recording was his daughter in action. Their immediate concerns seemed to ease once I explained how I'd captured the loud lyrics. Lonnie and I laughed for months about her infamy.

While Lonnie's Broadway rendition played on, my champion client's second competition drew nearer. Her frequent phone inquests continued to rub Tina the wrong way. At first, I felt our disputes were unwarranted because these daily phone queries were mostly related to the upcoming contest. However, I started second-guessing the innocence of SC's intentions. Her initial innocuous-sounding statements, such as "You are so unique," and "You are one in a million," played to my desire to be liked. Slowly, SC started saying, "I love looking into your eyes," and "You say all the things a woman wants to hear." Still, while I would have been concerned had a man spoken to my wife similarly, I dismissed them as platonic.

Ultimately, one Saturday evening, SC invited Tina and me over to her and her husband's home. Grudgingly, Tina agreed. SC uncomfortably sat me on a piano stool next to her and sat Tina on a chair next to her husband. As if the positioning were not awkward enough, SC began belting out to me a phenomenally talented version of "Something Was Missing" from the musical *Annie*. Her serenading vocal cords, just inches from my astonished and expressionless face, cavalierly displayed her enormous virtuosity and boldness. My flushed cheeks and forehead glowed like a lighthouse's beacon on a foggy night. I coyly peeked to catch erupting anger steaming from Tina's eyes at the back of my client's embroiled head. Her husband, seemingly incoherent to our internal fury, merely smiled, his head bouncing to the rhythm like a child watching *Sesame Street*. I wanted to disappear from the midst of the surreal dark comedy that encompassed us. I knew, though, that the ride home would not deliver much relief from this nightmare. Sure enough, Tina's every floodgate unbridled its full wrath for days.

I couldn't wait for Monday so I could question my client's intentions. SC asked me to join her in her car for an explanation. Once I was in the passenger seat, she placed a cassette tape into her stereo and asked me to listen. The speakers unleashed an incredible version of "Wind Beneath My Wings," as sung by my client. With tears dripping onto her lap, she articulated feelings for me that were profoundly deep and penetrating. SC revealed, "You are too good to be true. You are so, so much *more than* your *muscles!*"

No woman, including my wife of seven years, had ever expressed such intense attraction to me. She proclaimed an aching desire to be held and caressed by me. I figuratively had to pinch myself as she described me in such endearing and complimentary terms that I could only wish her words about me were true. As wrong as all this attention was, I did not want it to end. It was categorically sacrilegious, but it touched a dormant nerve that had lustfully craved such affection. Totally unprepared to counter such unfiltered sensuality, I sat in disbelief. Finally, after having sunshine and roses pumped into my thirsty brain, I asked with lamblike inexperience, "Does our relationship have to become physical? Why can't we just be good friends?"

She retorted, "I can't be around you and not have you!"

It became instantly apparent that something drastic needed to change. I gently explained that I could not live with myself if I betrayed my vows. My internal battle could not play to both directions, so we both agreed that we needed to be away from each other for the sanctity of my marriage. Although I fought off many desires that challenged my spiritual strength, she had awakened a sleeping giant. It was much more than ego. For the first time, my amorous and erotic sides became aware of their longing to unite. I did not want a meaningless tryst or adulterous affair. I agonized for passion to conjoin with pleasure. While I never saw her again, my perspective of an adult relationship was forever altered.

Weeks later, Tina received a letter in the mail from SC. The letter expressed remorse for falling for a married man, which only added to the ever-widening rift in our marriage.

Ever since my mother joined the workforce to compensate for my father's limitations, she tried to appease too many masters. Not content with being a perfect housewife, she extended herself to her employer's beck and call. As with all piling loads, eventually the weak link gives out. My mother began walking with a noticeable limp. When questioned, she shrugged it off as insignificant pain above her knees. Ignoring these tender areas only caused them to worsen. The pain became excruciating whenever she climbed into or out of a chair. She agreed to see a doctor. Testing proved that she had severe bilateral osteoarthritis in her hips. Other than accepting a degraded quality of life, artificial hip replacements were her only option. The agreed-upon plan was to schedule each hip repair separately, with a three-month gap in between the surgeries.

She was in her usual great spirits on the day of the first surgery. After five hours of waiting, the surgeon told us that the procedure could not have gone better. "Textbook!" was his description. Relief and happiness eased our concerns. It was late afternoon before we could see her in the intensive care unit, so we could only spend a little bit of time with her.

The next morning, we rushed to her bedside to greet her. We were surprised to find that she was not in her room, and a nurse advised us that Mom had gone for further testing. As a nurse finally wheeled my mother toward her cubicle, I noticed that her nose was crinkled as if she sniffed a rancid piece of Gorgonzola cheese. It was her nonverbal way of notifying us of a problem. She then informed us that the surgeon, attempting to feed too large a prosthesis into the bone, had split the shaft of her femur. I immediately roared, "What kind of textbook surgery was that?" My mother needed an entirely unplanned surgery to insert clamps strategically around the femur to prevent further splitting.

Following the spontaneous surgery, she was physically run down and drained. It was obvious that the compromised conditions of my father, mother, and grandmother, who lived with my parents, would require extra aid. Each movement of my mother's crippled body stressed my father and grandmother to their physical capacities. With my help and their combined contributions, we saw a daily improvement. The one person I never imagined languishing about was my Energizer Bunny mother. Normally like the Roadrunner, a few beeps and a trail of smoke denoted her presence. She was never self-absorbed or fixated on glamour, but she always took the time to at least apply makeup or have her hair styled. It was disheartening to see her in that condition. I arranged to have her primped as a way to enhance her mood. I also bought an electric razor and gingerly shaved her pathetic legs. She really seemed to appreciate that gesture, and she had emphasized the importance of that indulgence many times throughout the years.

With each passing day came an increase in my mother's mobility and another day closer to her second planned hip surgery. Just like her father before her, she never wavered or vacillated from the inevitable. She reminded me of a soldier awaiting his craft's launch onto an enemy beach as she said, "Let's get it over with." With that, my mother undertook her final episode of a hip replacement.

By the time she returned home, our family had a proficient system in place, and it operated like greased gears. My grandmother's maternal instincts were just as nurturing as they'd been when my mother was a child. Even Bella's newly acquired waitressing skills suppressed her normally brash style. The service my mother received was equal to that of a five-star restaurant. My father's ultra-masculine harshness was tucked away so that an unknown gentle man overwhelmed his testosterone with enough estrogen to tenderize his calloused touch. The soothing imposter fulfilled the emotional void that was part of the territory of being a spouse to such manliness. He uncharacteristically interrupted his chronically one-dimensional dedication to his trade as an appliance technician with numerous daily breaks at home to offer aid and comfort.

I was the plow horse that kept their household balanced. I carefully interpreted and shopped for the chicken scratch that constituted Bella's grocery lists. Her mix of slang, hieroglyphic drawings, and no-longer-existent brands such as Crystalline Bleach made shopping an adventure. I took on my daily list of chores with great pleasure. The very woman who had meticulously taught me the practical meaning of unwavering love since my birth deserved nothing less. While my mother ate, I replicated freshly vacuumed lines in her carpets, as she had always done when we were children. She had mastered the techniques of the best stadium grounds crews with a vacuum cleaner. I strategically sat next to her while she slept so I could assist each of her semiconscious movements. It was necessary because even minimal motion caused severe pain. I perched like a hawk waiting to pounce on the slightest motion. There were no setbacks or physician's miscalculations this time. Before we knew it, our Energizer Bunny had fresh batteries, and she was hopping to her old beat. She acquired a unique gait from her misaligned prosthetic implants, but she was happy with her restored independence.

Jim and Jamie from Master's Gym were national judges for men's and women's bodybuilding competitions. They consistently traveled to events and accommodated competitors from other states. In the course of their professional duties, they were privileged to unpublished and inside information about the sport.

One afternoon, while deep in thought about my mother's convalescing success, I overheard Jim's phone conversation about future rule changes. The sport of bodybuilding had been suffering in the public's view due to the freakish cartoon-like hyper growth from the effects of steroids. According to my ears, the monstrous proportions and excessively visible veins were considered unrealistic goals for the average spectator. Thus, the sport suffered significant financial losses at each competition.

When Jim hung the phone up, I was curious about the solution to the problems I'd overheard. I followed him to his car to inquire. Jim explained that women's competitions had all but died, and the men's contests were beginning to have diminishing appeal as well. The governing bodies had recommended the implementation of comprehensive drug testing. I asked if the testing would be only for females, as a desperate measure to fill their wallets, or if they were finally going to get serious and subject every competitor to the same scrutiny.

Jim smiled and said, "Now you might be able to get back into it." I questioned him further to confirm my hope. Always short on hyperbole and drama, Jim just said, "You'd better start training."

We can only suppress who we are for so long, until the right circumstances trigger us to our calling.

SEVENTEEN

The Greatest Love of All

(Being second can be good)

Can love be just as strong the second time around?

I FELT LIKE SECRETARIAT READY to launch from the starting gate. My eye was on the target, and I was raring to excel. First, I added chicken, fish, and egg whites to my already stringent diet. My protein-depleted muscles sucked it up just as I once slurped Bosco-laced chocolate milk in my high chair. I began to fill out and gain weight. My workouts had always pushed the envelope, but my added incentive drove me even more. Further inquiries into the initiation of drug testing tentatively pointed to the 1988 Men's National Bodybuilding Championships. That event was scheduled for September, so I needed to qualify for such a national contest by placing either first or second at a level-four competition before that date. Fortunately, a local promoter named Peter ran one of the premiere national qualifying contests in the country, the Southern States Bodybuilding Championships. A check of the Southern States date showed it to be about six weeks before the nationals, so the timing could not have been better.

As if my consuming passion to win were not enough of a motivator, other factors fueled me. Bodybuilding plugged the ever-growing void in my marriage. Free time meant too much introspection, which increased the mounting frustration and potential depression. Also, many of my friends and clients at Master's Gym had never seen me compete before. Eight years had elapsed since my last competition, and it was meaningful for me to live up to the respect that Master's members granted me. I developed a following of trainees and aspiring competitors who viewed me as a mentor. Young hopefuls such as Jeff Schwartzer came to me regularly for advice, and I wanted to set a good example for them.

I felt as though my wings had been mended and I could suddenly soar above the mountains again. It was invigorating to face down a challenge once more. Nothing stimulated my adrenaline as much as overcoming potential failure through the convergence of hard work, dedication, and pinpoint concentration. There was something about staring up at the glistening blade of the guillotine and managing to maneuver from its path just in time. In a way, that is what competition represented to me. I was generally a timid person, who once had a phobia of crowds. I once shied away from dealing with social pressure. Competition was my means of battling those internal ghosts and not only defeating them but also turning those weaknesses into strengths. It pumped my muscles, and it psychologically pumped me up as well. It was me against the world, and more importantly, me against myself. After all, I had always been my greatest nemesis, toughest adversary, and harshest critic. But if I could live up to the insanely high level of scrutiny I set for myself, then no other's critique would matter. However, there was an enduring obstacle that I had not conquered yet. Guilt! I carried unwarranted guilt from everything from the slavery that existed in our nation's past to culpability for having loving parents when others did not. Somehow, I felt fault for everyone's misfortunes, yet I also knew I had not contributed to their ills. Still, the stigma infused my every pleasure with negativity. Each personal triumph was always diminished by my gnawing predisposition to allow guilt to disrupt glory.

The thought of announcing my intentions to compete again initiated internal bartering propositions to alleviate my guilt. That stinking emotion slapped my face just as the smile of the spotlights warmed my soul. I prepared to concede nearly anything. I had an odd logic in which I believed that I always had to sacrifice something larger to gain something smaller. I was only comfortable when I was renouncing some kind of personal pleasure—never when I wanted something for myself. Of course, I knew I surpassed most parents' and spouses' efforts, but I was never satisfied with myself. I drove myself crazy at times, but there were instances where others seized upon my frailty for themselves. Logically, I was aware that others utilized blame and shame to manipulate my actions. Still, within me, I was captive.

At home, the conversation of divorce had become boilerplate. Neither of us knew how to resolve our issues because our answers were too trite. Somehow, the subject of the effects on Matt growing up without siblings became a hot topic for Tina. Its repetitious drumbeat triggered the "Big G" in me. In a peculiar ploy to get permission to compete, I conceded to Tina's demands. Before long, we were trying for another pregnancy. At that time, Tina convinced me that the notion of another child seemed like the answer for many issues. It surely would remedy the sibling debate. It certainly would remind us of the happier times when Matt was first born. And hopefully, it would allow us to grow closer. Oh, and of course, by giving in to Tina's desires, I would not have guilt festering within me. Or so I thought. Within weeks of the onset of discussions, Tina was pregnant with our second child. I was genuinely happy. Even though the timing was not to my liking, how could I not be ecstatic?

I had just completed the long, arduous task of scoring number one on a promotional exam, which alleviated some of our financial burden as well. The nightly multiple rescue alarms would positively not be missed. My promotion to a driver engineer's position, although much desired, meant that a shift transfer would remove me from my familiar crew and station. Still, it would be positive because it would be more conducive to another child and competition.

Once more, I found myself juggling various obligations. The increased size of Tina's fundus was representative of my increasing responsibilities. Matthew was a perfect little child. He made every moment beautiful. He loved his little G.I. Joes and being pulled in his little red wagon to go fishing. He was with me every moment that I was not working. He adored me, and I cherished him. Tina preferred not to work, so I continued to work many overtime shifts in addition to concert and drag strip details. Part-time employment at Master's Gym was not difficult, but it was an added commitment. Most days, though, Tina brought Matt to Master's while she worked out. During her sessions, Matt and I tinkered around the gym, and it made my time more fun.

My training continued while the rest of the world was in their REM phase of sleep. Previously, I had used very heavy weights during my workouts. It stemmed from my days as a power lifter. This time, I decided to refine my sessions around isolation, with slow, methodical contractions. Every movement guaranteed that I removed momentum by pausing during various positions of the concentric (contraction) and eccentric (lengthening) phases of repetitions. Instead of low to medium reps, there were days when a set would total fifty to one hundred controlled contractions. My workouts became longer and required me to get up even earlier than usual.

Due to Tina's previous C-section with Matt, our second child's birth was scheduled earlier than the due date. On the morning of delivery, all went well. The moment his little head slipped into our world, I fell in love all over again. While Matt looked like a serious little man, David had the adorable characteristics of chubby cheeks and the button nose associated with newborns. David was the perfect birthday present for me, as he was born just three weeks before my twenty-eighth birthday. Beforehand, I had doubts that I could love another child as much as my first, but those suspicions were nullified the instant I embraced David in my sterile scrubs. Nothing could confirm or legitimize belonging as much as the touch of my newborn's skin. His brown eyes awkwardly directed themselves toward the familiar voice that once spoke through his surrounding womb. His suckling lips tried to root on my constant kisses to his perfect little features. I'd lifted weights nearly my entire lifetime, but these six pounds suddenly meant so much more to me. Even his frustrated hunger-induced screams were as soothing as a choir of angels. From the instant our worlds collided, there was a harmonizing oneness. Whereas most fathers projected their happiness toward their newborns in the same context as having their favorite sport franchise win "the big one," my feelings were more maternal. David was much more than a trophy. He was the definition and palpable proof of my love. My eyes swelled with emotion each time I stared at God's gift to us.

Several issues with his premature esophageal valves prevented him from sleeping well at first, but it was resolved with the proper formula and time. Matt, who was just turning four, immediately welcomed his younger brother. I had another reason to excel now. Although they were much too young to know it, I yearned for the two most important beings in my world to one day be as proud of me as I was of them.

Several weeks before my competition, Gil and Nelli joined Master's Gym. It had been two years since I'd left Apollo Gym, and their reappearance justified my disbelief in the villainous rumors and warnings about Gil. Surely, if he were the felonious Corleone crime family killer described by Detective Damiano, they would have arrested him by now. Contrary to the popular sentiments shared by most of Master's members, I was happy they were at our gym. At my son David's baptism, Gil and Nelli brought my son a breathtaking crystal bust of Jesus. Once again, I was convinced that innuendo, rather than fact, misrepresented and maligned this gentle giant. As I watched my son sleep so contently in his arms, I could not fathom Gil leaving a trail of cadavers in his wake.

The Southern States Bodybuilding Championships drew large crowds of experienced competitors and spectators. I embraced the opportunity to choreograph a routine I would be proud of. After much deliberation, I chose the new Whitney Houston hit, "The Greatest Love of All," for my evening posing routine. Most male bodybuilders posed to either headbanging rock and roll or R & B dance music with an upbeat rhythm. I was much more comfortable with lyrics and a theme that tapped into my deep emotional consciousness. Posing, to me, was an expression of passion, love, and freedom. The first time I heard Whitney's smash song, I sensed that it had been penned for my new son, David, and me.

Even though I was dealing with many ancillary issues that most competitors don't have, I felt ready. My main weakness was a layer of fluid remaining predominantly over my quadriceps. The prejudging was long and arduous. While the Southern States had always been well run, it had so many separate divisions that it lasted for hours. The largely biased crowd definitely favored me. This was my home crowd, and many friends came to support me. The scuttlebutt among the audience was that first place was up for grabs between one other competitor and me. Sure enough, after the preliminary rounds at prejudging, it was too close to call.

Backstage at the evening presentation, I had psyched myself up to let it all hang out. I envisioned myself emulating great routines by Ed Corney. While I was not as crisp or large as I would have liked, my presentation, symmetry, and shape were superior to my main competition. When our division was called to line up, there was no sight of the individual battling me for first place. All the other contenders were pumped, oiled, and ready. The judges and backstage expeditors frantically called for the missing athlete. They decided to delay our stage entrance several minutes in order to conduct an all-out search of the auditorium. Still, there was no trace of him. The judges eventually commanded us to proceed without our phantom competitor. I pleaded with the judges to delay the competition because I would not have wanted to miss this opportunity if I were late. I suggested that maybe he was stuck in traffic or had a mishap. They refused my request and declared him a no-show.

As the first competitor hit the curtain, a sprinting figure bolted through the back doors and tore off his warm-up suit. The backstage expeditors gave the remaining competitors in our division the option to readmit him or have him remain officially disqualified. While other competitors saw his elimination as an opportunity to place higher, I lobbied for his reinstatement. In an unprecedented ruling, the judges and expeditors allowed him to compete. Before stepping on stage, I volunteered to put a coat of oil on my appreciative competitor.

My overdue comeback was a humbling experience. Many crazed friends whom I had not heard from in years showed up. They were louder than I had ever witnessed at a competition. In unison, they chanted my name until its echoes reverberated from the rafters. In many ways, reality exceeded my fictitious fantasies. I actually felt awful for my fellow competitors because judges' commands were muffled by the audacious roars and catcalls. As the crescendo pegged the decimal meter at ear-puncturing levels, we were thankfully ushered off the stage. It was time for the individual routine that I had practiced so diligently.

With the first note from Whitney Houston's heavenly voice, an intensification of "Joe! Joe! Joe!" squelched any chance that I'd hear the song I had memorized so well. I continued to an internal clock that had been set by repetitious rehearsals. My supporters' collective energy levitated me like a rock star, adorning my efforts with thunderous applause. As I completed my last pose, pandemonium hit an apex, triggering my involuntary reaction of punching the hollow stage. The drumlike percussion was my symbolic gesture to thank the crowd for its red-hot reception of me. It was a moment of sheer ecstasy!

As second place and my name were announced in the same sentence, the crowd started throwing trash and insults at the shocked judges. First place had ironically gone to the very athlete who had been disqualified as a no-show, whom my pleadings had reinstated. While I appreciated the unfettered support, I pleaded with the audience, through gestures, to respect the decision and the winner's moment in the spotlight. Backstage, the winner approached me and said he appreciated the classy way I handled the entire event. He recognized that he would not have won without my delay tactics and unselfish influence. Although I internally agonized over not having been victorious, I knew I was back where I belonged.

Each child, and thus each human, is as special and deserving of respect as any, because we all have unique qualities.

EIGHTEEN

Good Is Not Enough

(Being among my idols)

Is awe of others a good thing?

I SPENT HOURS REPLAYING THE activities and events of that evening in my mind. As much as I understood that I needed to improve to deserve first place, it still hurt to lose. High-level competitive bodybuilding exposes just about everything while a competitor is onstage. It is next to impossible to hide weaknesses or flaws. It is unlike the "real world," where we often compensate for our inadequacies through our choice of clothing or by shying from the spotlight. Therefore, losing has the tendency to feel as though one is being rejected wholly ... and while at his or her most vulnerable. That sentiment of disapproval may distress or torment even the most emotionally secure.

I grieved. *So close to the golden ring, yet still an embarrassment. About to discover the splendor of Mount Everest's summit, then suddenly the dank oppression of the Mariana Trench desecrated my dream. The sympathetic and obliging compliments were meaningless without the title and trophy.*

The more I thought about the ramifications of losing the Southern States competition, the more the soreness set in. As well intentioned as everyone was, I had let them down and devastated myself. Pity-filled handshakes and conciliatory hugs replaced high fives and halleluiahs. There were mournful statements intended to cheer up the disappointment: "Maybe next time, Joe." "I thought you had it." "You got robbed." "Second place is not that bad."

What was that? I thought. *Second place is not that bad? Like hell it's not!* I shouted in my confounded brain. *Second place was that bad!* It was not my objective, and therefore it was failure. Unless, of course, I learned and improved. Failure would have been guaranteed if I accepted the results of the Southern States as an end point. But there was no way that I would allow my journey to bodybuilding's summit to end at that time and place. While different in many ways from my initial degradation at the hands of the poop-painting pranksters, the results were the same. The only saving grace was that the first and second place winners qualified for a chance at a national title. I wanted to win. I had to win!

The next morning, my self-imposed punishment was a torturous quadriceps and hamstring workout intended to inflict pain upon myself. Lactic acid's burn became my closest ally. Without its allegiance and reminder, I would have deserved nothing more than second place. The nationals were next, and I could not settle for mediocrity. Several days later, I discovered that drug testing would only be utilized for the Mr. Universe qualifying portion of the Men's National Bodybuilding Championships. Those competitors attempting to qualify for the Mr. Universe portion must agree to anabolic steroid tests, but those satisfied with only the nationals title would not be subjected to such scrutiny. An odd stipulation, but I had no problem with complying. Thus, it would ultimately result in a contest within a contest.

As my national debut drew near, the quaintness of Master's Gym gave all the members a sense that they had a stake in my competition. The overwhelming encouragement was uplifting and appreciated. Jamie, always loving and thoughtful, arranged for a secret collection from gym members who wanted to assist financially for my trip to Atlanta for the nationals. I received a beautiful card signed by all the contributors, with enough money for a round-trip ticket. That act of kindness still touches my heart.

The day I was about to leave for Atlanta, I received a phone call from a Pembroke Pines firefighter. I was not too familiar with Norbert. We were certainly cordial to each other, but he was new on the job, and we had not yet worked a shift together. He requested a few moments of my time so that he could drive by my home to wish me good luck. It struck me as extraordinarily kind, considering our unfamiliarity. I was rushing to get to the airport, so our visit was brief. He quickly explained to me his tremendous admiration for my discipline and drive. He commented on how much he respected and appreciated the characteristics and virtues I displayed through my conduct. You could have knocked me over with a feather. I was just being myself. I wondered what I had done that kindled such undeserving compliments.

As we shook hands, he handed me a greeting card, which he asked me not to open until I was on the plane. Later, when I opened the card, a fifty-dollar bill fell out. It was charitable beyond words. I could not believe the degree of unselfishness that his unexpected gift showed. As if the money weren't uncommonly nice enough, his card exceeded any proportion or scale of thoughtfulness. I must have reread his flattering narrative five times during the one-hour flight. He alleged that his observations of me reassured him that goodness still existed in our crazy world. He went on to write that even from a distance, I inspired him to be a better person. I was personally moved by his humbling testimony. But the more significant lesson was that we all impact others' lives, both positively and negatively, in ways we may never even know.

Upon arrival at the Atlanta Ritz Carlton Hotel, my first thoughts were of how posh it was. We were greeted by doormen who wore top hats and tails with great panache. It was as if the Duke and Duchess of Windsor were expected. The lobby reeked of opulence. The ambiance surpassed any place at which I had ever lodged. My self-consciousness reminded me of my first day at Sts. Peter and Paul. The entire environment was so swanky that I felt like a small child visiting a castle. Walking through the halls was another overwhelming experience. I was amidst the national stars of the sport, whom I'd read about and dreamed of one day competing alongside. I saw myself as inferior and lucky to be among their company. But there was little time to waste, so I rushed to Lee Haney's Gym for a quick pump and sweat.

Seeing Lee Haney in person surprised me. He was hospitable, engaging, and an excellent role model. As I was obliterating my perceived weak body parts, he meekly asked if he could offer a suggestion. He extended a tidbit of guidance that has proven to be invaluable. His counsel, "Train smarter, not harder," has remained a staple of my training ever since. My memory of meeting Arnold Schwarzenegger was quite different. The arrogance and condescension with which Arnold spoke to me shied me away from approaching any other superstars of the sport. Lee Haney was the opposite of Arnold in so many ways. Lee renewed some faith within me that humility and kindness can coincide with accomplishments. I thanked him, although I did not comprehend the full impact of his recommendation at that time.

Weigh-ins involved the infamous drug tests. It was infamous only to those who feared being exposed as "juicers." To those of us who were unclouded, it was a minor formality. An unknown official followed us to an open stall in the men's room, where we were ordered to unceremoniously void into a sterile cup. Unaccustomed to voyeuristic companionship, it was slightly uncomfortable. Once I overcame my "stage fright" and indulged his commands, he sealed and signed my sample. Then my restroom escort casually grabbed my personal contribution with his gloved hand and abandoned me like a jilted bride at the altar. Typical guy! He took what he wanted from me and left me for another.

The prejudging was a venerable all-star assembly of the nation's premiere bodybuilders. I knew every flexing athlete from my many hours of reading about them. I was in awe of each popular champion. As we lined up for our mandatory poses, I knew that in this assemblage were many athletes superior to me. My last thought before our comparison round was that I had come this far, and I refused to go down without a fight. Two separate and taxing prejudging competitions took place. The first was for the national championship, which had me competing against anabolic steroid–enhanced athletes. While I was surprisingly called out to compare against the top competitors in the class, I was aware of the stacked odds. Even though I weighed in at the top of the class, several of the drug-using athletes' muscularity gave them the illusion of being twenty pounds heavier than I. The second prejudging removed most of the intimidating competitors. I gained confidence as I realized that I was an apparent frontrunner. One of the other odds-on favorites was a seasoned champion. He looked incredible, but I received just as much applause as he did. After the preliminaries, he walked over to me and nicely confided that he was impressed with me. *Imagine that—impressed by me,* I thought.

The evening finals had all the glitz and spectacle of a Hollywood award show. Women were in evening gowns, and many entertainers were present. Once again, as all the competitors lined up, I felt privileged to participate in such an event. As we were waiting to parade onto the stage, Isaac Hayes, a friend of Lee Haney's, sang the national anthem. In single file, we marched out for one pose each. Only the top eight finalists were called back onto the stage for their individual choreographed routines. As my name was included in the finals, I took a deep breath and recalled thinking that I was dedicating my routine for all the family and friends who had unselfishly supported me.

When my turn arrived, the world around me seemed to go into slow motion. It was like a Superman episode, where he turned the clocks backward by reversing the earth's rotational direction. The flickering flashbulbs reminded me of the childhood home movies cherished by my parents. The sound system gave me musical guidance to contract my proudest poses slowly. As I reveled in the words of Whitney Houston's "One Moment in Time," I truly felt as if I was "more than I thought I could be." I recalled looking at two judges whispering comments in the front row. Then I noticed one of their expressions and a head nod depicting an impressed acceptance of my presentation. It propelled me to a higher confidence level. Every movement felt crisp, with cheers and whistles encouraging me to continue. As I concluded my routine with my patented leg split, the energetic members of the audience rose to their feet. While less rambunctious and unruly than my Southern States ovation, Georgia cordially received me. Watching professional bodybuilders, movie stars, and judges vigorously applaud me briefly erased my natural tendency to feel insufficient or inconsequential.

While standing on stage, the final decision almost lost its significance. I positively wanted to represent the United States in Australia for the Mr. Universe competition. However, the affirmation from the sport's elite that I was worthy of their accolades transcended this competition. As it was announced that I had lost first place in the Mr. Universe segment by one point, I thought, *I'm not there yet, but I'm on my way.* Many cheers were audible from the esteemed audience for my placing. While walking offstage, a symbolic event represented this particular rung in my ascent. Unexpectedly, a magazine writer placed a microphone up to my drawn face and curiously asked, "How do you feel?" Without any forethought, I responded, "I am just happy to be here." It was an apparent subconscious acknowledgment that I neither showed up expecting a victory nor believed I deserved it. As I was climbing into my warm-ups, a higher level of awareness within me exuded more certainty about my future. I had viewed my competitors as larger-than-life figures whose press clippings and popularity were evidence of their superiority to me. Now having firsthand knowledge of their imperfections and vulnerabilities gave me the confidence that they too were human—and therefore beatable. As I walked away, I thought, *Now that I know I belong at this level, I will return to win.*

Many judges and fans approached each of us afterward. The

overriding attitude toward me was of confirmation and kudos. The laurels seemed sincere as I was encouraged to return. In the cab ride to the airport the next day, one of the judges shared the commute. He confirmed that I had, in fact, lost by only one point. He also informed me that I came within one point of a fifth place finish in the non-drug-tested segment. His advice was to gain some weight and move up from the bantamweight to the lightweight division. He insisted that he fully expected me to be a national champion one day.

Once home, I could not help but revert to feeling guilty. So many supporters had monetarily endorsed me, and I hadn't delivered the goods. I opined that from their perspective, my thanks and appreciation were just words. And I recalled the sacrifices I'd imposed on my children. While I spent more quality time with them than most fathers spent with their children, I was never satisfied with my efforts. I compensated for my training time by employing twenty hours of effort per day between work and nurturing my family at a superior level. Averaging less than four hours of sleep per night would not be conducive to long-term health. The oppressive tension in our home from continued marital issues and my intense overburdened work schedule took a toll on all of us. Thus, turmoil raged within me, between unfulfilled personal goals and trying to be perfect at everything. It became blatantly obvious that something had to give. Yet a ghost within me continued to haunt me with an insatiable spell to achieve greatness in bodybuilding. A framed illustration in my home embodied the crux of my anxiety. It read: TO BE GOOD IS NOT ENOUGH, WHEN YOU DREAM OF BEING GREAT!

**Each one of us holds the power to emulate
or surpass those we most revere.**

NINETEEN

All Things to All People

(Life can be a four-letter word)

How much of ourselves should we give to others?

As if my love-hate relationship with stress and pressure had not already begun to simmer, some additional burdens were about to be applied. I was the proverbial frog in the boiling pot. Some relative notoriety brought further commitments. Local and national bodybuilding publications began requesting articles and interviews. *Florida Muscle News*, a bodybuilding journal distributed throughout the southeastern United States, featured my training advice and monthly columns. Mike Bondurant, a well-known Florida promoter of drug-tested competitions recruited my services to write articles for his newly formed *Natural Muscle Magazine*. One local promoter of the Florida Bodybuilding Championships compelled my entry into his contest to heighten its prestige. He was Florida's head judge, having the power to bolster or sabotage a national competitor's triumphs and eminence. The coercion applied for my compliance was that it was an "offer I could not refuse." The option of waking with a figurative horse's head in my bed was not appetizing. While I had already surpassed the state level in competition, this squeeze was typical of how politics reared its repugnant head. So I couldn't say no if I yearned for higher titles.

Our expanding family required a larger residence. Tina insisted upon upgrading to a home with a garage, extra bedroom, and backyard. Of course, I wanted to give my family a better home, but I could not imagine working any harder or any more hours to attain such a home. As usual, though, I could not have lived with myself had I chosen to be selfish. We chose a brand-new community in the western part of town. The timetable for the home's completion was roughly six months from the initiation of the contract. Coincidentally, the expected closing date directly clashed with the date of the Florida Championship. As our exclusive income earner, it always fell on my shoulders to augment and maximize our economics. Criss encouraged me to begin charging clients for personal training sessions, which I had still been providing for free. At first, I resisted, but through necessity and ongoing skirmishes for my time, I acquiesced. As if I did not live at Master's Gym enough already, the unexpected inundation of requests for training sessions submerged my gasping head below the rising water. That initiated a seven-day-a-week work schedule that lasted the next seventeen years.

Gil and Nelli purchased an adjacent storefront to Master's Gym for their new venture of an aerobics studio. Their urgent desire to fill instructor positions with males, to attract female clientele, led to more duress and persuasion. It was their belief that my strong following and associations would assist with their success. After struggling with their request, I finally agreed to partake in their classes conspicuously, until my skills would allow me to assume the instructor's role. I asserted that if my name and reputation were to be used, I wanted to display excellence. So I approached aerobics with the same focus and attention to detail as my other exploits.

Simultaneously, a teenage competitive bodybuilder requested my assistance in his attempt at winning a national title. He'd had several previous unsuccessful attempts at such a title. He was also experiencing financial difficulties from the floundering home improvement business that he and his father owned. When he approached me, he was in a state of severe depression. He was so desperate for help that he offered me his services as a contractor, should I ever need them in the future. He promised to be at my disposal for anything from painting to tile setting. I accommodated his appeal at the expense of my own sanity and much-needed rest. Countless evenings were set aside as his personal trainer, psychologist, choreographer, chef, life coach, and parent figure. My charitable side saw him as destitute and an underdog. Long after my family had gone to bed, I remained by his side to spoon-feed him his championship. Ultimately, he did capture the title he sought. However, as soon as my last beneficial advice was dispensed to him, a sudden termination of phone calls took place. His title also gave him a sense of superiority, which caused him to look down on the rest of us. I guess I was no longer needed. But I knew it was not personal since most gym members told similar tales about our teenage champion. His choice to sever communications with me was at first confusing, but it gave me an enduring and unflattering lesson about human nature.

Passion usually fueled my decisions and directions. Although competing in the Florida Championship was neither my idea nor my desire, I still trained hard. I would not allow myself to approach my training with nonchalance. A secondary catalyst within me was my antipathy for embarrassment or humiliation. I did not want to look bad on stage. The idea of being trivialized as nothing more than the brunt of a joke or an impertinent "also-ran" was intolerable.

The combination of higher repetition training and regular aerobic dance classes initially hardened my muscles more than my previous efforts did. Once the positive feedback of increased muscularity and vascularity became evident, I fell into the "more is better" trap. Three high-impact aerobic classes per week grew into seven sessions. Several months of this approach manifested into a sensation of walking on broken glass. Each step became more painful. But my habitually obstinate trait was similar to the famous Russian chess master Boris Spassky, who once said, "When I am in form, my style is a little bit stubborn, almost brutal." I approached the soreness and throbbing as just another hurdle to overcome. At the point when I could no longer climb a ladder at work or squeeze my swollen feet into shoes, I figured I needed the advice of an orthopedic specialist. Unfortunately, X-rays clearly displayed bilateral stress fractures.

Due to my many obligations and commitments, I would not turn back. I remembered Kellen Winslow's heroics against my beloved Miami Dolphins—how he miraculously fought off humidity-induced cramps and single-handedly defeated Don Strock's greatest comeback attempt of his career. He refused to quit, and therefore I would not surrender either. I often thought, *Before I concede one inch, they'll have to carry me off the field as well.*

Eventually, my feet were placed into soft casts. I wore my "designer boots" as proudly as one with a shoe fetish would wear their handmade Donald Pliner shoes. I continued on, one agonizing contraction after another. Those orthotic boots became my badge of honor. Each time a concerned individual asked," How can you train like that?" I was emboldened to march through the adversity. I was going to show them how it could and would be done! Even though the slightest bit of medical intellect (which I had) should have prevented my stupidity, I proudly categorized myself as having "the heart of a champion."

With weeks left before my strong-armed competition, we were notified that a closing date for the completion of our new home was nearing. Normally an exuberating transaction, the closing could not have occurred at a less advantageous time for my competition. I was faced with the task of laying tile throughout my entire home within days of the Florida Championship. Such activity was not exactly textbook pre-contest advice. But then I recalled that while I was entrenched in my fatherly caretaking of him, the new teenage bodybuilding champion that I'd trained had offered to tile my new home. Since I had given so much time and effort to his successful title attempt, I went against my normal philosophy and requested his aid.

His response was shocking and a testament to the old adage "Let no good deed go unpunished." Even though I sincerely offered to pay for his expertise, he barked, "What do I look like, a charity service? I'm a bodybuilder, not a laborer anymore." Following the loud *click* when he emphatically hung up, I sat in disbelief for a few moments. Regardless, there was no time to sulk, even though his sudden repudiation of me deeply lacerated my soul. Hearing of this slap in my face, a firefighter, ironically named Angel, accepted my financial offer and greatly assisted me in laying the tile in my new home.

I had been depleted before, but following flooring, moving furniture, and decorating, I became emaciated. It was much too late to attempt putting muscle back on, so I had to forge forward with the embarrassing knowledge that I was a figment of my potential.

As I stepped on stage, I wanted the entire ordeal to be over. Although many complimented my hardness and posing routine, there was no mistaking that the real casualty was my cataclysmic muscle loss. Though my mind recognized my decline, I carried on with an artificial smile and contrived enthusiasm. When the dust settled, I once again found myself in the familiar position of runner-up. I could not escape the bright lights quickly enough. As I drove away from my Little Bighorn, I swore that I'd remember Lee Haney's advice to "Train smarter, not harder."

Most of my greatest hardships and failures had created the most lasting lessons and character growth within me. The Florida

Championship, like other events that I dreaded at the time of their occurrence, was no exception. I had become the image of my mother, spreading herself too thin for the benefit of others. While I would have loved to have been the best father/husband/son/employee/ friend, I realized that I could no longer be all things to all people. I began to feel used, abused, and disrespected. My emotive side had unintentionally made invalids and dependents of those around me. I had also unknowingly projected that it was perfectly fine to disregard my needs or worth. By asking for little and stretching myself to please others, I had learned how selfish people can be. The more I gave, the more some people had their palms open, expecting additional handouts. I sadly realized that many perceived my niceness as a form of weakness to pounce upon for personal gain. After the Mr. Florida debacle, I had grown bitter and resentful of those around me. I discerned that the fault squarely rested on my shoulders. Giving my sweat was fine, but I needed to maintain intellectual control in spite of my emotional tendencies. Still, I certainly did not want to relinquish my core ethics and kindness.

My single greatest attribute was my determination, and I cultivated that through overcoming the hardships and setbacks of life. Ironically, I had tried to insulate those closest to me from their hardships, which hampered their capacity for personal growth. Not only had I prevented them from evolving in fortitude, but I had also become annoyed at the results of my actions. Tina had become extraordinarily dependent upon me for everything as a direct result of my obsessive caregiving, yet I held it against her. I was also solely at fault for overdoing my concern and compassion for the teenage champion that I mentored, but I was resentful that I was used to such a degree. I fully knew that by removing the training wheels, some anger and bitterness would develop toward me; but just like Ms. L. had taught me, my motivation had to be long term, rather than for their instant gratification. Even so, I would remain in the wings, ever vigilant to assist when they actually needed me. Criss was correct when he said, "You have to demand respect or others won't give it." I had finally grasped that having everyone like me was fleeting and inconsequential. But creating respect was lasting and more purposeful.

While negative forces always dwelled, so too did a positive power. One such beneficial source that always kept me grounded was Padre's friendship. Regardless of whatever scheduling conflicts I encountered, I never turned down Padre's requests. On one occasion, he wanted me to drive with him to a mutual friend's home. That elderly supporter of the Oblates of Mary Immaculate, Padre's priestly affiliation, had baked a cake for one of her beloved brothers. She was visually impaired and was completely unaware that hundreds of tiny ants had infiltrated her love-inspired confection. As I was about to openly warn Padre that insects had beaten him to his slice of chocolate delight, he instinctively placed his index finger over his lips to curtail my alert. Padre's only concern was to make our friend happy, not to embarrass her. He miraculously ignored his well-being and exuded excitement while he consumed his entire piece of cake. Padre's choice seemed irrational at first, but it very much typified how he always thought of others before himself. His indulgent and compassionate act demonstrated that the most optimum lessons occur when we least expect but most need them. Padre and I never discussed that event because I feared humiliating him. But I did recognize that kindness was always warranted and should never be neglected for fear that others would not appreciate it. The timing of Padre's uncanny gesture snapped me out of the crankiness and self-pity I had exhibited.

During that era at the fire department, my new crew was learning about my idiosyncrasies and warped sense of humor. At the conclusion of each on-duty meal, I developed a habit that escalated to firehouse tournaments and tradition. Originally, my co-workers chided me about my ritual of crushing my aluminum foil that encased my home-cooked chicken breasts and then shooting it into the garbage can. I utilized it as a tongue-in-cheek prediction of upcoming New York Yankee or Miami Dolphin games. I would repeat the same annoying catchphrase every shift: "If this goes in, the Yankees (or Dolphins) will win tonight." If the attempt was a bull's-eye, I'd needle fans of other teams. When my basketball deficiencies resulted in a missed attempt, which was more often than not, I'd get lambasted for the remainder of the shift. Slowly, fans of other pro teams began repeating my antics for their respective teams.

Then a round-robin-style joust became the nightly post-dinner event. They came to be titled "shoot-offs." Within weeks, preposterous challenges where issued as a form of penance for missed shots. Eating concoctions mixed from old rotting food or wearing smeared peanut butter and raw egg yolks under one's armpits for the remainder of the shift became common. As different shifts rotated through our station and added their proposals and submissions, it ultimately proliferated into full-fledged sanctioned battles, with devastating ramifications for the losers. While most of the uncountable consequences of losing a shoot-off were dreaded, nothing elicited more fear or sent chills up one's spine like the "Joe T. goatee." It was named in honor of this spectacle's originator, yours truly. It was composed of pubic hairs (otherwise known as "shag hairs," like a 1970s shag carpet) ceremoniously shaved from someone and then glued onto the loser's face like a mustache and goatee. The loser had to wear his "mask" at lineup for the oncoming and leaving shifts to mock. Today, shoot-offs are still used to haze unsuspecting rookies, combat out-of-control egos, and test the limits of grotesque imaginations. As unlikely as it is that a civilian may find these bonding antics therapeutic, they effectively alleviate the post-incident stress with which firefighters struggle. Such outlandish and boorish comic relief counters the emotional upheaval very effectively.

I approached the nineties with renewed promises to myself. I vowed always to assess my motives and to be true to my faith and family, while never purposefully hurting anyone. An immediate test came in the form of an employment decision. My lifelong friend Bob sought to open a top-tier gym. He and his partner from the police department had grown disenchanted with their profession and desired a change. Neither of them had experience in the gym business, and they were familiar with my intimate knowledge. We met to discuss their goals and the possibility of their implementation. In South Florida, they wanted to duplicate the unparalleled atmosphere of the Gold's Gym in Venice, California. They explained that their choice would be to have me manage their dream facility, which would be the greatest Gold's Gym franchise outside of Southern California. In keeping with my self-made promise, I needed to discuss the option with Jamie since she had always been phenomenal to me. Following a month of internal strife and upheaval, I chose to make the best financial decision for my children. I expressed to Bob that I would take the position but would not engage in immoral undermining or sabotage to Master's Gym or any of its interests. He and his partner, Ed, shared my morality and logic, so we finalized an agreement.

We set out to gather the very best employees and optimum equipment to surpass all preconceived standards. As the grand opening approached, it became clear that we'd achieved most, if not all, of our goals. Before the doors even opened, we established a new benchmark. The buzz became monumental, and on opening day, we had lines of perspective members. Ed Connors from Gold's Gym's corporate offices, and director of Gold's franchises, could not believe the public's response.

As the fanfare and initial success stole the limelight from most other local news events, a long-approaching storm was about to undermine the celebration. One morning, a police helicopter had been hovering around the surrounding neighborhood without explanation. As its rotors tilted to steer it from view through Gold's front windows, I became enmeshed in my managerial duties. Within an hour, two members walked into the front doors with the most chilling and unnerving looks of discomfort on their faces. They hurriedly ushered me into the back office to eviscerate the last of my serenity. They reported that Gil and Bert had just been arrested by a swarm of police officers in cars and a helicopter for three counts of first-degree murder. Both members knew of my steadfast support and advocacy for Bert and Gil's innocence. We turned the television on to corroborate the harrowing and distressing scandal.

When they left, I lowered my bawling eyes into the palms of my sweaty hands. The unfolding events pulverized my seven years of faith in my friends. By the time I assimilated the actuality of this nightmare, the phone began to ring incessantly. Once it began, the intensification and upsurge would not stop. Person after person played town crier. It was also impossible to avoid the nonstop reports that were broadcast on local radio and television stations. It seemed as if the tragedy sucked the air from Gold's Gym as instantaneously as one collective gasp. Washed-out faces hovered on numb bodies as members mingled in small groups, whispering various *National Inquirer* headlines to each other.

Stunned as I was, I recalled thinking that poor Nelli had just become pregnant with their second child. As much as I tried, I was incapable of erasing the vision of my handcuffed friends. Nelli seemingly went into exile, as my many attempts to offer assistance went unanswered.

In spite of the circumstances of that July day, I somehow had to focus for another crack at a national title. With just weeks under my belt in a new gym management position, arrests of two friends on capital murder, and a marriage that was on life support, my goal was clear and concise. At three hours past midnight, the morning alarm aroused me to the reality that my world was crumbling. Still, I knew I had to be strong. As I perceived it, that was my daily chance at redemption. Nine weeks away was a self-imposed appointment for another national title attempt at the Los Angeles Shrine Auditorium, and I refused to miss it.

Be as kind to ourselves as we would be to others.

TWENTY

Thrilla in Manila

(Keeping my chin up in spite of difficulties)

Do tough blows mean we must change course?

ADVERSITY IS AS MUCH A part of life as prosperity and good fortune. Acquiring this concept prepared me for my second attempt at national recognition. Whereas my reverence of the elite athletes and the imposing environment marred my first experience, this time I knew I would be formidable. As most national or international level athletes discover, there are so many additional facets to contend with than just the task of their sports' performance. Success, at any level, may be separated from failure by the slightest of margins. Higher competition presents more superfluous components, such as crowd influence, media demands, and unfamiliar venues, which interfere with one's normal and customary training routine. Until people actually encounter those unique pressures and experiences, it is highly unlikely that they can anticipate their impact. After experiencing the burden of those outside forces during my first national competition in Atlanta, I would not be overwhelmed in Los Angeles. My second place finish in Georgia had qualified me for another go at my ultimate mission, so I was not about to squander that. I certainly did not take on conceited or egotistic traits, but I was not mesmerized or intimidated either. Previously, I had pondered *if* I could win, but now the only question was *when*.

In spite of my many challenges, I also had managed to gain significant muscle since my General Custer impersonation at the Mr. Florida contest. Enough lean weight had been accumulated that I'd moved up a weight class, from the bantamweights to the lightweight division.

During my contest preparations, our spousal disputes escalated to an impasse. Tina and I could no longer agree on which side of a gun's muzzle was safest. Each day, we engaged in superficial arguments as a cover for the underlying issue of profound emotional isolation. Most family and friends had no idea of the frigidity of our relationship, as we had both mastered the art of depicting the image of the perfect marriage. Our public persona remained what most would expect from "high school sweethearts." Yet we silently remained locked in our private penitentiary. The frequent comments and compliments about our exemplary bond further shackled and prohibited our ability to request help. Our image took on a life of its own. Neither of us wanted to admit to ourselves how futile our choice to remain was. We certainly did not want to devastate our families and supporters. Once the stress became tangible to Matt and Dave, however, we secretly sought counseling.

Our covert attempts initially gave me the sense that our placebo might keep us afloat. Within these sessions, her agonizing admissions of violations during her childhood heightened my guilt to unmatched levels. Had I understood the basis of her internal struggles, I would have certainly been more sympathetic and sought help sooner. I hurt so much for her, as surely the weight of her isolation and pain excused any of the complaints that I verbalized. Our counselor sadly confided that so many walls had been established between us that only a miracle could save us. The suggestion of a trial separation temporarily jarred us into a false sense of complacency. The fear of the unknown made our familiar conflicts seem like the better alternative. Though worlds apart, we agreed to remain with the status quo until after the approaching holidays and the national championships in Los Angeles. A silence, so obtrusive, draped our home in an armistice as flimsy as Korea's thirty-eighth parallel. We continued with our daily routines, refusing to stare the inevitable directly in the eyes. Brooding in shame and loneliness, I continued toward the showdown at the Shrine.

No matter what occurred at home, I had the uncanny strength to summon enthusiasm and zeal toward my training. Emotionally, I felt as though I had survived the "Thrilla in Manila," but I stood for each bell without considering throwing in the towel. Unpredictably, increased muscle size and definition caused me to look better than I ever had. The day before my transcontinental flight, a sweet girl from Gold's Gym offered to wax my upper body to achieve a smooth, hairless look. About one minute into the hour-long ordeal, I knew I had made a monumental mistake. Never having experienced such a procedure, I was ignorant to its potential risks. With each tug of my dark Italian follicles, layers of skin were torn from my once uniformly complexioned torso. Other than the pain of the process, my first red flag was the crimson blotches that camouflaged my muscularity and reminded me of a jaguar's irregular spots. By the time I went to bed that evening, I was swollen and developing tiny clusters of scabs.

Traveling alone only served to agitate the resentment that simmered within my mottled skin. Due to drug testing, all athletes were mandated to arrive four days in advance to allow for potential delays in laboratory results. The sanctioned hotel would not provide guests with any essential items required for preparing food. Therefore, my depleted body was required to haul a litany of equipment like a pack mule. Through airports and lobbies, I dragged a microwave oven, an assortment of pots and pans, a travel burner to heat the pots, pre-contest packaged food, a tiny refrigerator, and a week's bundle of workout clothing. By the time I arrived at the hotel, I was exhausted and dehydrated.

When I first removed my shirt to assess the trip's consequences, I was sure a dermatologist would have panicked. I had developed tiny boil-like inflammations known as folliculitis around my hair follicles. The solution should have been cleansing the infected area and the use of antibiotic ointments. However, in lieu of medication, the application of layers of artificial tanning agents was necessary for the competition. Needless to say, my condition was exacerbated by the skin dye.

The next morning, following the athletes meeting, random drug tests and weigh-ins were ordered. I was the first name called to undergo the familiar process. As soon as I removed my shirt, the scale attendant's eyes bounced off my blemished chest as if he'd stumbled on smallpox. Even my old acquaintance who'd accompanied me on my last urine specimen at the previous nationals shunned me like a date with genital warts. Determined to find a solution to my quandary, I took a cab to a pharmacy before going to the gym. As anticipated, there was no immediate resolution that was also conducive to my competitive needs. Once at the Venice Gold's Gym I immersed myself in the liberation of my training. Pumped up in warm-ups, I nearly forgot about my plague.

While dialing for a taxi, a breathtakingly beautiful Shari Belafonte look-alike approached me. She offered to drive me back to my hotel.

She immediately expressed an attraction and a desire to accompany me to my room. While flattered beyond words, I refused to be unfaithful. Besides, even if I were single, my shirt's removal would have prompted her to reevaluate her lustful intentions. I courteously advised her of my marital status and respect for its vows. She scarcely slowed down enough to drop me off by my hotel, and then she sped off. Within a few hours, an enormous bouquet of roses was delivered to my room. The card attached was a complimentary invitation from my Shari Belafonte doppelgänger admirer, wondering if I had reconsidered her enticing proposition. Although I recalled wishing that someday I'd receive such advances from my wife, I still felt as guilty as if I actually had cheated.

A few hours later, a knock on my door interrupted my attempt to coat myself with another layer of tanning dye. It turned out to be a friend from Miami who was also competing. He was in a different weight category. He and his girlfriend requested use of my makeshift kitchen and well-thought-out provisions. They bartered an arrangement for us to "paint" each other. Unfortunately, the strategy became completely one-sided. Once I applied two coats of DY-O-Derm stain on him, he and his companion became embroiled in a *War of the Roses* scenario that would have made Michael Douglas and Kathleen Turner envious. A spontaneous competition ensued between them—to destroy or throw out each other's finest possessions. The all-night escapade involved the police and walking the streets to find my friend's missing partner. I ended up counseling their maniacally uncivil relationship for the remainder of the week. The nightmare terminated with her decision to leave my friend for a one-night stand she met while straying along Venice Beach. As embarrassing as it was to step on stage with my blemishes, it was a relief to get away from such a chaotic and dysfunctional relationship. I promised myself that if my marriage failed, I would never partake in the kind of disrespect that I observed that week.

Seeing the countless stars of screen and television among the dignitaries made me self-conscious about my speckled skin. I had done my best to finagle my blotches into a positive by coloring my upper body darker than usual. Contrary to the natural instinct to fold my cards and come back for another tournament, I chose to face my demons as if I were flawless. I absolutely refused to quit as I had done so many times in my youth. I decided that I would not just go through the motions, but I would do it with my head held high. As I walked on stage for the prejudging, I was bearing a heavy heart for the imminent demise of my marriage, but I would be damned if a soul would know. I convinced myself that I would reflect dignity and poise. After all, the real battle raged inside me, and I was determined to win that feud.

By the time the finals occurred, the unlikely result of much of my calamity was tremendously positive feedback. In spite of the subcutaneous fluid from the folliculitis, I was once again a finalist in the Mr. Universe qualifying event. Many of the sport's best complimented my radical improvement in muscle mass and stage presence. The seductive verses of Mariah Carey's "Vision of Love" were ostensibly composed to stimulate both of my compelling cravings: a championship and companionship. Far more than simply a series of poses, my prayers and loneliness came alive through my muscular contractions. The judges received my choreographed routine very well, and several of them said it was one of the best performances of the evening.

When the curtain finally dropped, though, I was just points from traveling to Germany to represent the United States. Of the drug-tested athletes, I was once again the runner-up. As much as I despised not winning, I recognized that by refusing to quit, I established myself as a favorite for future competitions. Vince McMahon of wrestling fame approached me about joining his neophyte professional bodybuilding association. California, where Tina and had I endured the toughest financial times when we temporarily relocated, was now welcoming me. More importantly, I defeated some internal foes. The trip began with adversity and scourge, but my persistence had turned the tide.

The pleasure of returning home to my children was quickly overshadowed by the blatant realization that a separation was the only logical step in our marriage. We both understood the fact that continuing our charade would only prolong what had already proven to be delusional. With the most intensive and extensive torment I ever experienced, our inevitable separation took place. Sleeping away from my beloved children that first night taught me how much I truly adored them. Although my marriage had failed to endure, I swore that I'd never relinquish my desire to be the best father possible. I pledged that

I would not only live up to the standard that I had received as a child, but I would exceed it.

My first move was into a bungalow owned by the mother of Gretchen, one of my favorite personal training clients to whom I'd grown extremely close. Gretchen's mother was kind and compassionate in renting her mother-in-law quarters to me. She wondered, though, to Gretchen, how it was that a man could be "so warm and kind yet still be straight." I made the miscalculation of mentioning Gretchen's mother's commentary to Jeff Schwartzer. While mentoring Jeff, we often confided in each other.

One day, about a month into my stay, he decided to stop by and play a practical joke on me. Jeff's intentions were to erase, mockingly, any ambiguity that Gretchen's mother had about my sexual orientation. While I was driving my boys to their mother's house, Jeff suspended a large pink sex toy from my doorknob, along with a carefully crafted sexually explicit note. The phallic toy, labeled "Angel," was reminiscent of the pushmi-pullyu llama in the 1967 movie *The Voyages of Doctor Doolittle*. This colossal coital object was a tandem appliance whose design implied that two heads truly are better than one.

When I saw the object on my door, I simply removed it, intending to replay the buffoonery on him in the future. At first, because my quarters had an entrance separate from the main house, I did not know that Gretchen's mother had already discovered "Angel." However, one phone call from Gretchen made it clear that Jeff's gag had worked perfectly. While Gretchen found this entire episode hilarious and priceless, her mom was convinced that her revelation was authentic and irrefutable. Following that, I could barely look Gretchen's mother in the face since her strong Christian values and lifestyle could not comprehend or appreciate such vulgar levity. To prevent any further uncomfortable circumstances for her mother, or unnecessary scrutiny for Gretchen, I decided to move from my temporary "love shack" into an apartment. While that transitional dwelling had only lasted a few months, it delivered infinite laughter for Gretchen, Jeff, and me.

No matter how many times we fall, we must stand back up.

133

TWENTY-ONE

A Tale of Two Cities

(The day naïveté was put to rest)

Why do we sometimes blind ourselves on purpose?

WITHIN SIGHT OF GOLD'S GYM, my new apartment helped establish some semblance of order in my life. I rented one with a second bedroom for my boys and for when I was assisting in the caretaking of my grandmother. While we adored Bella, her increasing dementia made the task of overseeing her similar to babysitting a small child. Her memory loss, increasing disagreeability, and Tourette's syndrome–type vile language made every day intriguing and sometimes entertaining. While my mother and father assumed the massive responsibility of Bella's impediment most of the time, I alleviated their burden and pressure for the balance. It worked well, though, because Bella's maternal instincts were beneficial for the rearing of Matt and Dave.

My boys, seven and three years old at that point, were in my care and custody every non-duty day. They were adjusting beautifully to the divorce, while excelling in school and sports. I coached their baseball and football teams, allowing an extraordinary bond to form. We were close before the divorce, but we became an even more cohesive unit after. Tina and I had the constraint of our facade removed, which allowed us to get along better than ever. She began dating, which I sincerely advocated. She deserved to be happy, and if someone delivered that pleasure to her, I always offered to facilitate her dates with the appropriate flexibility in custody arrangements. She was the mother of my precious children, so I saw her as special. She and I would sit together for our children's events, and it provided tranquility and a smooth transition to the boys. On the few occasions when Tina dated someone, I always respected and welcomed him. After several short-term companions, she began a relationship with an individual, Dan.

At first, he seemed cordial, and I had no reason to believe we would not continue to get along.

At about that time, I became fond of a girl who was a competitive bodybuilder from Gold's Gym. We first met when she went on two casual dates with my friend Bob. Neither of them was enamored with each other, nor did they seem to have anything in common. Conversely, Amy and I became instant friends. We spent hours discussing training and all aspects of our common sport. Amy had been a national champion gymnast, having won the all-around gold medal in the AAU Junior Olympics. There was an unspoken connection through our respective shared eating and athletic lifestyles. While neither one of us initially sought more than our bodybuilding alliance, a phenomenal amount of mutual respect and admiration formulated the basis of our attraction.

The first time Amy visited my apartment nearly destroyed any potential for our evolution. Fifteen minutes after her arrival, my phone rang. A soft-spoken male voice, sounding as if it were in disguise, said, "Hey, Joe, this is ... *Dick*."

I'm no fool, I thought. I was certain that Jeff was pranking me, just as he had at Gretchen's mom's house. So I jumped ahead of the curve. Mimicking his articulation, I retorted, "Yeah, well, if you're the *dick*, then I'm the *nuts!*" Proud of the fact that my quick wit momentarily muzzled Jeff into silence, I boastfully chuckled in a victorious fashion.

After what seemed like twenty seconds, that same modest voice responded, "Seriously, Joe, this is Amy's father, Richard. May I speak to her? She's expecting my call."

The instantaneous flushed sensation of complete and utter mortification accompanied pronounced nausea. As I handed Amy the phone, I wasn't sure if pleading insanity or jumping out of my apartment window would have been the more appropriate exit strategy. I spent the next hour trying to convince Amy that my dimwitted display had a logical explanation and was more of an aberration than a precedent. Knowing Jeff's warped playfulness, she appeared to accept my clarification and apology.

About an hour later, while we were preparing dinner, I heard a familiar growl from Bella's room. My first thought was, *Dear God, this cannot be happening to me.* Amy never flinched, so I pretended to ignore it. I continued slicing chicken breasts for our stir-fry. Moments later, another distant eruption broke our culinary silence. Thinking fast, I began whistling and trying to duplicate the muffled tone with my sneaker on the kitchen's linoleum floor. Amy barely tilted her head toward the direction of the fracas, so it seemed that my counterfeit squeak caused her to second-guess her ears. Then, just as I was convinced of the success of my covert actions, a series of explosions sounding like Hiroshima and Nagasaki echoed from the bedroom. My humiliated head just drooped as if I had been caught red-handed, and I prepared for Amy's warranted revulsion. But no, she just smiled and continued slicing tofu with her pleasant demeanor unaltered. I wondered if Amy had serious hearing deficiencies or if my CIA tendencies were that proficient.

Then a grand finale was unleashed on an unparalleled scale. The eruptions guaranteed that Amy was seconds from exiting my apartment for the first, and last, time. I turned to her for the tirade that I believed she was about to launch. Rather, in the most unbelievably unaffected manner, she looked toward me and asked, "Why didn't you tell me that Bella played the horn?" Waiting for the punch line, I was flabbergasted at her oblivious inquiry. For the second time in one evening, I searched for the words to undo the unexplainable dilemmas thrust upon this sweet girl. So, with nothing else to lose, I was brutally honest. I was forced to explain the legendary flatulence from Bella's diverticulitis and how my boys would hysterically instigate her musical sessions. As Amy left that evening, I honestly believed our incipient flame was extinguished by the events of the night. While she seemed unfazed, I felt embarrassed and was sure she would never be back. In the slight chance that she returned, I had the solemn knowledge that she would tolerate just about anything.

While my personal life had been augmented, some impending justice lay in wait. As the frenzy of South Florida's trial of the decade was nearing, I received a subpoena, as expected. I was called to testify at a pretrial hearing on behalf of Bert and Gil. The initial shock of the spectacle wore off quickly as I saw the toll this eight-year ordeal had taken on the families of the accused. Each ragged, depleted stare reminded me of newsreels of concentration camp survivors. They had been to hell and back and seemed prepared for the worst. Nelli halfheartedly smiled at me, apparently not feeling the emotions of the cordial exchange. Who could blame her, now raising two children on her own?

The opening statements were like the first chapter of *A Tale of Two Cities*, by Charles Dickens: "They were the worst of men. They were the best of men." The prosecution painted a picture of an organized crime syndicate capable and culpable of heinous crimes. The defense countered with a depiction of the men I knew—outer mystiques that were macho and burly, yet compassionate family men inside. The state's star witness was a well-known South Florida strongman with a reputation for brutality and a record of convictions for petty crimes. The prosecutor's story would have the jury believe that their eyewitness had participated in multiple murders along with Gil and Bert, but now his remorse caused him to flip on his co-conspirators. How was it possible that a known criminal could simply confess to three homicides and have all charges absolved and pardoned for his testimony against Gil and Bert? There was something inherently wrong with handling the same accusations so differently. Two suspects were potentially facing capital punishment, while one would be placed into a witness protection program. The incentive to blame everything on the suspects was undoubtedly and immensely strong.

Mike, the flipped informant, explained that he had arranged a phony drug deal. As the trusting dealers entered the home where the exchange was to transpire, Gil and Mike pulled weapons on the unsuspecting minor criminals. The three lower-level dealers were then tied up and taken to a remote dirt road in the Everglades. There, the story continued, Gil walked the blindfolded victims into the canal one at a time, as they begged and pleaded for their lives. At that point, Mike claimed that Gil put a handgun to their heads and executed each of them. An irony of the story was that Gil purportedly suffered an eye injury from bullet lead. I recalled that Gil did have a corneal abrasion around that time, which he stated was from clanking dumbbells together during a gym session.

Although Mike's version of events seemed to tie many unexplained past events together, I had difficulty comprehending how the jury could believe such a desperado. I was only a character witness, and when I took the stand, lawyers asked me to verify the types of positive attributes Bert and Gil presented, which would cause the prosecution's story to be deflated. All was well until the prosecution's attorney manipulated my words so they sounded dishonest. It was a display of fancy legal experience versus a sincere yet ignorant witness. When I finally stepped down, I was confused and filled with guilt for how little I'd done to help. While I was not present for the verdicts, I had faith that the jury's deliberations would be prejudiced by Mike's history and the deal arranged for his potential exoneration.

When a bulletin flashed across the television screen announcing guilty verdicts for both Bert and Gil, I wept for the children and families of all involved. Whatever truly happened became irrelevant, as their saga had destroyed so many lives. As the criminal justice system celebrated its victory, I wondered how they failed to comprehend that they had also released an admitted murderer. While Gil and Bert faced the ultimate penalty, an emancipated killer was sanitized and given a new identity through our tax dollars. Before that jury's decision, I had believed in the death penalty. For the first time, I began to question my position.

In an odd form of leniency, both Bert and Gil were sentenced to three consecutive twenty-five-year sentences, which equated to seventy-five years before eligibility for parole. They were spared the death penalty but would likely remain in prison the rest of their lives. In fact, Bert's already frail health finally succumbed after several years behind bars. Many people said, "I told you so," and they were quick to berate me, for trusting in them, following their incarcerations and convictions. Regardless, I had to base my opinion only on what I had witnessed.

The conclusion of that enigmatic turmoil caused me to cling that much tighter to the people and ethics I held dear. I reaffirmed the value of family and loved ones. Vowing to protect and serve all who were mistreated or demoralized, I became much freer with my hugs and overt affection. I was no longer hesitant to tell my friends I loved them. Mostly, though, I promised that nothing would prevent me from insulating and safeguarding my children. Both Gil's and Bert's kids were left fatherless and at the mercy of a large and lonely world. Thus, protecting Matt and Dave would be subordinate to nothing and no one. It became apparent that my boys needed an environment that was more secure than the apartment complex by Gold's Gym. At that point, I purchased from Tina the home that we had built during our marriage. Since the boys were predominantly with me, it made sense to have the backyard and extra space for them. In a peculiar way, Bert's and Gil's influence would prove to have profound effects on my children's lives.

One such consequence was my decision to pursue a national championship one final time. On the surface, it might have appeared that I had lost my drive. However, two distinct reasons challenged that premise. First, always allowing the same excuse—that I would "get them next time"—justified my tendency to spread myself too thin. I pledged that my last attempt would shame all challengers, for I would push the limits of physical tolerance beyond any effort they could generate. Nothing would be accepted but first place. I would alleviate all nonessential constraints and take no prisoners. Although I would never admit my adage until after the nationals, I reminded myself of this daily: *Everyone else will be a prop for my special day. They'll all be competing for second place.* That was my attitude, and nothing was going to stop me.

The second, and more important, reason for making this my last competition was my refusal to one day look back and reminisce that I had neglected my children's youth. Seeing Gil's boys and Bert's daughters without the protection of their fathers accented the significance of involved parenting, and I appropriately prioritized my role as guardian.

**Honesty is difficult and painful, although
it is essential for growth.**

TWENTY-TWO

It's Showtime

(Victories occur before we ever step on stage)

Must we be willing to step outside the box?

EIGHT MONTHS BEFORE THE UNITED States Championship, I began my seven-day-a-week regimen. It was evident that without the aid of anabolic steroids, I'd require every edge possible. If I were to overcome my disadvantages, I had to think beyond traditional methods and utilize unconventional techniques. In essence, I could no longer emote. From the third-person perspective, I would view my body as an inanimate mechanism. There would be no room for fears, trepidation, or excuses. Either it would respond to the extraordinary stimuli I was to impose upon it ... or the wheels would fall off.

Previously, I had not been exact in weighing my food intake 100 percent of the time. For this competition, every meal was placed on a gram scale, and it was precisely portioned to the tenth of a gram. Also, I required a massive increase in calorie consumption to compensate for the bombardment of exertion demanded of me. I ordered cod by the case and divided three and a half pounds per day into seven evenly portioned meals. I ate a total of eight meals per day, each consumed two hours apart.

My first meal was composed of one dozen egg whites, which bodybuilders tend to consume since the yolk contains most of the fat content of an egg, and a concoction of protein powder mixed into pancake shaped patties. The protein source for every meal beyond that was derived from a half pound of cod. Within a week, I smelled like low tide at Orchard Beach and gained popularity among the neighborhood felines as I strolled by. At the pinnacle of my intake, I additionally ingested five pounds of sweet and baked potatoes, combined, per day. Capping off my meals were green beans and broccoli by the bushel.

An alarm clock alerted me to the fuel requirement I needed every two hours.

While I endeavored to preplan and solidify my routine, fire department alarms sometimes slightly disrupted or revised my schedule. When clusters of alarms hit like a Sugar Ray Leonard combination of punches, I adapted with contingency plans. The fire service's mantra became my personal credo: "Improvise, adapt, and overcome." I tucked my ever-present cooler beneath my bunker gear, making nourishment perpetually convenient. During many fires, I was eating meals while pumping multiple hose lines to mystified firefighters.

One such occasion was a multiple-alarm town house fire. Several chiefs and administrators arrived on the scene. An overweight chief walked by my clattering and screaming fire engine as I was inhaling fists of green beans at the same time I was calculating friction loss. We had an affable and ribbing relationship, so he proceeded to mock my mouth-stuffing techniques with great delight. Later that shift, our crew was eating dinner, and that same stout officer crept up behind me to deride me for the crew's entertainment. While impersonating me, he comically said, "Hey, Troccoli, they couldn't pay me enough to eat the way you do." He proudly glanced around the room to delight in the several snickers his wit elicited. Pointing to his bouncing potbelly, I responded, "I understand exactly what you are talking about, Chief. I eat this way because you couldn't pay me enough to look like you." Everyone exploded in humorous disbelief. Totally humiliated, he roared, "Go f--k yourself, you little troll!" And he stampeded away from the uncontrolled cackling my comment caused.

There had been a series of on-duty injuries to firefighters in the preceding years while engaging in makeshift deadlift competitions. So our administration responded by removing all fitness equipment from our fire stations. That required me to keep a stationary bicycle in my car and bring it into the station between calls. Before shift, I rode a bike at home for one hour, immediately upon waking. When I finished the morning bike ride, I ate the first meal of egg whites and protein powder pancakes. Then it was off to Gold's Gym for my anaerobic assault for muscle growth. Once at the firehouse, I consumed a second meal before my shift began. Around midday, I brought the stationary bicycle inside and pedaled for another hour. When I was off duty, I utilized the StairMaster for one hour instead of the noon biking session.

Finally, between my last meal and bedtime, I implemented another one-hour biking period. I totaled three full hours of cardiovascular output per day. Time had become such a rare commodity, so I was forced to multitask whenever possible. During my biking activities, I studied videos incessantly and obsessively. I had ordered videos of all of the preeminent national competitors and studiously memorized every one of their moves and their stage routines. So fervent and devoted was I to this task that I could discern every body part on all of my competition. My fanaticism reached the point where I knew their assets, music preferences, vulnerabilities, attitudes, and reactions to both positive and negative audience responses. I likely knew them better than they knew themselves.

An unheralded asset that absolutely contributed to my inner sanctuary was Amy. While I had always had some assistance, nothing had ever approached this level. First, having a proven champion believe and trumpet my virtues added a level of courage and pugnacity that exceeded my previous heights. I admired her competitive excellence, and her reciprocation of those sentiments augmented my already notable fortitude. Her unselfish contributions of weighing and preparing meals removed much of my burden and time restraints. Her genuine involvement with the nuances of the sport's intangibles alleviated much of my guilt and resentment. I never felt that she was disinterested or reluctant when I dragged her along. She actually enjoyed my sport, while others had just tolerated it.

Other invaluable advocates from the gym contributed more than words could ever describe. Criss always viewed me as capable of unlimited success, and his confidence in me drove me never to disappoint him. By providing certitude and unconditional friendship, Bob never wavered in his psychological support. Ralph placed me on an undeserving pedestal that kept me reaching for higher achievements.

Oh, and wonderful Sally! She was a national champion whom I respected immensely as a competitor and a moral person. She was the rare individual whose greatness was never subverted by unbecoming arrogance or conceit. She stood as an excellent role model for any lucky enough to follow in her steps. Thus, her backing mattered tremendously to me.

One day, she and I were discussing my upcoming contest. Certainly not meaning any disrespect or dishonor, she casually stated, "Your legs will keep you from winning." While she nonchalantly continued as if her previous statement were insignificant, the impact of her words became the rallying cry for inconceivable self-torture. When I was a child, I owned an old Nancy Sinatra record of "These Boots Are Made for Walkin'," and it had a scratch on it. That imperfection caused certain words in the song to repeat monotonously, until I was forced to manually stop it. Much like that old vinyl record, Sally's cynical phrase replayed itself in my mind continually. It provided me with an energy source more plentiful than Saudi Arabia's oil reserves. It was no longer just desire. Sally had unknowingly converted this battle into one of honor.

I reduced my personal training clientele to facilitate more training time for myself. Two separate one-hour posing periods were stuffed into my already brimming day. I added two additional thirty-minute sunbed sessions to my initial two appointments, and it changed my complexion tremendously. The unconscionable pace sucked up calories so rapidly that I added another dozen egg whites and more cod to my diet, just to maintain my body weight. Every day, more muscular definition emerged on my increasingly chiseled muscles. Six weeks prior to competition, my skin was as thin as tissue paper. Skinfold calipers were no longer able to measure my evaporated body fat. Even with the massive amount of calories I consumed, I lost weight rapidly and yearned for energy. The zombie in me begged for any spark. For the first time in my life, I began drinking black coffee immediately before my workouts. Whether the coffee was only a placebo or if it actually gave me a slight kick of energy to make it through my workout, I grew dependent upon the caffeine's efficacy. Even with coffee, my outward appearance resembled that of a corpse.

Thinking outside the box, I originated a psychological trigger. Every time I consciously conceded how tired I was, I utilized a phrase intended to convert a negative thought into a positive action. I verbalized, "It's showtime!" It was intended to evoke the notion that when the curtain is about to rise, all doubts and dilemmas must be put aside for the performance. As I explained to Criss, I had driven myself so hard that I constantly felt as if I had a virus. Sympathetically admiring my fortitude, he expressed, "Based on the way you train, you'd think the prize was a million dollars." I responded without forethought, "They could pay me a million dollars not to win, and I would not accept it. This means way more than money!"

With less than four weeks to go, I could not comprehend anything other than first place. Still, though, I was not satisfied. I turned to a diet guru named Joe, who had quite a national following. I only requested some minor fine-tuning. So, with three and a half weeks remaining, we met, and he assured me that the only issue between the title and me was a small amount of superficial fluid. He and I decided on the final diet adjustments to perfectly dial my body into contest shape. As each twenty-four-hour cycle elapsed, a new and improved butterfly emerged from the cocoon in which I slept. Never one to be overconfident, I began to visualize my dreams materializing. Each tanning booth session turned into deep meditation. I had managed to conceptualize the entire competition in my mind. I envisioned everything from the sensation of my bare feet on the cold metal scale before the event to the warm, perfumed embrace of Amy following receipt of my first place trophy. My visualization took on a clarity that replicated the minutest details.

Tom, a television broadcaster and a friend from Gold's Gym, asked me if he should arrange to fly to Los Angeles for my competition. He cautiously worded his question, "Is it worth flying out there?" Do you really have a chance to win this time?" While I understood his financial inquest, my atypical affirmative response proved to me that this time would be different.

The night before Amy and I left for Los Angeles, we finalized all preparations. Amy was to help me remove the last remnants of hair from my physique. To prevent a repeat of the rash-type folliculitis of my last national competition, we diligently engrossed ourselves in the process. I refused to entrust my fortunes to a stranger's well-intentioned miscalculation again.

That evening, the completion of Amy's assistance was the application of Nair to my buttocks. She carefully read the directions and had full confidence in her actions. As my naked and Naired body lay prone on a towel, Amy answered the phone. It was her sister calling to wish us good luck. As they engaged in their normal repartee about family and feminine subjects, my fatigued body drifted to sleep. While I speculated that I only dozed for a second, I was awakened by a blowtorch charbroiling my gluteus maximus. My rattled reaction to my chemically peeled bottom caused Amy to remember, distressingly, the task of which she had lost track. Moving like a mongoose, she vigorously rubbed the dried hair remover from my sautéed derriere. As her tear-filled eyes took on a look of revulsion, I realized that her appraisal matched my discomfort.

Running to the mirror, I was met by the vision of a cherry red bottom. Amy pleaded with me for forgiveness, as she believed that her lapse of time would cause my trophy to vanish along with my hide. Somehow, I did not panic or harbor anger. I had a sense of tranquility that shielded me from the normal gamut of pre-contest emotions. Amy was upset, so I held her in an ironic attempt to comfort her. Rather than chastise her as she fully expected, we embraced for a while, and I reassured her that I appreciated all her positive contributions. The pain was nothing, considering the road I had endured. For the remainder of the evening, she proceeded to apply, conscientiously and attentively, coat after coat of DY-O-Derm.

Conventional wisdom only brings conventional results, while extraordinary planning and forethought deliver extraordinary results.

TWENTY-THREE

Life Is Beautiful

(The third time is the charm)

Can good guys ever finish first?

A SUPERVISOR FOR DELTA AIRLINES, who was also a friend from Gold's Gym, greeted Amy and me at our departure gate. His good luck gift to us was a free upgrade to first class. While we greatly appreciated his kindness, the other paying passengers were the real beneficiaries of his benevolence. Those who would have had the misfortune to be in close proximity to me undoubtedly gained the most. One of the unpleasant techniques, or tricks, to enhance the "glowing" stage presence was to withhold showering for several days before competition. While it certainly achieved the desired effect of oily skin, it also created pungency that only Pepe Le Pew would be attracted to. When coupled with the non-concealable fishy aroma that the radical consumption of cod produced, quarantining me would have been best.

Arriving in Dallas for a layover turned out to be eventful. The severe dehydration that is required to achieve total muscle definition was taking its toll on me. The constant feeling of having a virus, also a side effect of having an unhealthy low percentage of body fat, coupled with dehydration's telltale vertigo, made it arduous to stand. As we walked from one gate toward our connecting flight, I could have sworn Dorothy, Toto, and the Wicked Witch swirled around me a few times. I had to sit on the floor and regroup. For a few moments, we contemplated requesting a tram ride. Remembering my trigger—"It's showtime!"—elevated me into a standing eight count. Then, with the magnanimous actions of a saint, Amy entered my malodorous personal space and propped herself under my arm. My new crutch, along with sheer willpower, pushed me onto our decisive flight toward fate.

That was my third time in Los Angeles. The City of Angels had not always been so gracious. As I chaffed with Amy about Los Angeles, "This time she would either welcome me with open arms or I'd bash her door down." Tom met us at our hotel. He and Amy were in the midst of a meal in the lobby restaurant when Tom kindly asked me, "Are you allowed to eat anything on the menu?" Thinking to myself that I'd allow nothing to get in my way, I responded to Tom, "I'm allowed to eat anything I want. I choose this lifestyle!" With that, a competitor in the next booth interjected, "I have never heard it put that way. What a good answer."

After lunch, we drove to the Venice Gold's Gym to scrutinize the physical effects of the flight on my body. We were given permission to utilize their posing room. Within minutes, a crowd of inquisitive gawkers shoved into the tiny stage duplication. The increasing oohs and aahs drew an overflow crowd to investigate the reason behind the ruckus. The feedback was incredible. My first thought was, *Los Angeles: the third time is definitely going to be the charm.*

The rest of the evening, I focused on losing ten more pounds of superficial water weight before the arrival of morning weigh-ins. After Amy applied several more coats of tanning dye, I climbed into a rubberized sweat suit and went to bed. Around three o'clock in the morning, I awoke in an attempt to drain the last particles of fluid from my parched and burning bladder. I glanced in the barely lit mirror and exposed my abdomen, only to catch a glimpse of the most startling transformation that I had ever witnessed. The person in the mirror, duplicating my motions, surpassed any of the cutouts from my teenage "collage of champions" that painstakingly covered my walls. My crackling voice yelled to Amy's comatose body for verification that I was not dreaming. By now, my disrobed body was slowly demonstrating the positions my body would project from the Santa Monica Civic Auditorium's dais. Her twinkling hazel eyes were all I needed to realize that Tom had not wasted his money. Amy and I hugged for several minutes. We never said a word, but we were fully aware that we were witnessing a sneak peek of history. Amy grabbed the camera and immortalized several private photos of someone the bodybuilding world would soon remember.

I did not sleep another wink. Although the battle of my life was imminent, my anticipation and excitement energized my previously languishing body. I must have thanked God a million times for delivering me to this point in my life. Then I drifted into a deep introspective period as my thoughts turned toward my grandfather. Here I was, possibly about to earn the title of Mr. USA as a direct result of my Italian-born grandfather's sacrifices. I would be the one potentially receiving the applause and accolades, but his unequaled heroics would remain obscured from everyone else. It seemed so unfair. I promised myself that I would never forget my origins and foundation. I knew I would not be alone on that stage; I was only one of many who had manufactured this prestigious opportunity. This unbelievable privilege was directly attributable to the lonely, cold, and daring nights Giuseppe Bencivenga experienced on the distant docks of New York.

Regardless of all the physical and emotional preparations, walking backstage gave me a jolt. I had been so ready and willing, yet, instinctively, the sight of the great Mercury Morris Claiborne intimidated me. He was phenomenal in every aspect of the sport. I admired and revered his legendary career. He was the Joe Louis of lightweights, and certainly the favorite. However, I remembered that I had a secret weapon: I was not alone. I went into a desolate corner, closed my eyes, and proceeded to exorcise most of the demons from my innermost core. I prayed for the strength to show no fear and perform in such a way that my children would look back with pride. Although they were back in Florida, I wanted to be able to make that special phone call to them in the morning. As I stood up, all apprehension and anguish were gone. I was at peace.

The judges summoned all lightweights to an area for instructions and pump-ups. The pump-up area is a makeshift backstage gym where bodybuilders lift light weights to pump blood into their muscles immediately before stepping onto the stage. In addition to the physical advantage of pumped-up muscles, bodybuilders are notorious for trying to psych out their competitors while pumping up to gain a psychological edge. I saw Mercury staring at my improved muscularity with concern. My quadriceps began cramping as I flexed blood into their striated fibers. I refused to show vulnerability. I continued as if everything was perfect, pumping my muscles like a peacock claiming territory. Just then, I noticed that Mercury began having cramps in his abdominal muscles, which projected as concern and distress on his face. As he squared his shoulders off with mine, he began to show outright alarm because he likely did not expect any of his challengers to be his equal.

As we filed onstage, the warmth of the bright lights bathed me in a soothing comfort. My peripheral vision could not help seeing an uneasy discomfort from my adversary, who clearly recognized the confident paladin within me. The first comparison was between David and Goliath.

I quickly assumed the first place position in the center of the stage, which left Goliath reeling for an appropriate retaliation. He stepped onto the X that was reserved for the second place finisher. We gave each other peculiar looks, as if to wonder if this moment foreshadowed our futures.

As the head judge directed the first poses, my well-practiced routine subconsciously took the reins. Methodically, with a grin erupting from my soul, I commanded the judges' attention. Conversely, the giant's mortal wound had already landed. Going through the motions, without the brashness he usually displayed, he withdrew into an unfamiliar defensive posture. Each comparison pose dripped more blood from the champion's fading hopes of repeating his claim on the title. I gripped each position with the tenacity of a hungry tiger. I tasted the blood and relished it. It was showtime!

As we exited the stage, two expeditors rushed toward me and exclaimed, "Wow, you looked great!" Mercury, a few steps behind me, obviously heard the exalted statement, which must have added insult to injury. I hugged Mercury and kept the mood light by telling him how fantastic he looked. Never a mean person, he just appeared subdued.

In between the prejudging and the finals, I filled my ravenous stomach with much-needed sustenance and lacking water. Many well-wishers called our room with praise and kindness. I refused to get cocky, as I knew Mercury was formidable and would not go away without a fight.

Backstage, before the finals, a completely different atmosphere existed. Like the true champion he was, Mercury looked invigorated and ready to reclaim his first place status. His attitude was once again lofty and representative of the many victories he'd earned. The champ had not been knocked out, and the battle would rage on. The lineup once again formed for each finalist to perform his individually choreographed routines. First up, the impressive and consummate

Mercury Claiborne would have the spotlight to himself. He received a well-deserved ovation. The other finalists then took their turns entertaining the crowd. None, however, received the level of crowd support that Mercury had.

Then, as the first few notes of Patti LaBelle's "There's a Winner in You" welcomed me, a roar of approval leapt from the audience. I slowly emerged from my kneeling position to savor the tangible sensation that I had ached for so many times before. Each chorus of lyrics, which I adored, almost foretold the epilogue to my incredible odyssey. Once more, the hunger that drove the shy young child from meager beginnings lapped up the wonder of the event. I never wanted the song to end because tucked in the back of my mind was my promise that this was my last national competition. As my muscles coiled into my last pose, thunder echoed from Mercury's home state crowd. They rose to their feet at the same time I did, and I wanted to scream out, "Thank you!"

Before I could celebrate, the top five winners were brought out for the presentation of awards. The fifth place winner was announced and then stepped toward one side. Fourth place was given to another competitor, who was quickly placed opposite the fifth place position. The third place winner was a handsome fitness model, who had incredible shape and stage presence. Mercury and I moved directly next to each other, in the center of the stage. The tension was incredible as a rumble of devout and fervid accolades were hurled toward us from opposing advocates. We grabbed each other's hands while waiting for the ultimate announcement. I remembered looking toward heaven with one last prayer. Tremors began within me, as if choking back the forthcoming eruption of Mount Vesuvius. I barely heard the first syllable of my name as I was swallowed in a moment in time that I will cherish forever. The release of every emotion that I had ever experienced seemingly fused into one mighty atomic blast of radioactive energy. I fought to preserve the masculinity that I had just earned by sucking back projectile tears.

As Laura Creavalle held my arm up for the official victor's pose, my swollen tear ducts obscured the blur of lights and faces. Walking off the stage, I yearned for a clearing where I could finally unleash my thanks. The first recognizable voice I encountered was Tom's while he embraced me. An immediate weakening of my knees corresponded with all that I had temporarily withheld. I could not stop the uncharacteristic ecstasy from turning me into a sobbing sack of elation. The first words I could formulate to Tom and a host of magazine reporters was, "Life is beautiful!" That came to be Tom's and my trademark slogan from that day on.

I rushed toward the pump-up area to clothe my disgustingly smelly body. I dashed to meet Amy for our long-anticipated celebration. I honestly think she was as happy as I was, because her blubbering display of bliss was priceless. We hugged so hard and long that our hearts permeated into oneness.

Numerous media personnel and bodybuilding officials surrounded our jubilation with calls for photo shoots, magazine interviews, and invitations to the post-contest party. They informed us that the margin of victory was a scant two points. That was perfectly fine with me since losing by one point in the past had been much worse. Knowing it was my last competition, I cordially turned the media down for immediate interviews so I could fly home to share the joy with Matt and Dave. I did arrange, though, for several select phone interviews with a few premier writers from bodybuilding's paramount magazines. But those negotiated interviews would have to wait until I returned to Florida.

Amy and I quickly retreated to our hotel so I could shower to tame the abominable smelling beast that had become me. We remained in our room and feasted on various long-forgotten treats that Amy had devotedly prepared for the rest of the evening. Our celebration was brief and subdued, though, because our plane was set to leave early in the morning.

At about four in the morning, I awoke to what I thought was Amy jumping on the bed in a celebratory dance. Opening my eyes, I realized that she was still asleep. By the screams and commotion from the adjacent neighborhood, we perceived it must have been an earthquake. Sure enough, as we gleefully classified it, the gods were celebrating our victory. We gathered our belongings and headed for the airport, where a second earthquake rattled the windows of the terminal. We agreed that it was a finale for the perfect weekend!

While waiting to board the plane, I took the time to make that newsflash of a phone call to my beloved boys. As Matt enthusiastically dispensed the news to David, a sudden and obvious uneasiness seemed to overcome Matt. I inquired why there was such an abrupt change in attitude. Matt cautiously and quietly explained that Dan barked out from the other room, "I am not afraid of your father; I wrestled in college." Sensing Matt's obvious misunderstanding of Dan's facetious wisecrack, I comforted my unsettled and confused son, wondering what rationale there would be for such a comment from Tina's live-in boyfriend.

Arriving at the Fort Lauderdale airport was reminiscent of a mythical conqueror's return from battle. Amy and I were surprised by our welcome as we disembarked from our plane. A crowd of many family members, friends, and gym members cheered and chanted, "USA—USA—USA!" They had a homemade banner, signed by many people, reading CONGRATULATIONS, JOEY, MR. USA! I was so honored at the outpouring that I hugged each person and officially declared, "Life is beautiful!"

If we cling to our morals and stay the high ground, we will always be winners.

TWENTY-FOUR

I Did Not Know What
I Did Not Know

(Winning cannot solve everything)

Is the view clearer when you are king of the mountain?

JOHN ELWAY, THE HALL OF Fame quarterback of the Denver Broncos, was asked if he would have had a satisfying career had he not won the Super Bowl. I related to his response perfectly. To paraphrase him, he quipped, "When I did not know what I did not know, I would have answered yes, but now that I know what it was like to win, my career would not have been complete without winning."

Winning the United States Bodybuilding Championship (Mr. USA) was one of the most fulfilling and self-indulgent experiences of my life. Had I retired from competition before my ultimate victory, my survival instincts would have rationalized or compromised my mind into contentment. However, the previously unfathomable euphoria has since anointed me with tremendous gratification. My numerous losses, coupled with the many years of chasing one particular dream, exponentially compounded the elation of my achievement. Thus, my internal bliss suddenly made handling general issues more manageable. The joy was strictly personal, however, as attention and notoriety were never motivating forces to me. While I understood how insignificant my personal victories were to humankind, new champions were always of interest within the confines of the bodybuilding world. Tradition and protocol had always included the national victors in the post-competition editions of the sport's periodicals.

As mentioned in the previous chapter, I prearranged a select few interviews. One such memorable appointment and subsequent conference was with my favorite writer, Julian Schmidt, from *Flex*,

153

bodybuilding's preeminent magazine. The resulting article was first published in the January 1993 tenth anniversary special edition of Flex magazine. Lessa Acosta of Weider Publications kindly granted permission to reprint that article, which so well captured my palpable jubilation, as only Julian Schmidt could have done. The entire article, entitled "Holy Troccoli," is as follows:

Holy Troccoli!
Bodybuilding is a four-dimensional life for the
new USA lightweight champion

Listening to the pressing tempo in Joe Troccoli's voice when he speaks of giving back to people, of serving them when they are at their most vulnerable, of having his hands in the feces of a dying victim or helping a screaming mother bring a new life into the world, that's when you feel the inspired passion that touches those blessed few who burn with enough intensity to set fire to the whole world.

The rhipidate vitality in this young man spans urges from the physical to the aesthetic, and he follows them all with what he describes as "a hell-bent attitude to do the best job possible." Joe is powerless to do anything less. As a result, he is considerably more: a Renaissance man with heart and humility.

No career can harness him, none alone can satisfy him. From the moment he discovered bodybuilding at 15 and began shellacking collages of Ron Teufel, Carlos Rodriguez, Robby Robinson and their contemporaries on a big wood board to hang on the wall of his Florida home, he clung to his dream of someday winning a national contest.

Ordained with omnibus capacities, Joe was acquiring para passu such superlative grades in high school that graduation arrived a year early amid a spate of scholarship offers. After a circumforaneous academic journey that included the University of South Florida and the University of Miami, he was also graduated from college a year early with a degree in journalism and a 3.96 GPA.

Rare is the person whose career ever allows him to follow his bliss, but at the seminal age of 20, Joe was able to combine two of his: bodybuilding and writing. Muscle Digest magazine needed an editor, and Joe, they said, was the man they wanted.

Too good to be true? Alas, yes. Joe made the trip from Hollywood, Florida, to Hollywood, California, only to find the magazine moribund. It was the first pothole in his life, but in the process he lost his literary virginity and hence developed into an accomplished lyricist as well as a feature writer for Flex, Muscle & Fitness *and other publications.*

Even this wasn't enough. Back home in Florida, Joe felt still another call. "I've always truly enjoyed helping people," he says, "so when the opportunity arose to become a paramedic with the fire department, I took it." As might be expected, he was also valedictorian of that class.

It was an odd anastomosis of interests — the cerebral writer, the catonian bodybuilder, the Samaritan paramedic — but Joe can handle them all; and if they leave a lacuna in his day, he can always fill it with his perennial duties at Gold's Gym in Pembroke Pines, Florida, where, as contest coordinator, he has taken the Gold's Classic of South Florida from a bush league event to a very successful level-four contest.

While the mind boggles at his operosity, to Joe it's all routine. "When I become involved with something I enjoy, there is nothing else on my mind. I've had to train myself to do that, because ever since I was young, I've had to switch hats from one advanced course or gifted program to another, and doing so has taught me how to focus. What's more important, however, is that I love each of these endeavors.

"As a writer, I'm the type of person who has to express himself. There's so much in me struggling for an outlet that, when I write, I cannot hold back. I'm even trying to be less expressive with my feelings, but I don't think that's possible. I have to let them out."

The fire department offers plenty of opportunity for that. "Being there for someone in a crisis situation has always been the most rewarding feeling I've known," is his explanation. "In addition, it's a team effort, which I've always enjoyed. You work together and either fail or succeed together. It's almost as if I'm involved in another sport. In addition, I enjoy the camaraderie with my colleagues; but most of all, I truly am fulfilled from helping other people."

Place his pied life in perspective, and a balance emerges. "I live several contrasting lives," he admits, "but I believe they all complement each other."

After a day of having his sensibilities pummeled by tragedy, it's understandable he would find a counterpoise in bodybuilding. "It's something I can totally control, and while there may be subjectivity in the competition aspect of it, there is no subjectivity in the gym. If I don't get my legs as cut as I wish or if I don't get the biceps I want, it's my fault and not that of cruel fate or some other person. Bodybuilding enables me, for the moment, at least, to take the bull by the horns and be the controller of my life. It's a physical challenge that pits me against the known physical odds of the weights. I'm not in this sport for the glory. If that were the case, the steroid issue would be totally different, and so would my bodybuilding."

As it is, Joe must train for weeks without a break, 20 to 40 sets per bodypart, reps from 25 down to max-singles, ignoring persistent expostulations that he's overtraining. Still, he doesn't complain. This is his chosen consequence, denegating as he does all anabolic assistance. Steroids vitiate the sport and the competitor, but Joe is in this for the pride of excelling. In 1992, that conviction became his greatest virtue when he journeyed to Los Angeles and brought home not only the USA lightweight championship but all of his honor. Few bodybuilders have demonstrated Joe's resolve in pursuit of a dream — indeed, the 17 years it took him to reach it are the equivalent of the career lifespan of the average bodybuilder — but that makes his triumph all the more heroic. Joe reflects for a moment on a Whitney Houston song: "There are a few lines in 'The Greatest Love of All' that admonish one to never walk in anyone's shadow and to set your own standards. That's my motto in life. If I look toward others for motivation, I will always be disappointed."

As he was a star pupil in school, so has Joe learned from life. "I love the sport of bodybuilding," he says, "but if my body were to fail tomorrow, or if I were to be crippled in an accident, the one thing that will remain is what's in my heart, and I think that's far more important: the giving of myself to those who are less fortunate. That turns me on to be able to do that for people."

Dare we name anyone more qualified than Joe Troccoli to lead bodybuilding into the Age of Enlightenment? He sublimates it above the crass quest of ego and defines it in multi-dimensional human *terms that leave its former solipsism appearing empty and dead.*

"One thought should be on everyone's mind when he decides to take up bodybuilding," Joe reminds us, "the same as with boxing or any other so-called 'individual' sport: namely, this is not an individual sport. Forget that fact for a split second, and all balance in your life is destroyed. That's what I realized two years ago when my marriage failed after 11 years and two children.

"Anyone who says he's done it on his own is extremely selfish and self-centered and really doesn't understand how many sacrifices other people make for him. I'm going to use as an example the woman who is with me now. Her name is Amy Tubif [sic], and I know for a fact that, without her, I would never have done as well as I have. She not only went to the store and got all the food but weighed everything and pre-packed it for me so all I had to do was sit down and eat; she was that much help. Emotionally, she was always there during those times when I was very depressed. She was exactly what I needed.

"Neither can I forget others, especially Vince Taylor, who trained at my gym and was unselfish in his critiques and tips, and Joe McNeil, my diet miracle maker. It's for those people and especially my parents that I'm driven to succeed, because my satisfaction is solely derived from knowing what those achievements do for them. To come home with straight A's or college honors, and now the USA championship, and see the looks on my parents' faces is extremely fulfilling. They are a part of this, so when I win, it's a tangible victory of their labors. It's our way of sharing something."

Source: Reprinted with permission from Weider Publications, LLC. Copyright © April 1993.

I genuinely appreciated Julian Schmidt's flattering article, which brought me some credibility and high-level notoriety. The positive slant was that my personal training business surpassed my capacity to serve the increasing number of requests. While I was neither a more competent trainer nor a more superior mortal because of my title or crown, I certainly was treated with more respect. So many individuals who ignored my daily kindness and universal friendly greetings suddenly initiated fellowship or conversations. Before my victory, I was the equivalent of a knockoff purse, and afterward I was an official Louis Vuitton.

The spotlight also brought about some unforeseen repercussions. My expanding associations made it difficult to decipher the opportunists from those with sincere intentions. Some unscrupulous entrepreneurs apparently tried to capitalize on my newfound "celebrity" status by exploiting society's lust for labels and titles. Several attempts were made to contractually bind my name and likeness for cunning and deceptive purposes. Those business offers varied from pyramid-style Ponzi schemes to pornographic movie roles. I actually laughed aloud at the hilarious mental picture of me in a porno! Boy, would they have lost money on that deal.

Another unanticipated change was that international recognition presented complexities that were normally nonexistent. I suddenly began receiving notes and inquiries from Japan, Germany, England, and various other corners of the earth. It was originally enriching to receive letters and calls from fans and zealots of the sport. Bodybuilding was cultish in its limited appeal, but I recall wondering how real celebrities, with names and faces that are instantaneously recognizable, dealt with it. At first, I attempted to express appreciation to all those who took the time and effort to contact me. I diligently wrote out heartfelt responses to all who initially offered congratulations and praise. Some of the numerous innocuous requests were invitations to travel with strangers and give seminars. Some bolder inquiries were money orders to purchase my sweaty underwear following workouts, a man with a foot fetish desiring tracings of my feet, and women confident enough to ask openly for sexual favors.

As increasingly bizarre behavior escalated, I had to end all correspondence to protect my family. One brash guy had tried to earn my trust through a series of letters about competition and training. Once a rapport was established, his nightly phone calls became demanding and burdensome. He sent me naked photos of himself in an excited state. He began calling at all hours of the night while openly engaged in self-gratification. But when implied threats toward my children were expressed to me, I was left with no alternative other than law enforcement's involvement. Stalking crimes, and thus associated laws, were not drafted as of that time. As the local police explained, they could do little to impede such behavior. After the agony of Adam Walsh, I could not idly stand by. My children's safety made such potential threats intolerable and excruciating. (However, to protect my boys emotionally,

I never let them find out about the ongoing erratic antics.) A close friend in law enforcement eventually utilized unorthodox methods to curtail the interloper from continued assaults on my family. Once our safety was reestablished, my afterglow manifested into a period of heightened enjoyment. The bland was made pleasant and the fun enhanced. While life brought its challenges, it truly was beautiful.

Several years of much personal growth and almost complete happiness followed. My evolving confidence gave me the backbone to speak up amid situations in which I would have previously remained silent. A crucial awakening occurred during my son David's First Holy Communion. Saint David's Church was overflowing with proud parents and family members. Empty seats were scarce, consequently placing strangers unusually close to each other. Luck had me sandwiched between Uncle Henry and a woman with an infant suckling her shoulder. I sheepishly compressed myself against Henry's spherical belly and snickered as I imagined mythological lightning bolts from heaven as retribution for Henry's presence in the house of the Lord.

As the celebration progressed, we became more comfortable with those unknown worshipers around us. The infant next to me discovered my smiles and kissing gestures, which caused him to laugh and desire more interaction. His mother became aware of my cordiality and acknowledged my actions with reciprocating smiles. She then recognized that Henry and I were as crowded as sardines. She also must have noticed that his profusely sweating body had stained the entire right side of my shirt. In an attempt to be neighborly and alleviate my apparent discomfort, she asked, "Would you like to come closer to me so you can spread out?"

Before I had a chance to respond to her kindness, Henry blurted out amidst the momentary silence, "I'll come over there and spread you out, I will!" Henry's disturbing misogynistic statement drained the celebratory mood through the soles of my feet. As I felt a boiling rush of blood flushing my exasperated cheeks, I saw Henry, with his contorted teeth, making an animated biting action toward that same woman. If there was a chance that his words could have been innocently dismissed, Henry's Hannibal Lecter chomping erased any doubt of his intent. Although it was his uncouth and primitive attempt to project sexual flirtation, he came across as a diabolical ogre.

The poor woman clutched her baby as tightly as possible and flung herself around so her back faced us. In a state of total humiliation, I reprimanded Henry as if he were a small child. I told him how disappointed I was that he'd reverted to his old ways, similar to before his daughter was born. A convoluted and boyishly confident grin remained on his face; it was as if he actually believed his lascivious behavior made a positive impression. Once outside the church, I demanded that he apologize to the cowering woman that he had disrespected. I was just as surprised at my overt admonishment of Henry as he clearly was. Like so many other milestones, it seemed to delineate my transition to an authority-like figure.

My sympathy and compassion, although always present, became more acute during that period. I once again resorted to instinct rather than intellect. On occasions when I became aware of others' hardships or misfortunes, I spontaneously responded. A single woman from Gold's Gym told me that she was financially incapable of sending her son to summer camp. That very evening, I gave her the funds for her son. Another trainer's electricity had been disconnected because she was delinquent with her payments. Upon learning of her hardship, I paid her overdue balance and the next month's electric bill. I voluntarily purchased school supplies for a struggling gym member's children. A male gym member who routinely commented about my actions and often complimented me about lifting more than professional football players noted aloud, "Your good deeds are legendary in the gym. You are the one in a million that is nice because you want to be, definitely not because you have to be. But I do pity the fool that mistakes your kindness for weakness."

A female client of another personal trainer in Gold's Gym approached me one morning. She explained how she had observed my behavior since becoming a member. She explained how my "depth of character and compassion" astonished her. She went on to volunteer, "You are definitely not the stereotypical bodybuilder. You are *more than* just *muscles*." Although such favorable remarks felt good superficially, I never considered them warranted. Whether others perceived my actions as good or bad was secondary to the fact that I was merely doing what my conscience demanded.

Padre knew of most of my virtues and flaws, as he was my ever-present spiritual adviser. He urged more monetary caution, as he detected that my kindness had become a convenient resource for the conniving. Criss advised me that before I felt too proud of my generosity, I should be aware that charity begins at home. When he asked me what I had done for my family's financial security, I stuttered to answer, understanding his point well. Even though Criss had admirable intentions, I felt completely humiliated. He suggested that it was time to devise a long-term fiscal strategy. After buying out Tina's portion of our home and paying the legal fees of our divorce, I was left with little residual savings. Once I secured Matt's and Dave's prepaid college funds, I was essentially penniless.

Further evidence of Criss's timely advice was recognized with the discovery of Amy's father's bladder cancer. In addition to the colossal emotional and physical hindrance of Dick's diagnosis, we found ourselves under a mountain of debt. To augment my finite financial offering to Amy's parents, I utilized my medical skills to aid Dick by tending to his many requirements, from Foley catheter insertions to diaper changes. The deplorable seriousness of cancer continually haunted us for the next seven years. While I was only capable of minimal monetary contributions, such as replacing their car's transmission, I imagined how much more chivalrous I could be with fiscal security. I remembered how difficult it was when my father underwent his health issues. Criss advocated two specific suggestions to enhance my economic security. Using himself and Vivian as an example, he explained the stabilizing effects of becoming mortgage free. With his help, I devised a payoff schedule to achieve that rapidly. His second idea was to live frugally and invest as much as possible for my children's future. With that advice and my already prudent behavior, I sacrificed most self-fulfilling purchases and obsessively invested in the stock market. I read about it and invested habitually. I applied the same dedication and determination from bodybuilding and academia to my savings tactics.

A variety of unexplainable concerns about Matt and Dave transpired. The boys placed an eight-by-ten photo from my Mr. USA Championship in their room at their mother's home. They proudly intended to show their friends. To my boys, that personalized photo was their Michael Jordan. After about a month, they returned it to my home, stating that Dan, their mother's boyfriend, would not allow it at their home. According to my boys, Dan stated, "No pictures of men in underwear are allowed in my home." Believing Dan must have been using his increasingly confusing sense of humor, I urged the boys to ignore such witticism and leave the photo at my home.

While Matt and Dave were at my home the majority of the time, another peculiar sign began when they were at Tina's. In the evenings, from their mom's, Matt began to call in a secretive and whispering fashion. Our ritualistic twice-daily prayers were usually accomplished during these conversations. Mistakenly, I believed that Matt's seeming attempt to engage in our prayers secretly was a result of sudden bashfulness. But then Matt began repeating an almost exact script-like dialogue. He would begin each session the same way: "Dad, you know how you say wherever two or more are gathered together in prayer, God will be there?" And I always answered, "Of course, honey. God promised." Then Matt would inquisitively ponder, "He will protect us, right?" I always reassured him, and that appeared to preserve his need for comfort. This custom continued for a few years, but with increasing urgency.

With each passing month, the boys' eagerness to spend time at their mother's home declined. At first, my ignorance wrote off their desire to remain at my home as a passing phase. Upon questioning my boys, discomfort with the subject became obvious. Not wanting to add stress to possible inconsequential immaturity, I chose not to press further. Along with Matt's requests to stay exclusively at my home, David began exhibiting more signs of withdrawal. I decided that it was essential to express my concerns to Tina because the children's emotional certainty waned. She and Dan chastised me as if I were meddling into their privacy. They claimed that I was a "troublemaker." Questioning my own observations, I left their home filled with guilt and humiliation.

Shortly thereafter, an intercom message to report to my captain's office interrupted a routine tour of duty at the fire department. My captain's wife, who was on a speakerphone, felt "compelled" to inform me of issues that were bothering her. She and my captain were friends of Tina's and mine when we were married. Since our divorce, she had continued her close relationship with Tina. Somber and gloomy, she implored me never to divulge the contents of her call. Of course, I agreed because I had no concept of what was to follow. She sadly explained how, through conversations with Tina, she learned of a plot by Dan to systematically harass and cause turmoil for Matt and Dave.

She specified that Dan planned to instigate an undisciplined response from me. The intention, according to her, was to "get in my face" through the kids. She stressed that Dan believed my profound love for them would be my weakness. It was his concept that my unrestrained retaliation would lead to such a seemingly hostile act that it would result in Dan suing me for ownership of my home. According to my secret adviser, one of Dan's beefs was that he hated that I had purchased Tina's half of our co-owned house and felt that Tina should never have agreed to such a sale.

As nefarious and disgusting as that conspiracy sounded, I agreed to keep our conversation a secret from Tina, while remaining vigilant for my boys. The correlation between my children's uneasiness and Dan's peculiar actions suddenly seemed to make sense. I confidentially sought a consultation from an attorney, who informed me that my captain and his wife would need to testify about Dan's threats or their information would be considered hearsay and therefore inadmissible in a court proceeding. I strongly requested (it was the only time in my life that I actually begged anyone for anything) such testimony from my informants, but they absolutely refused to assist my children in an open forum. They chose not to get involved. It struck me as odd that loving parents of their own children could be so "compelled" to inform me, yet not want to actually prevent those threats from becoming reality. After they refused my pleas for my children's safety, I was no longer able to respect my captain and his wife enough to continue any kind of friendly relationship. Because of their lack of cooperation, I did not hire an attorney at that time because I had no evidence to back such incomprehensible allegations.

One day, while preparing for a shower at my home, Matt requested a private conversation with me. He unloaded a filing cabinet full of persecution, misdeeds, and tirades that Dan directly perpetrated upon himself and Dave. He begged me not to speak to Tina about our discussion. Some of Matt's descriptions of Dan's actions crossed many ethical boundaries. Aghast from this information, I did not know how to remedy it. Finally, feeling as if I had no alternative, I attempted to speak to Tina about it. She lambasted me and grew highly agitated. Feeling pressed into a corner, I contacted the Florida Department of Health and Rehabilitative Services (HRS). That was the former name of what was later retitled the Florida Department of Children and Families

(DCF). Their highly unprofessional and biased response did absolutely nothing to resolve the issue. They barely introduced themselves to Matt or David, and they never came to me for clarification. After exclusively listening to Dan, an HRS worker concluded that I was still "hung up" on Tina, and that I was engaged in retaliatory measures from a jilted romance. This preposterous conclusion served to embolden Dan and suppress the boys' faith in a system that was clearly established to protect them. More depressed, Matt and Dave grew resigned and conceded that such vexing matters had to be tolerated.

Although Matt was normally an exceptional student, his school contacted me. They relayed their concerns for his increasingly overt malaise and melancholy mood. While I was horrified and concerned, I was also relieved because I believed that the school's involvement meant Dan would no longer be able to prevent an investigation. Matt's school petitioned for both boys to have a counseling session with a child psychologist. Within twenty-four hours of their first conference, HRS arrived at Dan and Tina's house to investigate the children's stories. Although the counselor refused to divulge whether he called investigative services, logic and timing made it obvious. When all signs pointed to the counselor's concern for Matt and Dave, Tina canceled further sessions at that facility, prematurely hindering the investigation.

From that point on, a severance of nearly all communication and cooperation between Tina and me prevented any chance of mutual resolution. She issued a verbal edict, which was blatantly illegal, demanding that all correspondence about our children had to be exclusively structured and governed through Dan. In essence, she unilaterally knighted Dan as the sole authority over Matt and Dave. If Tina's ruling went uncontested, I would be nothing more than a spectator to Dan's atrocities. Such a one-sided decree was contrary to any custom or prevailing law.

With all confidence gone for any governmental authorities to intervene on behalf of my boys, I did my best to compensate by fanatically nurturing their domestic tranquility at my house. I recalled the sacrifices my grandfather had made for our entire family. I remembered how my parents had been like Fort Knox in protecting my brother and me. With extraordinary paragons to epitomize, I swore that my children would always have a sanctuary with me. While probing all potential options to end my children's desperation for an emotional asylum, I forged several meetings with Dan. I caught him during a more sensible and receptive mood on one occasion, and he actually projected a conciliatory attitude. I calculated that Dan's figurative truce was not sanctimonious or deceitful, and therefore I chose the peaceable route over the scars of conflict.

A slight improvement in Matt's schoolwork and an ebb in his outward stress allowed a temporary détente to take hold between Dan and me. Dave, at nearly eight, was still too young to stand up for himself with contrasting opinions; he was more of an appeaser. As part of my attempt to reconcile our biparental discrepancies, I bought a town house close to Tina. I hoped that by selling the object of Dan's vitriol, my home, his scorn would also vanish. The new and closer proximity, I gauged, would serve two additional purposes. First, it alleviated any logistical hardships during custodial exchanges. Second, and more importantly, it created within my boys the confidence that a hospitable shelter was always close by.

Be careful what you ask for because success brings about its own unique issues.

TWENTY-FIVE

Vision of Love

(Discovering the meaning of my life)

Does once happy mean always at peace?

UNDOUBTEDLY ALREADY HEAD OVER HEELS in love with Amy, I
decided to consummate our amorous and passionate relationship. I also
speculated that a loving marriage would set an example of stability for
my children. After requesting permission from her parents, I proposed
to the woman with whom I yearned to spend eternity. Thank goodness
Amy had a severe lapse in judgment and common sense, as she accepted
my proposal. Amy and I settled upon a simple marital ceremony. Amy
understood that we had both recited vows previously, and that choosing
the correct soul mate was far more significant and intelligent than
decadent festivities. My brother, a yacht captain, was kind enough
to offer the services of a yacht for our sacrament, but Dick was in no
condition to endure the ocean setting. We settled on marrying in her
parents' recreational room in their apartment complex.

With wedding plans complete, Amy moved her personal items
into our town home. The boys were excited about our home's addition.
Unlike me, with my unostentatious wardrobe, Amy was an apparel
addict. The amount and caliber of her sublime clothing mesmerized
us. That is what caused my confusion when Amy suggested that I
deliver two bags of "old" clothing to the local Goodwill store. We had
just placed her items in our house and everything appeared classy and
elegant. Unsure of her rationale, I questioned, "Are you sure you want
to get rid of your clothes? From what I saw, your stuff is gorgeous and
looks new." She assured me, "Trust me, this is old junk that *needs* to
go." So I was off to Goodwill.

Upon arrival, I clandestinely offered a young female employee
first dibs on the astounding bounty of petite wear that her luck was

about to deliver. I elaborately explained that fine materials and designer fashions were hidden in my two Santa Clause sacks. Her excitement for her grandiose gifts was evident through her sparkling innocent eyes. Expecting childlike thrill when I intimately gave her a peek in one of the bags, I was surprised when her face went blank. I quickly turned to see the focus of her disappointment. Wanting to vanish instantly via a *Bewitched*-style nose wiggle, I should have climbed into the bag and hid. Before my stupefied and appalled eyes were two bags of *my* old Dickies pants, Zubaz genie workout bottoms, and tiny early 1980 vintage gym shorts. We both stood silent and dumbfounded. With the agility and haste of a cheetah, I released the bags from my sweaty palms and sped off in embarrassment. Amy chuckled for many years whenever Goodwill was mentioned.

A few days before our wedding, I offered to deliver Amy's wedding dress, jewelry, and assorted wedding items for the festivities to her parents' house. I loaded all the special day's necessary components into the trunk of my new Honda Civic.

At about three forty-five in the morning, a loud knock at our door echoed me out of a sound sleep. Running to the door, with adrenaline forced into every inch of our bodies, we heard the words, "Police, open up!" A stern Plantation police officer asked me if I was the owner of a green Honda Civic. I affirmatively replied and proceeded to walk outside with the intention of proudly displaying my new vehicle. To my astonishment, an empty space remained where my automobile had been parked. Abruptly, Amy screamed in agony as she realized that everything, from our wedding music to my grandmother's pearls, was also missing along with my stolen vehicle. The officer informed us that a neighboring city's patrol officer had stumbled upon my stripped and abandoned vehicle in their city and had notified the Plantation police.

It set off a scramble to remember and replace all the essential articles in time for our sacred and solemn pledge. Even with Amy's incredible wardrobe, she lacked the appropriate dress for our wedding. The unforeseen misfortune caused much distress when Amy finally reconciled that she had to marry in a black dress rather than in the traditional off-white of a second marriage. Trying to add some levity, I teased, "I told you we are unique. We'll be the only bride and groom ever to marry in all black."

Our goal was to make my children, by catering to their whimsical desires, feel as if the wedding was as much their special day as it was ours. Instead of the time-honored custom of having adult bridesmaids and groomsmen, we had our families' children partake in the ceremony. Matt, Dave, Anthony, Peter (my brother's younger son from his second marriage), Jessica (Henry's daughter), Gregg (Amy's nephew), and Sarah (Amy's niece) made our ceremony the sweetest and most unpretentious event that one could imagine. It symbolized a union of our family's future.

Amy was stunningly beautiful, as usual. Her fair skin contrasted beautifully with her delicate and tasteful black dress. Mariah Carey's "Vision of Love" was scheduled to be our wedding song. Unfortunately, however, our music was stolen along with my car. As fate had it, when my mother dashed from store to store on the morning of our nuptials, she successfully restored our first dance. The "sweet destiny" of Amy's companionship finally allowed me to "feel so alive." As Mariah's pristine vocal cords serenaded us, the ultimate sensation of mutually passionate affection blessed my cravings.

While clinging to her breathtaking radiance, I remembered thinking that this "vision of love" was worth the many years it took to find. Nothing had ever come easy to me. But I recognized, by refusing to allow my dreams to deteriorate, that the fruit grew sweeter with time. This was the instance in my life where so many questions were answered, and I finally understood my purpose. I was the culmination of generations of sacrifice and martyrdom so I could represent persistence, perseverance, and dedication. Nothing was meant to be easy. The master plan called for many agonizing tribulations and battles in the depth of the dankest valley to earn and appreciate the wonders and majesty of the mountaintop. Yet my purpose was not to gloat or revel in my present ecstasy; rather, it was to act as the Giuseppe Bencivenga of my generation. An entirely new era of impressionable dreamers required that I act as their beacon. I was now the rock that all at my wedding clung to for their foundation. I was the one who gave confidence and reassurance to the meek and timid. Until then, I had never been prepared for so much astonishing responsibility, but the cauldron containing posterity's instructions was now assigned to me. The comprehension of such dependence no longer smothered me as it once had. Fate decided when the time was appropriate, and judging by how I felt, I concurred that it was the right time. But undisclosed, within the isolation of the folds of my brain, I continued to question whether I was worthy.

The remainder of the wedding was simple yet endearing. In keeping with our modest nature, we did not have a honeymoon. Rather, we chose to take Matt, Dave, and my nephew Anthony to Lion Country Safari, an animal theme park in West Palm Beach, the next weekend.

Barely acclimated to the ring on my finger, I was back at both jobs. One morning at the gym, while training a female client, another member advised me that someone was taking photos of my automobile in the parking lot. Since my vehicle had just been returned from the insurance company after being stolen, I assumed they were the ones taking the pictures. I stepped outside to find an unknown woman by my car. I introduced myself and asked if I could assist her. In a hostile and confrontational manner, she began an inquisition one would expect under the bright lights of a police interrogation. At first, I thought someone was playing a prank on me. However, her acidy demeanor never wavered. She persisted in questioning me about my whereabouts the previous weekend. Stricken by nerves and surprise, I stumbled to answer her demands. The more aggressive her insinuations became, the more my discomfort prevented convincing responses. She finally showed me a badge and declared herself a police detective investigating a rape.

In the midst of her cross-examination, Terrence, a friend of mine from another fire department, pulled into the parking lot. As is always fire service custom, there is never an inappropriate time to antagonize each other. Just as the officer was snapping a picture of me, Terrance satirically yelled out to the undercover officer, "It's about time you caught that pervert!" There could not have been a more damning deposition on his part. His mischievous one-liner was the *aha* moment she hoped for. This Pink Panther-esque discovery assured Inspectress Clouseau that she had found the culprit she was looking for. No further evidence was necessary for her to conclude a verdict. She was probably picturing "Old Sparky" thrusting megavolts of retribution through my reprehensible criminal body. She demanded that I turn myself into her custody at the police station. She refused to allow facts to interfere with her conjecture, and thus notified me of my impending arrest.

Perplexed from this nightmare, I entered the gym to explain the circumstances to my client and reprimand my fellow worker's untimely epigram. Like a slap across my already furious cheek, my client stated to another gym member, "You see, you never really know people." I was incensed by her assumption that the trainer she'd known for years was capable of such heinous activity.

The "How was your day, dear?" from my new bride elicited a response she didn't enjoy hearing and I didn't enjoy explaining. We immediately decided that hiring an attorney was our best option. As we found out, the actual crime occurred while we were at Lion Country Safari. The story was that a bodybuilder served a "Mickey Finn" to a young woman on the night in question. That same man attempted to rape the female victim in a vehicle that was similar in description to mine. Jumping ahead of the accusing officer, my attorney pressed for my vehicle to be impounded and demanded a photo lineup to clear my name. While waiting the few days for the police to arrange such a lineup, an ambulance rushed my mother to the hospital with chest pain. The stress of her son's wrongful accusation caused her body to mimic symptoms of a heart attack.

Waiting throughout the weekend for the results of the photo lineup was like watching an oak tree grow. Knowing my own innocence was not enough. I thought back to Bert and Gil and imagined the upheaval that they and their families endured. Then my mind wandered to irrational and unthinkable scenarios. "What would happen if this stranger, who was apparently under the influence of a drug that was slipped into her drink, wrongfully believed my face resembled the actual perpetrator of the crime? How could I prove my innocence? What if she somehow chose me? Not only would my life be ruined, but so would my children's, my parents', and Amy's. Could I trust my future to the criminal justice system?" I wondered how many innocent people confronted these same questions. Because circumstances are not always what they seem to be, I pledged to myself that I would never prejudge someone. The death penalty that I had begun to doubt during Bert and Gil's ordeal now seemed cruel and discreditable. I suddenly became enraged at the possibility that the rape victim held so many of our lives in her hands.

On Monday, as we had hoped, the victim exonerated me as soon as she glanced at my "mug." Although relieved, I was indignant over the turbulence that had arisen so unexpectedly. When I requested an explanation from my attorney about how such an injustice could eventuate from total guiltlessness, he urged me to move forward and not look back. It was an unfortunate lesson that taught me the ease with which life can change without fault or notice. The distress lingered within my mother for quite a while. I promised myself that I would avoid the criminal justice system if possible.

A resulting sidebar from that near cataclysm was that I dropped my client whose comment questioned my character. While I was far too involved in the distress of the debacle at the time of the accusation, I cut all ties with her after the smoke cleared.

Doing the right thing does not assure positive consequences or prevent the unexpected.

TWENTY-SIX

That's the Way It Is

(Innocence denied is innocence lost)

At what cost should we stand up for our principles?

As the finale of one fiasco eased some tension, another unsavory ordeal appeared. My fire lieutenant staunchly supported my bodybuilding endeavors. Although eccentric and unconventional to most, his intentions were reputable. My prompting and reinforcement helped Lieutenant Bobby overcome his insecurity of entering a hard-core gym. Being frail, the initial teasing caused him to be menaced by the muscle-filled environment. He resembled David Bowie, and fire department personnel felt obligated to remind him of that consistently. His affiliation with me, plus some forceful urging on my part to the gym bullies, provided a new hobby for him.

While I was mentoring him in the gym, he began confiding in me about some of his personal problems. He too had child custody issues and discrepancies with his ex-wife. He complained that his protracted legal squabbles had left him with little more than a life insurance policy for his son. Bobby initiated some uncomfortable conversations about undetectable methods of suicide. He spoke of some exotic cocktail of common household items that, when mixed with dry ice and ingested, would quickly dissipate and become undetectable in an autopsy. The context of this conversation was wrapped up in the idea that Bobby was worth more to his child dead than alive, due to that insurance policy. Not truly grasping the serious nature of his words, I relegated it to just another example of his quirky digressions or overly analytical disposition.

One afternoon, while I was in the office at Gold's Gym, Bobby extended his head through the doorway and requested a moment of my time. Swamped in paperwork, I asked if he could wait a few moments. Being completely honest with myself, I abruptly forgot about his request. Several minutes later, Bobby whispered, "Joe, I can't wait any longer because I have to go." Recognizing my own short memory and its appearance of insensitivity, I jumped up and asked him to please come back later to talk with me. With that, he said, "Just call me Mario Scenario," and he casually walked out of Gold's. His statement referred to a well-understood and uncomplimentary nickname given to Bobby at the fire department. It was related to the incessant and peculiar "scenarios" that he concocted to test his subordinates' reasoning and problem-solving skills. Again, I failed miserably to detect the underlying anguish that caused his parting phrase.

The next shift day, Lieutenant Bobby did not report for duty. After several unanswered courteous phone calls to alert him that he might have overslept, we sent a rescue crew to inquire about his status. The goose bump–inducing radio transmission of the crew's discovery was a low point in my career. As shocking as the detection of his corpse was, the sudden realization of the level of his depression overloaded me with guilt. As it turned out, I was the last person to speak to him. In retrospect, the signs were there, but once again, my mind was AWOL. As if that weren't enough to remind me of my dereliction, our crew's non-coincidental secondary finding cemented my liability. Cued up on Lieutenant Bobby's fire department office radio was a cassette of his and my favorite Elton John song: "Funeral for a Friend." I felt I was the target of Bob's directed message. Any remaining wind was gut-punched right out of me.

Later, the cause of death from the autopsy was worded rather indecisively, but it was not listed as suicide. Regardless of any medical or legal findings, I knew what really happened. In an odd and difficult to justify expression of love for his son, he voluntarily made the ultimate sacrifice. I was relieved that Bobby's son would never know the magnitude of his father's depression. Yet I was distressed that his son would never know the breadth of Bob's love for him. It began with Gil and Bert, and now there was Bobby. None of their children would have the protection of their fathers in this confusing and sometimes dastardly world. My children were fortunate, and only my actions could assure the continuance of their protection.

My personal brush with the law had taught me so much. Among the lessons from the rape allegation was the potential for unforeseen results. A small inaccuracy or misunderstanding could have had devastating and lasting consequences. With that memory firm and fresh, I abhorred venturing back into an imperfect court system. Also, Bobby's recent passing reminded me of the fragile nature of life and relationships. However, fate now summoned me to harbor my vulnerable boys.

The avoidance of legal issues required cooperation from all parties. I tried to prevent it, but Dan continued his disturbing behavior. The threats that my captain's wife had once shared about my boys returned to torment them. Also, for the first time, indicative bruises and physical markings were noted on Matt and Dave. The contusions were associated with tales of Dan's out-of-control temper. The children developed such egregious fear of Dan's presence that they refused to return to his rage. That cemented the nearly decade-long dilemma that had become our family's cross to bear. As redundant and unwelcome as our judicial skirmishes were, they were necessary. Repugnant actions against the innocent could never and should never be tolerated or left unchecked. However, the memory of the effect that Gil's and Bert's irrational choices had on their children's lives helped prevent my instinctive and aggressive retaliatory response. Additionally, the heads-up warning by my captain's wife served as a forward reconnaissance similar to an old political adage: "I learned long ago, never to wrestle with a pig. You get dirty, and besides, the pig likes it." So, in a deliberately undemanding fashion, I requested one last cordial meeting with Dan to express my concerns and draw a line in the sand. Within that exchange, I established clear and concise boundaries for acceptable methods for disciplining Matt and Dave. Or so I thought.

Dan sadly and mistakenly perceived my harmonious tactic as evidence of impotence. What should have been little more than conversations reiterating common sense between adults unilaterally became a battle of Dan's will. There was never a desire to control Dan's individuality or freewill, as he contended in future court proceedings. Regardless of his alibis or extenuations, the preservation of my children was my only purpose. Following my numerous sincere and unsuccessful attempts to negotiate a rational agreement to end the physical and emotional torment, I hired an attorney. Had I not grasped the enormous risk to the boys due to Dan's continued escalation of hostilities and threats, I would have never introduced such a detestable solution. I concluded that if I made a mistake, my error would be on the side of caution in order to protect my children. I recalled my grandfather's words of warning: "Those that fail to act must live with the consequences …" Many people had let us down, and it became evident that if I did not respond accordingly, "no one else around me would have."

My protective instincts were impassioned because I fully realized that my children's safety, tranquility, and future were at stake. As physically taxing and all-encompassing as competitive bodybuilding was, the custody ordeal was the epitome of emotional distress. No words or adjectives could possibly convey the degree of pain and agony that a parent endures at the thought of his children suffering. One can only comprehend such desolation if they have endured similar circumstances. I related to and acquired strength from the courage that John and Reve' Walsh demonstrated throughout the horrific nightmare of losing precious little Adam. Another fortitude builder was the lyrics of Celine Deon's "That's the Way It Is." During one memorable moment, I was driving alone in my car, correlating our issues to the lyrics, when a flash of divine inspiration flooded me with the gallantry and resolve to sell everything I owned to assure my children's salvation, if need be. Yelling with sanctified boldness at the top of my lungs, I swore to all who were looking over me from the heavens that my last breath would be spent protecting my kids. It was comparable to the aftereffects of the motivating conversation I had with Sally before the U.S. Championship.

As the children grew older, their words took on much more significance in the eyes of the law. As a young teenager, Matt expressed himself well. Even David spoke in terms that left no doubt as to his opinion. Under unrelenting pressure from the judge, court-appointed personnel, our children's consistent testimony, and my refusal to back down, Tina was forced to sign a settlement. That agreement gave me primary custody, and Dan was no longer allowed anywhere near my boys. While I would have found a certain degree of satisfaction watching the judge bang his gavel in a powerfully worded ruling against Dan, the settlement had the same repercussion. Matt and Dave were liberated from their injustice.

Amy was incredibly supportive during those dark days. Not only had she suffered through our custody issues, but she also agonized over the debilitating effects of cancer on her father. Cancer is a viciously unrelenting affliction that destroys families. It robs any serenity from all the loved ones of the stricken. However, out of even the worst moments, some positives can occur. Amy's mother, Paula, demonstrated a degree of grace and honor that demanded respect. When most of us recite our wedding vows, we dwell on and expect the best to occur. Paula's devotion and adherence to the "in sickness" and "for worse" segments astonished everyone. The unselfish execution of spousal dedication touched and inspired me. So often we hear of abandonment in similar circumstances, but Paula refreshingly did the opposite. However, regardless of Paula's fidelity and our allegiance, Dick's degrading condition was steady and sure. During the entire era when my children's preservation and Dick's health were in question, we formulated an essential kinship and support system. Once more, I found myself as the infrastructure upon which all relied.

During all these trying events, I continued delivering care to strangers in my career as a firefighter and paramedic. Each shift, as always, remained a mystery as to the multitude of predicaments or emergencies that would confront us. Each alarm presented unique challenges that required proper judgment and decisive actions. Alarms occurred throughout the day and night.

Early one morning, the usual sound of our Zetron alarm system instantaneously shattered the temporary stillness of the firehouse. All the employees quickly mounted their assigned units and prepared for the potential complexities that confronted us. Sirens wailed through darkened streets, competing against the ever-ticking dispatch time clock. Our westbound trek took us a few blocks to a shopping center, where a bagel shop owner had stumbled upon an abnormal and noteworthy finding. His predawn revelation of legs dangling from the vent above the stove caused him concern. The proprietor was unsure if the trapped adult male was still alive. Upon our arrival, I saw that the police had already surrounded the building. They discovered that the entrapped male had attempted to burglarize the restaurant by squeezing down the exhaust vent. Time was essential for the burglar because the narrow vent could have had the same effect upon his breathing as a boa constrictor wrapped around his chest. We determined that two fire personnel had to enter the premises to ascertain the patient's condition.

I immediately volunteered, along with another employee, to attempt the rescue.

Once inside, we found that the patient's lower extremities were mottled and lacked a pulse. Without further investigation, a complete determination of the patient's fate could not be concluded. We had no access to the patient's upper body. A collective decision was made for me to stand on the commercial stove and lift the victim to allow his lungs to expand and possibly initiate spontaneous respirations and a pulse. Immediately upon movement, an unexpected explosive discharge detonated into my unprotected face, blasting me off the stove. My subconscious gasp and gulp caused a massive inhalation of fire suppressant and other unknown chemicals. I was momentarily bewildered as I scrambled to understand our unprompted misfortune.

Later, an investigation determined that the tank containing the extinguishing agent had its nozzle embedded in the back of our patient. That nozzle was strategically placed at the bottom of the vent system. As his body asphyxiated and became limp inside the vent, he descended until the nozzle punctured itself into his torso. Unable to breathe, he succumbed quickly and passed away. Movement of his corpse then caused the linkage to break away, resulting in the instantaneous discharge of chemical agents. It was established much later that inadequate record keeping made it impossible to trace the exact contents of the tank. It was surmised by our fire inspectors that proper hydrostatic techniques were ignored by the agency responsible for cleaning out the tanks. By not fully adhering to such standards, numerous unknown chemicals remained within the tank from previous fillings and resulted in a toxic chemical cocktail.

My rescue partner and I navigated through the chemical cloud and crawled from the hostile and suffocating environment. By the time we gained visibility, pasty white powder inundated my mouth, nose, and lungs. My gag reflex violently revolted against the chemicals. I looked like the Pillsbury Doughboy with a cloud of powder surrounding me. Our crew quickly lifted and shuttled us to the safe confines of our rescue truck. My crew's rapid intervention and excellent care had me oxygenated and heading for a hospital within moments. Even though my airway was irritated, my first cognitive thought was how lucky I was. Although still breathing uncomfortably, I believed that once I coughed and spit the remaining silt from my orifices, I would be fine.

Within a day, I thought a severe lung infection had replaced the smothering sensation. Follow-up physician visits elicited prescriptions for antibiotics and reassurances that I "looked fine." The doctors did not administer any further testing, and I simply learned to deal with the irritation and difficulty breathing. Subsequent complaints of lingering effects at my annual physical exams resulted in no ancillary or supplemental testing either. Unknown at the time, my superior cardiovascular condition and relentless resolve only prolonged the burning fuse of a life-altering diagnosis. My partner quickly developed severe hypersensitivity to most common chemicals and was forced to retire from the fire service.

As the physical effects of the explosion persisted, they also served as an impetus to preserve my children's well-being. Sadly, though, our long court campaign burdened too many years of my children's youth. Even David was becoming a teenager by the time our legal issues were winding down. However, an uncanny awareness of the entire legal system brought about Matt's strong interest in becoming an attorney. He wholly rejected injustice. During some surrealistic and vigorously influential testimony, Matt had directly contributed toward his and Dave's emancipation from Dan's antics. Matt and Dave's corroborative affirmations amazed the court-appointed psychologist and guardian ad litem. This empowerment further fueled Matt's motivation toward his future career. Again, out of each negative event, some positive byproducts surfaced.

While my sons' declarations eventually succeeded in their release from contact with Dan, it had the concomitant effect of dismantling any remaining relationship with their mother. Tina's staunch support for Dan caused the resentful estrangement between the boys and her. While I have certainly done my best to provide a healthy, stable, and productive environment for the boys, some mutually accommodating maternal contact would have been beneficial. I prayed often that Tina would reconcile within herself and with her boys her misjudgments and erroneous decisions. My heart always had empathy for her, as I wholeheartedly believed her insecurity and childhood caused an otherwise praiseworthy person to make poor choices.

As soon as the court proceedings concluded and all parties had signed the documents, we arranged an unprecedented family vacation. We chose Las Vegas because it had undergone an evolution toward a more family-friendly atmosphere. Additionally, we wanted to visit my uncle at the Southern Nevada Veterans Memorial Cemetery. My boys, Amy, my mother, and I traveled with great anticipation for a much-deserved hiatus from stress. Although breathing was quite difficult at that high altitude, I managed the flight without overly alarming my family about my complications or obstacles. However, my secret struggle to oxygenate my traitorous lungs had left me exhausted.

Upon landing, the enormity of the hotels and the unexpected area's natural beauty astonished us. Our first full day was replete with a comprehensive agenda. After an early morning tour of the wondrous Hoover Dam and an emotional visit to my uncle Butch's gravesite, we immediately journeyed to the top of the skyscraping Stratosphere. I refused to capitulate to my lungs' mutiny, but I did agree to stop by our hotel for a few moments of rest before our next venture. We were totally unaware of how that decision would alter our plans.

Hatred is more a reflection of the hater than a statement about the hated.

TWENTY-SEVEN

Last Hurrah

(Interrupted celebrations)

Is there such a thing as the inevitable?

OUR BREATHING SPELL IN OUR MGM Grand hotel rooms was expected to last only ten minutes. The arid August heat wave demanded some rehydration and added to the need for my lungs' reprieve. Matt and Dave went into my mother's room, while Amy and I slumped into our adjoining quarters. Amy entered the bathroom to freshen up in preparation for the balance of the day. Our next destination was going to be the muffin stand in the Star Lane shops. The concierge had told us that their fat-free/sugar-free blueberry muffins were overloaded with fresh berries and melted in your mouth when served warm. While I've always fancied blueberry muffins, I've rarely indulged because of my strict diet regimen. Then we were planning to visit the Liberace Museum for my mother. She looked forward to the extravagant outfits and nostalgic experience. After that, we were supposed to proceed to the MGM Grand Buffet for a gut-busting feast before our concluding Cirque du Soleil show, Mystère.

As I retrieved our show tickets from my carry-on, I noticed the message light blinking on our room's telephone. *My kids must have discovered a way to entertain themselves and undoubtedly left a prank message,* I thought. The message turned out to be from a captain at my fire department. He had apparently called our hotel room around the time we were exploring the Stratosphere Hotel. I felt ashamed that I had assumed such notions of my kids. *But why would Captain Joe call me here?* Then I realized that that very day was slotted to be my routine duty day, and some schmuck had obviously made a scheduling mistake. Out of respect, I decided to call him quickly, while Amy was still touching up her makeup.

Captain Joe's conciliatory disposition immediately gave me the impression that he was reluctantly about to give me a verbal reprimand for a vacation snafu. I outwardly snickered, as I had kept my vacation request form handy and knew that I had appropriately followed all procedures. But when his disposition became overly demonstrative and concerned with whether I was seated, razor-sharp clarity replaced my sun-induced lethargy.

Just then, Amy casually walked out of the powder room and gently whispered, "Who are you on the phone with?" Before Captain Joe could even reveal the reason for his out-of-character compassion, I knew Amy was trying to decode my emotions. I consciously tried to erase all expression from my face, but the involuntary tugs of distress forced my lips together unnaturally. The closer Amy got to me, the more her perception and intuition recognized my incongruous look. As Joe began speaking, Amy repetitiously repeated, "Joe, what's wrong? Joe! Tell me what's wrong?"

Captain Joe softly asked, "Is your wife standing by you?" That was the second that I totally understood the nature of what I was about to hear and then be forced to explain to Amy. Joe went on. "It's her dad. I am afraid things are real bad."

Trying to slip my question under Amy's radar, I asked, "Did he make it?"

Too familiar with me to misinterpret my grief, she exploded like a little girl, sobbing hysterically and screaming, "No! No! No!"

Through the chaos of my tight embrace and Amy's collapsing body, Captain Joe concluded, "No, Joe, I am so sorry to tell you he died."

I gripped Amy's inconsolable, spasmodic body like a vise and continued softly repeating my extreme sorrow into her unstable ear. At that point, further information was secondary to Amy's brokenhearted despair, so I told Joe I'd call him right back. Amy was wailing and heartsick as I carried her ruptured soul into my mother's room. Matt and Dave were startled from a playful mood to one of immediate alarm. My always sensitive and compassionate mother thrust her arms around Amy and me, clairvoyantly recognizing Amy's loss. I gave a quick explanation, and I immediately called Captain Joe back in Florida to ascertain the remaining details and to place Amy on the phone with her mother. During the two minutes of their cooperative and agonizing commiseration, I had our suitcases repacked for our impromptu return home.

While "shocked" would be an inaccurate portrayal of the emotions following a seven-year engagement with the malevolence of cancer, we never anticipated such an abrupt conclusion. The rawness of Amy's tearful, heart-wrenching distress was far from conventional. Cooperatively, the boys and my mother picked up their personal items and packed their bags rapidly. Moments after the barrage began, we were headed back to McCarran International Airport, where we stood by for the first available seats. I spent the entire red-eye flight—or as my mother unintentionally twisted it, the "dead-eye"—holding Amy and listening to her fondest memories.

With respect for Amy's Jewish heritage, we made arrangements immediately upon our arrival that next morning. As Criss had so prepared me financially, I was able to defray half of Dick's funeral costs. Although it was a sad time, I was pleased to have the capacity to contribute. Once the hypersonic pace of Amy's loss decelerated, she felt awful that the circumstances prematurely ended our family's very first vacation. As my mother so well said, "Families stick together during good and bad times." I reassured everyone that since we'd all enjoyed our brief stay in Las Vegas so much, we would return during better times. Meanwhile, I coordinated placing Amy's mother, Paula, into a comfortable and much-desired senior residence. It was like a resort catering to senior citizens who did not require physical assistance.

Our accumulating assets, like most investors during the turn of the millennium, suffered significant decreases. More significant than mine was my mother and father's financial loss. Nearly overnight, the stock market misappropriated all the security that their half century of labor had produced. My ailing parents were forced to return to work as a direct result. It sickened me to witness my father and mother exerting themselves for menial wages just to survive. The sudden volatility of the stock market contrasted with my fiscally conservative philosophy and became intolerable. So I sought other avenues for replacing my parents' funds so they could retire for good. That was the driving force that caused my research and analysis of every financial transaction, speculation, and venture possible. Remembering the beauty of the Las

Vegas valley, I subscribed to their local newspaper in hopes of educating myself on properties and values.

Over time, I became familiar with areas of interest and further explored through the Internet. I eventually established some contacts. Two unaffiliated land acquisition specialists, Ken and Steve, made me the most comfortable. Through continued and in-depth dialogue, some potential investments presented themselves. Ken, a courteous and honorable man, allayed most of my fears by sending me an abundance of facts and details from a myriad of sources. I stressed to him the amount of accountability and anxiety that investing my parents' remaining monetary assets elicited. Professionally and sincerely, Ken handled our due diligence as if we were family. We ultimately became interested in a forty-acre parcel of land in the direction of population growth. Then I arrived at the conclusion that two goals can be simultaneously fulfilled. In addition to my need to inspect the forty-acre parcel, Bella had always wanted to visit Las Vegas. After consulting with my mother, I surprised Bella with tickets for the first vacation of her life.

Traveling alone with Bella raised many legitimate concerns. Her Alzheimer's disease presented many unforeseen challenges. Fully comprehending the risks, I chose to fulfill Bella's dream of seeing the Las Vegas lights. During lucid moments in her later years, her sense of humor had become keen. In spite of her condition and constraints, I knew we'd have fun.

The evening before we left, our entire family came together to share in Bella's anticipation and excitement. When everyone else was occupied with kitchen tasks, Bella secretly removed what she thought was ice cream from the freezer. It was actually a frozen dog treat called Frosty Paws. She stealthily devoured the contents of the clearly marked dog treat. When my mother noticed the empty container, she realized that the modus operandi could only be that of one culprit. When asked, my grandmother used language that would have made the proverbial drunk sailor blush. Her unyielding denials tended to be emphatic and laced with expletives ferried from several continents and dialects.

While she was in the midst of her rage, I coyly and prudently told my mother a fabricated story about an imaginary patient I'd tended to on duty. That made-up victim, I stated, consumed Frosty Paws also. My hoax went on to say that such animal treats caused severe stomach damage if left to digest in human beings. Although I never made eye contact with Bella, it was obvious my elaborate story alarmed her. After a moment, she burst out with, "JoJo, I ate the dog food! Do something, fast!" With that, my mother and I laughed hysterically at Bella's change of heart and sudden confession. Of course, as she realized she was caught lying, she added extra emphasis to her spiced-up Italian profanities.

Moments later, I pretended to make a phone call to the airline to confirm our reservations. Again, with a phony look of concern, I explained that we needed to arrive extra early at the airport to have our parachutes and goggles personally fitted. As predicted, Bella's phobia of flying became visible. Sensing the hook was about to be set, I complicated the fiction with technicalities about the rigors of flying in a vintage 1920s open-cockpit, propeller-driven plane. I explained how riding in a crop duster would save much money compared to an airliner. After swallowing her excess saliva along with the hook, line, and sinker, she yelled out, "I'm not riding in any f--king crotch-duster!" Once again, our laughter provoked Bella's patented obscenities. But that time, she even accentuated her words with unmistakably obscene Italian sign language.

During our first evening in Las Vegas, I suggested to Bella that she make sure she used the restroom before our morning tour. I wanted to prepare her for our long off-road trek the next day. She acknowledged my advice and went to take a shower. After an extraordinarily long time, I noticed water seeping from beneath the bathroom door. I knocked to see if she was safe. She sheepishly said, "I think I have a problem." When she opened the door, I could not fathom the amount of water saturating every inch of the walls and floor. She had removed the handheld massaging showerhead from its harness and allowed it to dangle. Because of the excessive water pressure, the showerhead spun like a runaway garden hose. It took two hours and multiple calls for more towels to clean up Bella's calamity.

The next morning, Ken could not have been more accommodating and helpful with my grandmother's limitations and difficulties. Our pace was exclusively established by Bella's comfort and convenience. As if it were planned, as soon as Ken's four-wheel-drive SUV reached a point far from paved roads, Bella's stomach began roaring like a lion warning of impending peril. At first, everyone ignored the vicious beast as it reverberated for attention. Finally, out of concern, Ken asked,

"Bella are you hungry?" Trying to enshroud her always-gassy stomach in secrecy, I said, "Yes, she did not eat enough breakfast; she must be hungry." Bella, with the innocence of a child, corrected me. "No, JoJo, I took a physic!" It must be understood that the term "physic" was commonly used by Italians of Bella's generation for medication to purge their intestines. Today, most people refer to them as laxatives. She perceived her daily use of laxatives as a panacea that guaranteed good health. Is there any wonder why her bowels constantly rebelled? I was humiliated for both of us. However, her decreasing cognizance left her unaware of shame as she repeated over and over that she'd taken a physic.

We rushed to the exact location to inspect the vacant land of interest before Bella had an "accident." I coaxed Bella to be the first to stand on the property for good luck. Petrified of snakes, she cautiously lumbered onto it and then hurried back into the safety of Ken's vehicle. The land was far more beautiful than in pictures. Totally satisfied with all conditions, Ken and I shook hands to consummate the land transaction. Then Ken kindly expedited the return trip to our hotel to facilitate Bella's medicinally induced business.

Once she completed her personal issues, I took her to the casino to indulge in the slot machines. I placed her on the center machine in a group of five adjacent one-arm bandits. She plugged her casino club card into the machine's appropriate receptacle. Figuring she actually would be hungry at that point, I offered to take her for a memorable dinner to celebrate the purchase of our land. Instead, she wanted to eat matzo ball soup while playing the slots. When I returned with her soup order, I saw that she had moved one seat to her left. Her card's line was now stretched like a rubber band ready to rupture. It was still inserted in the center machine by its phone-style elastic cord. I asked Bella if there was a specific reason for her changing seats. In her familiar liberalization of facts, she repudiated my "ridiculous lie."

A young woman was sitting at the far right machine, three slots from Bella. Within moments, the machine's flashing light and alarms notified her that she had won the jackpot. Always out of the loop, Bella asked, "What's that racket?" When I explained that the woman to her right had just won twelve hundred dollars, Bella blurted out, "Some f--king people have all the luck!" As colors from embarrassment flashed across my face faster than the lights on the slot machines themselves, I unplugged Bella's card and escorted her rapidly away. I scolded her and explained that her foul language insulted people. She looked puzzled, as if I'd lectured her on the structures and substructures of the genomes. When I asked her if she understood why her statement was offensive and unacceptable, she responded, "Go f--k yourself."

Several hours later, I took Bella to MGM Grand's acclaimed stage production "EFX Alive." The headliner of the show was the multiplatinum recording artist Rick Springfield. Less than ten minutes into the elaborate production, I faintly heard a snoring sound through the loud music. Sadly, Bella had fallen asleep with her mouth just inches from the ear of the person seated next to her. Hovering on a floating disc above my slumbering grandmother, swiveling his hips and singing "Rhythm of the Beat," the megastar continued his performance. Sadly, Bella slept through the entire myriad of special effects, fire-breathing dragons, blaring rock 'n' roll, and suspended aerialists twirling on spinning hoops.

The next morning, as we were preparing to leave for the airport, I once again brought up the insensitivity of her statement, and the problems it could have caused. At that time, she had no recollection of the woman winning a jackpot ... or even of matzo ball soup. She also swore that I was "full of sh-t," when I mentioned that she dozed during the show. Although I cringed at the predicaments from her bizarre comments, I cherished our journey together. Recognizing the degree of her decline, I was aware that her first vacation was also her last hurrah.

You can't teach an old dog (or person) new tricks unless he or she chooses to learn.

TWENTY-EIGHT

The Greatest Generation

(The end of an era)

**If we truly believe in the afterlife, why do
our losses hurt so damn much?**

AN UNPRECEDENTED ESCALATION IN PROPERTY values around 2005, particularly in the southwestern United States, eroded much of the hesitation and misgiving that had preceded the purchase of my initial forty acres. Doubling the property's appraisal within a few years gave me the courage required to invest more capital on land purchases. Matt was turning twenty-one, and that milestone gave me further motivation to create the wealth for my boys that I never had. Ken had been fantastic, but my continued investigations determined that locations outside of his expertise were also excellent investments. I contacted Steve and used his services to purchase an additional forty-acre parcel of vacant land. Several brief scouting expeditions to the Las Vegas areas by my entire family also produced a desire for longer visits to the region. In keeping with my investment strategy, we also purchased a condominium just a handful of miles from the Las Vegas strip. Over the next few years, I also acquired other large parcels of prime real estate. Nearly each month, either Ken or Steve called to advise me of the incredible rising values of our properties.

My continued difficulties with breathing forced alterations in training and my lifestyle. Still, I managed to withhold the severity of my medical issues from family and friends. At that point, the significance of my short but enlightening conversation with Lee Haney over a decade earlier became valuable. It became physically impossible to train harder, so I employed a more intelligent and cautious approach in the gym. I continually brought my complaints to the attention of fire department physicians during our annual physicals. Unfortunately, my outward appearance overshadowed and excused my declining test results. I appreciated the compliments about my physique, but I failed to impress upon the physicians how my deteriorating pulmonary function tests related to my daily descent. The outright dismissal of my physical grievances forced me to compensate in many areas in order to continue actualizing a productive lifestyle. I incorporated a steady increase in the type and techniques of aerobic exercises.

I questioned whether the aging process simply had brought about a decrease in my cardiovascular fitness. So I increased my efforts with the hope of eradicating my continued downturn. I became the quintessential laboratory rat who was always on a treadmill. It became such an obsession that several firefighters began referring to me as "Cardio Joe." There was a certain amount of covert fear within me of not living up to my reputation for having superior fitness. I was considered the epitome of health and fitness, yet the intrinsic knowledge of my growing imperfections caused much turmoil. The training strategies I had so successfully employed for myself and many clients did not yield the results that they always had. Then, when palpitations became an invariable side effect of my daily post–fire alarm recovery, I knew my frailties surpassed a StairMaster's antidote. After returning to the firehouse at the conclusion of each alarm, I isolated myself by my bunk to slow my pulse rate and calm the annoying palpitations. Again, my annual physical examinations failed to replicate enough signs and symptoms to cause alarm among the fire department physicians. That further increased my frustration. With so many obligations and dependents, I had no options other than to continue nullifying my needs to serve those around me.

One Tuesday evening, which was normally pizza night at my parents', Uncle Henry never arrived. We later learned that he was in an auto accident. Hospital staff discovered that he had lost consciousness prior to the collision. He hadn't wanted to burden his beloved daughter, Jessica, but he had secretly been battling a medical condition that caused internal hemorrhaging. Within a few days of his accident, Henry's organs failed due to the irreversible effects of the blood loss.

His departure marked the opening salvo of numerous losses that wiped out nearly an entire generation of my family. When I was less versed, I'd rebuked Henry's crusty lectures and incorrigible behavior.

Time and many experiences tempered my perspective. While Henry's boisterous exploits could not be excused, he demonstrated that good people could do bad things and vice versa. I did not have the right to condemn or censure his rigidity or jagged edges. The era of his upbringing presented more turbulence than the average person in my age group could have handled. In Tom Brokaw's *The Greatest Generation,* he chronicled the harsh environments that caused that generation's struggles. The majority of my peers have few equivalent encounters from which to formulate judgments on those who survived such ordeals.

Henry's father had abandoned his entire family when Henry was a small child, and he was forced to survive on the mean streets of New York. Henry often told stories of how he would lie when his teachers asked what he ate for breakfast. He'd fabricate a bountiful bacon and egg delight. In fact, he had never eaten such delicacies. He actually had to steal food to survive. He ultimately volunteered for military service just to have three meals a day. When Henry returned from the horrors of World War ll, rehabilitation and psychiatric assistance did not exist. Nor would many of the vets have accepted such intervention due to their pride.

"Today," he'd volunteer, "we whimper and medicate nearly everyone with anxiety over their soggy Corn Flakes." Henry was proud of his unselfish and incredible sacrifices that defeated fascism and kept communism in check. He was disgusted how some within my age group promoted and embraced governmental control. Henry pointed out that Machiavellian politicians issued "handouts," which surreptitiously stole our freedom. "Those entitlements," he voiced, "only make us *feel* better. They actually trap the people they are supposed to help in a perpetual underclass." Henry detested the notion of dependence on any government for security and life decisions. He felt such personal weakness created the atmosphere that allowed political tyranny to flourish. His words always caused me to recall the famous quote perplexingly attributed in several forms to both Thomas Jefferson and Benjamin Franklin: "Those who would give up essential Liberty to purchase a little temporary Safety deserve neither Liberty nor Safety." Henry was not isolated in his hardships and resulting attitude.

Comparable to Henry's convictions were those of one of my heroes, named Cory. As a child, he was sent to a local store to purchase a loaf of bread for his mother. During that errand, he was enslaved by German soldiers who had invaded Cory's native Holland in May of 1940. He became a Nazi prisoner of war and was placed in a labor camp, where he was forced to build railroads with little more than his bare hands. He remained their captive until his liberation by Allied forces. Early in my career, I was fortunate enough to have the honor of working with Cory at the fire department. He was as tough as anyone, yet he had developed tremendous compassion toward others' pain and suffering. On numerous occasions, I observed him either blowing an indigent's nose or cleaning an incontinent senior's backside. He consistently alleged, though, "Joey, we'll never win the next war!" Cory meant that as a society, we had become too soft. His conclusion was that our youth had made a mockery of his generation's sacrifices. Often Cory would lecture, "Those who believed that their rights were due without the responsibility of giving great effort were destroying society."

Both Cory's and Henry's observations and accumulated wisdom made perfect sense to me. But I did not want my recognition of society's decreasing caliber to sour my disposition. Because I was able to sympathize with Henry's encounters and resulting grievances did not mean I wanted to mimic his attitude or personality. I resolutely chose Cory's approachable posture and philosophy as the preferable alternative to emulate. It was, in fact, Henry's passing that turned out to be the catalyst for the discovery of much of my profound guilt. The answers to why I "needed" to become valedictorian or produce financial security for my entire family lived in my capacity to pay homage to those who preceded me. It was my reverence for past generation's toughness and tenacity versus my perception of our relative comfort and leisure that forced the recognition of so much shame. I understood that the reason my grandfather came to the United States was to make life easier for his descendents. It was apparent that he wanted to give us relative comfort and the chance to excel to the best of our abilities. But I always questioned whether I had seized those opportunities and pushed forward hard enough. No matter how much I did, I always felt as if I fell short of my ancestors' efforts. It finally made sense why I was never satisfied with myself unless I engaged in self-inflicted torture or flirted with excellence. Comprehending some of the rationale behind my nearly terminal case of "guilt fatigue" was one step, but I still had to sever its omnipresence. I couldn't continue with such a self-loathing stigma.

Padre, as usual, helped me dig through the clutter while introducing a spiritual component. He understood the profound empathy I acquired from my mother and also witnessed the character I had developed from having fallen on my face so many times. He cautioned me not to allow my grit to blind my compassion. He spoke about trusting in "divine justice." Padre detailed, "It was God's place to hand out the penance, and your obligation is to be kind." He urged me to hold *firm* to my core values and beliefs while always remaining *fair*. *Fair and firm!* Hmm, now where had I heard that before?

Within months of Henry's demise, we experienced several other losses, but none caused more of an impact than that of our Alzheimer's-suffering matriarch. Bella suffered a massive stroke several days after Thanksgiving. For three weeks, her ninety years of experience wilted under the care of inexplicably wonderful hospice workers. Although she lost all ability to vocalize her thoughts to us, we faithfully provided her with round-the-clock affection and tenderness. The hospice workers did not experience Bella's F-bombs and cantankerousness, but I surprisingly yearned for her to direct one more ethnic profanity toward me. I was so thankful for the opportunity to express my appreciation and devotion as she slowly transitioned to the afterlife. All the words and feelings I never previously had the maturity or courage to utter now effortlessly illustrated and unraveled the imprint she had indelibly engraved upon my morals.

My daily vigil included the many services that she had so magnificently performed for me when I was a small child. I was blessed to have fed her tiny spoonfuls of ice cream and wiped her parched lips like she and my grandfather instinctively had done for their grandchildren. Just as throughout her entire life, she expected nothing and requested nothing. The circle of life was reaching its completion as her apoplectic affliction ultimately slid her into a coma. As her final few days brought a placid and serene atmosphere to her hospital room, an undeniable presence became tangible. It was as if God himself were anointing her for her inevitable journey. With her daughter holding on to the remnants of her precious mother, Bella joined my grandfather just days before Christmas.

I felt privileged to arrange all her final services and burial plans. While not overly opulent, her mass and homily honored the importance of her relative obscurity. She never lived her life for recognition or fame; she simply did what she believed was right. I spoke at Bella's funeral about the significant contributions that each of us bestows upon each loved one's lives, regardless of status or class. As I had learned from my grandfather years earlier, I said, "Fear exists in all of us." I added, "Only a fool would not be afraid." However, I explained how proud I was that Bella was fully aware of her grave prognosis, and through her spiritual convictions and unwavering faith, she consented with dignity and grace. I publicly acknowledged that those we often dismissed as trivial or inconsequential were the real heroes of our lives. I stressed that it was their impact that most directly influenced our acquired habits. My words were said to have touched many of our relatives, but my goal was just to reintroduce my grandparent's ideals to my children. I had to pass on and endow the next generation with the concept of *passing love* forward. *I had to act.* Still, though, some remaining deep-seated guilt caused me to wonder secretly if I had appropriately honored my grandfather's last words to me: "If something happens to me, please take care of Grandma."

The aftermath of our loss ironically provided an unforeseen gain. Similar to when I was a young child, Bella's zeal for the Lord reacquainted me with my faith. Staring in the eyes of death, she never blinked. Tragic events such as the shock of Adam Walsh's kidnapping and Gil's and Bert's arrests had eroded the core of my childhood tranquility that Padre had warned me about. But nothing pulverized my purity as much as one adult's betrayal and abdication of his role in my boys' lives. Throughout my children's tribulations, Dan's self-proclaimed "man of the house" status transposed such a position of responsibility and guidance into one of control, demands, and domination. There was the assertion, by Dan, that discipline had no boundaries because he was "born again," and therefore following God's word. While I do recall the biblical teaching "Spare the rod and spoil the child," I certainly never believed it to mean "Rule with an iron fist and impunity." The Bibles I had read never implied that crushing of a frail child's hands or malicious and humiliating insults would assist in nurturing obedience and good manners. I had wrongly blamed the painful and forsaken terror to which Dan subjected Matt and Dave on God. I allowed my innocence to be polluted with toxic bitterness. I had lost a segment of myself that had previously symbolized my personality.

Bella was quite different. Never once, regardless of her life's ordeals or infamy of the church, had my grandmother altered her trust or faith. Once again, one of "The Greatest Generation" exemplified trust and stability to the "intellectual youth."

My children's misfortunes were not God's transgression or culpability. Rather, they were obvious samples of man's frailties and blemishes. I have had my own warts to contend with as well. It was no longer acceptable to talk the talk of religion without walking the walk by personifying devotion. The time had come to exemplify forgiveness and clarify to my boys that life and happiness must go on, in spite of our losses. The result was a renewed appreciation for the many chances God had given us to rise over our obstacles defiantly. Although it was clear that life was not always fair, it was equally evident that life was worth living!

As hurricane season approached, the notion of my parents in their trailer home tormented me. As usual, my mother had converted the interior of their mobile home into her own personal version of the Taj Mahal. However, their safety was my concern. Neither of them was healthy enough to withstand the loss of their humble castle. I repeatedly expressed my desire to purchase a structurally sound home for them, but their unselfish and modest lifestyle initially prevented them from accepting my offer. At that time, Ken advised me of an opportune and serious offer for my original forty-acre land parcel. While I'd not intended to sell that property, the deal was poised to gross more money than I had cumulatively earned in my entire life. I determined that the amount of good deeds and gifts that I could offer my loved ones could increase profoundly. The substantial offer brought about a change of heart. After much deliberation, I sold my property to a prestigious West Coast developer. The net proceeds allowed for the purchase of a home for my parents and the acquisition of an even larger parcel of land in California.

Unknown to my parents, I began the search for the perfect home for them. Once my fanatical expedition isolated our options down to two potential residences, I surprised my parents with the choice of either home. Once they overcame their stubborn pride, one of the happiest moments of my life occurred. They chose a tremendously sturdy and quaint home in an adult subdivision. Padre had suggested the adult-only environment because of his awareness of my parents' increasingly fragile health conditions. The best component of the equation was, as the result of my cash purchase, my parents had no mortgage payment to stress over. Uncomfortable as they were accepting such a gift, all of us knew that hurricane season would not be so nerve-racking. The one missing ingredient that my new financial security could not replace was Bella's unique personality in the second bedroom.

There is nothing more cherished or powerful to human beings than the relationships we create.

TWENTY-NINE

Day of Infamy

(Discovering my mortality)

How relevant is our attitude during trying times?

THE PEMBROKE PINES FIRE DEPARTMENT possessed a Class 1 rating, according to the ISO (Insurance Services Office). Approximately sixty fire departments in the nation held that prestige. The prominent classification was earned through an elaborate system of scoring. Factors including dispatch, water supplies, personnel, training, and equipment were considered to procure such a distinction. Tremendous pride and responsibility came to those who delivered the highest possible level of fire protection. As with the title of Mr. USA, expectations were abnormally heightened. Each employee had tasks and accountability that needed to be executed proficiently for the elevated cohesiveness to be maintained. Inspecting and testing personal safety devices such as our self-contained breathing apparatuses and bunker gear were among our morning routines. Additionally, those personnel assigned to fire suppression units assessed and analyzed the condition and function of all tools, equipment, and the fire pump itself. That scrutiny began each shift for many years.

One oppressively humid August morning, the breeze was still, and the air felt excessively thick. Each inhalation required more conscious effort than usual to expand my lungs. My assignments as both a driver engineer and paramedic were extensive, and a leisure pace was intolerable. Although the exertion needed to satiate my oxygen requirements caused profuse sweating, I mused how a cool shower and clean uniform would solve that issue. The added heat of the fire engine's clattering diesel smothered me as if I were breathing through a wool blanket. My vehicle and surrounding items began to weave and vacillate. It was as if I were hallucinating a belly dance of tools. Growing more stupefied by the second, I wondered if the beltlike pressure around my chest was my imagination—or if I was actually having a heart attack. The swirling and undulating setting also made me conscious of my face potentially planting into the steaming pavement. I recognized my instability and paused to sit on the tailboard of my vehicle.

Eddie, one of my co-workers, paused to tell me how awful I looked. I managed to joke that he could have used that line any day with a gruesome face like mine. Ignoring my wisecrack, he stressed how unusually white and colorless I appeared. I suggested that a moment in the shade would work wonders. Then my familiar palpitations began a rhythm much more intense than usual. Before long, several of my buddies were stripping my saturated uniform off my shoulders in the air-conditioned kitchen of the firehouse. I, who drove to work to assist others, had paradoxically become the recipient of Class 1 rescue service. Dazed and embarrassed, my last words as they loaded me for transport to a medical facility were, "Please don't tell my wife if she calls. It will scare her."

Numerous preliminary tests were administered at a local hospital. A boyish-looking affable physician also suggested that I should be sent immediately for a cardiac catheterization. His testing had revealed that there was fluid and scarring in my lungs, my left ventricle and mitral valve were enlarged, and my pulmonary arterial pressure was significantly elevated. He explained that while he was not prepared to make a conclusive diagnosis without further analysis, all signs pointed to pulmonary arterial hypertension and the possibility that I had had a myocardial infarction. As a paramedic, I was aware of PAH, but not infinitely familiar with it. My concerned countenance must have caused his response: "I wouldn't worry because it is so rare. But believe me, it's the last disease you'd want to have." As he strolled out of the room, I immediate prayed. *Dear God, please give me anything but lung cancer! I promise I will handle any other illness with grace and strength, just please don't make it lung cancer!*

Our city's workers' compensation personnel arranged for an appointment at their designated physician's office. Regrettably, that follow-up visit was with a doctor who was much more concerned with whose financial burden the illness was, rather than seeking a remedy. As several days had transpired and my chest pain and shortness of breath worsened, I requested a cardiologist. After a wasted appointment with an apathetic and pompous doctor of osteopathy, I was extremely fortunate to have been examined by one of the most empathetic and thorough cardiologists in South Florida. He tested and evaluated me for five hours. Amazingly, he called back one of his technicians who had left for the day. Several highly definitive assessments were administered to confirm a diagnosis. While I waited for my test results, Dr. R. was in an adjoining exam room with a distressed elderly African American woman. I overheard that her completed testing distinguished her medical problem as hypoglycemia. In a unique and highly commendable display of humanity and tenderness, he proceeded to seat her in the staff kitchen. He then boiled and served her spaghetti while verbally reassuring her. His abundance of knowledge and innovative medical equipment did not impede the most essential of elixirs: compassion. I remember thinking that if I had lingering medical conditions, the only physician I would want is Dr. R.

When he reentered my exam room, he had a litany of results. He confirmed that I did have pulmonary arterial hypertension, scarring in my lungs from the chemical explosion I experienced on duty, and I'd had a recent heart attack. PAH is a rare disease. It occurs when the pressure within the pulmonary arteries elevates, and it may become life threatening. It may cause moderate to severe shortness of breath. In many cases, a lung transplant is the only countermeasure for its symptoms. My first thought was, *At least it's not lung cancer!* As odd as it is to admit, I was quite relieved with the diagnosis. Before that, I had known for several years that my health was diminishing, and now I knew why. Dr. R. had me back the next day for an additional battery of exams to conclude that I had moderate to severe pulmonary hypertension and chronic obstructive pulmonary disease (COPD). He repeated numerous corroborating exams to validate findings and coordinate treatments and medications. I had brushed aside an impending illness long enough. Now the entire cat was out of the bag. I could not help but wonder, though, *Is this punishment for something I've done wrong? Can it be that my illness is a form of payback for having unintentionally abandoned loved ones, such as my grandfather, when they needed me most?*

I pleaded with Dr. R. to at least allow me to return to a desk assignment at the fire department. He clarified that my fluctuations from medicinal side effects and oxygen dependency made my request disagreeable and medically insupportable. At first, I continued to beseech him, until one of my common near-syncopal episodes reached a pinnacle. My startled wife found me unconscious in the shower. Though I did not remember it well, she stated that a "ton of bricks" sounded like it dropped on the tile floor. Before my condition stabilized and we established my therapeutic dosages of medicines, there were several times when I passed out indelicately onto the floor.

As obstinate as I had been, even I had to admit reluctantly that my firefighting career was over. That was the first time in my life that physical restrictions were placed on me. I felt as if I had lost my independence and liberty. Tethered by a length of oxygen tubing, I moped around as if I had been sentenced to life in solitary confinement. Even though I yearned to cut my umbilical cord and reenter societal bliss, I knew my condition would not grant me that flexibility. In unfamiliar territory, I did not know how to respond. I longed for the relationships I had developed and the goals I had assisted my clients with while I was a personal trainer. I craved the bantering and friendly antagonizing among my peers around the firehouse. I coveted the pumped sensation of my flexing muscles as I hoisted dumbbells and barbells. I ached for the camaraderie and professionalism as a paramedic, thinking how our split-second decisions saved lives. My thirst for activity with my children and eventual grandchildren had not been quenched. *And what of the hunger for shared passion with my beautiful wife? Will that be taken from me?* I wondered.

The worst portion was the possible deterioration of my mind. Although I was unable to exercise my body, my intellect and creativity still required stimulation. Then I remembered the pact I had made with God. He had fulfilled his end. I could not allow myself to sit around with a sulking or sour mask. I reconciled how God had placed seemingly unrelated circumstances before us for a reason. A longtime female friend of mine had married a determined and energetic paraplegic gentleman. He was quite inspirational. He partook in scuba diving, piloted a private plane, and rode WaveRunners. His introduction into my life made me recall that anonymous maxim "Friends are for a reason, a season, or a lifetime." He was certainly brought before me to prepare me to accept my limitations with the grace and strength that I had promised God. Previously, such circumstances would have shaken my faith, but my experiences had entrusted me with the belief that

God had a reason for everything. So I promised myself that God's will would be respected and followed with a positive attitude. Even though I fully comprehended that I had restrictions, I refused to view my life negatively. How could I complain? I still had the best children any father could ever dream of. And my wife was the one woman on the entire planet with whom I would choose to spend my life. The parents and grandparents with whom I had been blessed gave me a foundation that every child should be so fortunate to have. As I first exclaimed to Tom in Los Angeles, "Life is beautiful!"

I learned how far I was capable of pushing my body without risking further harm. While there are conceivable hazards in every endeavor we engage in, I refused to die on the couch. I coined a phrase that Criss loved: "I'd rather die trying to live than live waiting to die." That had become my new mantra. After all, ever since I came of age, I wasn't about to have others set my ceiling. Although I missed many of the friends and activities that I once took for granted, again I had established a host of future aspirations. Rather than gripe and brood over my children's unfortunate experiences, I decided that I'd champion their cause and deliver advocacy for abused children. Selfishly, I decided to embark upon my long-neglected desire to continue composing lyrics. I had written well over two hundred and fifty lyrics. But I had not yet collaborated with a musician to create an actual song.

I had also had the natural desire to write a fitness or training manual. An unfortunate effect from the fitness boom was that nearly everyone who had either lost two belt sizes or driven by his local gymnasium had self-titled himself as an exercise "guru." It seemed like each so-called expert wrote his version of an exercise manual. Those of us whose passion existed long before the "experts" stopped inhaling Marlboro cigarettes or devouring Cheese Doodles never saw our sport as a means to an end. Despite sounding like sour grapes, I had never engaged in activities for the sole purpose of chasing the almighty dollar. Maybe that's why I had excelled in most of my ventures. My motivations had always commenced from my convictions and devotions rather than money. With the awareness of the glut of workout "bibles" crowding the shelves of Barnes & Noble, I still considered composing such a manuscript. Ironically, at the time I was jotting down notes to construct such a book, a tragedy impeded my path.

One Saturday evening, Amy and I decided to go out to dinner.

Just as we entered the restaurant's parking lot, I received a phone call from Padre. While he was advising me of his exact arrival time for his vacation, Amy decided to call her mother simultaneously. The following day was Mother's Day, and Amy wanted to arrange to spend time with Paula on their special day. Upon completion of our calls, Amy advised me that Paula had mentioned that she was in the mood for some eggplant parmigiana from a local Italian market. So Amy decided to surprise her mother the next morning and fulfill her craving.

Early morning on Mother's Day, Amy rushed about preparing to visit Paula to celebrate their family bond. Still unaccustomed to the minutia of my home medical treatments, I was delayed. Amy was excited about seeing her mother, so I suggested that she leave without me. While driving, Amy tried numerous times to call her mother from her cell phone. She grew alarmed that Paula unusually failed to answer the telephone. Amy repeatedly called me to voice her concerns. After attempting to settle her thoughts, I quickly called my old crew at the fire department to request their assistance. Even though I chided Amy about her constant worrying, my premonition was strong. Although I was unable to move as rapidly anymore, I still hurried to my car to Amy's destination. I called Amy back and demanded that she not enter the premises alone. At the same time that Amy arrived, personnel from my fire department pulled up. I was just moments behind.

At the exact time my crew exited Paula's apartment to advise Amy that Mother's Day was to be her "day of infamy," I stepped from the elevator. From the length of the hallway the slow motion and chilling crumble of Amy's knees was like a scene from *Romeo and Juliet*. As I watched my Juliet collapse, I cringed that I could not catch her in my vicariously trembling arms. Once by her side, I wept for her and clutched her. Her precious heart had been decimated by the horrific discovery, and I could not bear to release my tight grip for fear that her pain would take her also. While pulling Amy close to my heart, I glanced down to notice the words "Happy Mother's Day, Mom" encircled by a heart that was written on the card we had chosen together. The envelope, along with Paula's surprise feast, was positioned so that Amy's tears were dripping directly into the lovingly sketched heart. That enduring symbolism seemed to capture that moment better than any words.

As always, my parents hurried to help. Although Amy was consoled with comprehensive tenderness and concern, there are certain losses whose associated despair never subsides. Amy expressed penetrating regret that her mother passed away all alone. If Amy only knew how much I truly understood her sentiments! That was one more reminder of our most precious gift: each other. No matter what our status among the world's hierarchy, or what possessions we acquire, life and love trumps all.

Nothing good lasts forever, so we must appreciate things before they are gone.

THIRTY

My Life Is My Message

(We are the authors of our legacies)

What do our choices really say about who we are?

Perplexed over how to remedy Amy's lingering distress on the anniversary of her Mother's Day bereavement, I turned to the faithful Padre. He was on his annual pilgrimage to Hollywood Beach, and his motel room stood as our Greenbrier Bunker during times of angst. One hour of deliberations was usually the equivalent of a year of tutelage under Sun Tzu. Our conversations always began with Padre's unique way of spawning the appropriate atmosphere for in-depth subject matter. He designed his analogous stories to reinforce character and morality along the line of *Aesop's Fables*. At the conclusion of one or two mythos, he would segue effortlessly into current news events and their relevance to his intuitive reading of the day's topics. Historically, his anecdotes had already sired solutions in my head. And this time was no different.

His self-reflective story about his need to migrate south to recharge his battery to better serve his flock sparked an idea. *Amy would benefit greatly from a change of venue,* I thought. When I mentioned a possible brief vacation to Las Vegas, he concurred, as if I had concocted the idea alone. He was great at making others take credit for his instigated notions. He added that Amy's customary morning phone calls to her mother were a part of her established daily ritual. By breaking her pattern of automatically dialing while preparing for work, there was a chance that the distractions would terminate the cycle. It was my "Tooter Turtle" briefing from Mr. Wizard.

Even with such a seemingly simple solution, there was a major obstacle. Padre's growing dependence on medical care for his uncontrolled diabetes meant he could not be left unattended for more than a few days. When he was home in Boston, a staff of nurses in his retirement infirmary took good care of him. When in Florida, I was his only caretaker. Padre insisted that with some extra preparations, he would be fine for the days I'd be away. I was initially uncomfortable with the plan. So we placed all his supplies, such as syringes, insulin, and his glucose meter, on the table and wrote out an exact meal strategy. I revised Padre's technique so he could manipulate the plunger and syringe to inject himself. His shaky hands made me tentative, but his fear-allaying confidence proved victorious. Padre was always appreciative of even the minutest of favors and could not express enough gratitude for my "elaborate calculations and scheduling." With our well-planned resolution established, we were left with plenty of time to stray into alternative subjects.

Padre had become much more sentimental in his later years, and he would get chocked up quite often. He painstakingly recalled some of the kindness and service I had given to him over the years. He declared, "You've always been truly much *more than muscles.*" I had always perceived my actions more as compassionate friendship and reciprocation. Although I was touched by his complimentary axiom, I deflected it with farcical comebacks. He brought up how I always had a newspaper, with a television guide, ready for his yearly arrival. "The only reason was so you'd have no excuse to miss my Yankees crush your Red Sox on the tube," I quipped. Then he reminded me of how I always ran to be by his bedside when he was in the hospital. Jeeringly, I corrected him by explaining, "I was only there to interpret your Kennedy-like Boston accent to the poor English-speaking hospital workers." He thanked me for how I compassionately whispered that his toupee had shifted during an airboat ride without embarrassing him. "My rationale," I joked, "was just in case we needed to make a run for it if the snake I attempted to catch became angry." He expressed appreciation for inviting him to witness my many bodybuilding competitions. I mocked, "As bad as I must have looked when I first began competing, there was a tremendous need for divine intervention, and I selfishly hoped you had a pipeline to the boss up above." He could not put into words how much it meant to him to be part of my family's personal parties. I coyly dismissed those invitations to him as "a simple need for the presence of a good Irish gentleman who might have brought luck as a direct result of having kissed the Blarney Stone."

Padre then became emotional over the length and depth of our friendship, telling me how much he respected the man I had turned out to be. He explained that, much like Job from the Old Testament, he felt awful for the tribulations I had endured. He cited the arduous custody case for my children, saying how I never uttered a mean or disparaging word about Tina throughout the entire ordeal. How, as a single father, and then with the help of Amy, I managed to raise such fine young men. Then he reached for a handful of tissues as he wiped his eyes over his distress at my health issues. He opened his innermost secrets as he shared how my illness had angered him. Surprisingly, he stated that my health made him bitter at God for a while. Padre hinted that his faith had been tested over how a decent person like me could have suffered such an illness from my 9/11-style heroic act. His unexpected confession reminded me of the guilt that had consumed me over my quick-tempered fury at God, following Adam Walsh's departure and my children's anguish.

Just then, a cacophony of keys and banging suspended Padre's revelation. A maid, totally unaware of the room's occupancy, opened the door to Padre's room. I instantaneously remembered our legendary Orlando escapade's calf-raising interruption. My explosive burst of laughter seemed far merrier than one would expect, had this disruption not had such a sidesplitting precedent. It possibly also represented a tension release from Padre's emotions, and I simply could not contain my outburst. The maid was clearly flustered from this encounter and collected herself to ask, "Guten tag, Father, und towels for you?" This further contributed to my uncontrolled hysteria. Looking at me as if I belonged in the Amityville insane asylum, she retracted her cart and wheeled away.

Padre, always easily abashed, asked me with his crimson face why I found her entrance so comical. Through barely paused hysterics I began repeating, "Oh my God! Oh my God! Oh my God!" Padre immediately seemed to recall the horror of many years earlier, appearing to cringe as if hiding behind an imaginary bullfighter's cape. I shouted out, "Good thing we weren't doing donkey calf raises again!" At that point, two blundering imbeciles convulsed in a raucous mixture of humiliation and hearty laughter. After five full minutes of gasping for air and cramping abdominal muscles, we finally regained control of ourselves.

Trying to assert his composure and change the subject, Padre asked me if my family would be interested in a day trip to Key West when Amy and I returned from Las Vegas. He wanted to use the junket as a form of congratulations for Matt's graduation from law school and Dave's increasingly good grades. Naturally, I expressed our desire to go with him.

Time had breezed by, so I once again reiterated and reviewed Padre's meal schedule with him before I gathered my belongings. Padre reached into his Felix the Cat bag of tricks and pulled out some astronomy packets for my kids. One of his many hobbies was astronomy. He had passed on that interest, years earlier, to my boys. He also retrieved a beautiful calendar intended for my mother. At the conclusion of our visits, Padre always sent me away with sentimental bounty for my family.

As we strolled to my car, his hypersensitive emotions once again began to project. He spoke of his childhood and his yearning for our nation's patriotic camaraderie again, similar to during World War ll. He interrupted his tears as he fondly reminisced about how his parents brewed beer back then. He explained how slamming doors in their home would ruin the fermenting process. That flashback elicited giggling, and he seemed to transform into a vigilant young Donald, acting out his and his sister's tiptoeing to avoid their parents' wrath. The mention of brewing beer triggered the thoughts of his penchant for sweet drinks such as Harvey's Bristol Crème and his favorite, a Harvey Wallbanger. With one hand on my shoulder, he slowed our forward progress and expressed his comprehension for his drinking's contribution to his diabetes. Then he associated his drinking pattern with the example set by his parents. As his head seemed to dip shamefully, he grew silent.

When we reached my vehicle, he made several kind statements about my parents. Padre and my parents had a respectful and equally benevolent relationship. In an almost introspective analysis, Padre's conceded, "I know your father took a while to really trust my intentions with you, but I can rest happy knowing I have his complete faith now."

Once again, he turned to me and began a dissertation on how I had set an excellent example for my children. He furthered that point by enumerating disappointing professional athletes and their devastating effects on today's youth. He felt the impact of their highly publicized improprieties and iniquities directly contributed to the decrease in today's morality.

Suddenly, his pensive logic harkened him back to recall one of his favorite heroes, Mahatma Gandhi. He pointed out that Gandhi lived a modest lifestyle. The fact that one simple man's message of nonviolent civil disobedience had ultimately led to the independence of India mesmerized Padre. From his photographic memory, he recited his favorite Gandhi quote: "My life is my message." He loved how the simplicity of that quote had such bottomless depth. Padre interpreted and expounded its meaning in this way: "Our bodies of works and deeds are far more important than our words." Surprisingly, he attempted to draw an analogy between Gandhi's simple examples and mine. He mumbled something about Gandhi's quote being the perfect inscription on my tombstone.

I was extremely flattered, but I believed it bordered on blasphemy. I countered, "That type of praise should be reserved for real heroes such as my grandfather, who led through his actions." While I desired Padre's respect, I was fully aware of my many flaws and felt it was an insincere compliment to compare me to someone as great as Gandhi. I explained to Padre my discomfort with such a statement because I still carried so much guilt from my parting encounter with my grandfather. At first, I mistakenly thought he ignored my woe, for he responded, "Gandhi was a normal man too." He went on to express a profound sentence that still lives with me today: "From flawed men come great deeds!" His illustration of that quote was that no one was born great; only through discipline and choices did a man go on to do great things.

Stepping aside, he explained that he was fully aware of my many flaws from all the years of hearing my confessions. Padre assured me that my lack of precognition or prophesy powers only proved that I was normal. He whispered, "Neither your grandfather nor I could have predicted the future. You did the best you could with the information you had at that time. Hindsight is always twenty-twenty. Don't you think it's time to forgive yourself?" He clarified that a manuscript of my life would serve as an excellent diagram of how consistency, sincerity, and dedication can overcome humble beginnings and numerous obstacles without selling one's soul to the devil. Then he turned back toward me, shook my hand, and said, "Have you ever thought about writing a book that would show that winners don't have to be jerks?

Sunshine, there are so few role models nowadays. Your story would show that nice guys don't always finish last. Kind of like chronicling the events that have shaped you into the adult you've become. Without a doubt, your attitude and character are what cause you to stand out. Nobody handed you your character, and nobody can take it away. I have flaws, your grandfather had flaws, and so did Gandhi. Believe me, Sunshine, your motivations are second to none. If something happens to me, please think about writing that book. I'm serious! Will you promise me that?"

With my affirmative promise, we said good-bye, and I proceeded home. While driving away, I observed Padre in the rearview mirror and thought, *Now that is a great man.*

Halfway home, I recalled Padre's request. I then connected it to my long-held desire of transposing my feelings onto paper. *But*, I appraised, *what in my life could I possibly write about that would benefit anyone else?* Then I quickly dismissed the fulfillment of my commitment to Padre as being many years away. My contemplative mind-set flashed all the sterling examples of mentors that had crossed my path. Then, almost as if Padre were whispering the notion in my ear, I credited myself with having chosen such enlightenment, by embracing my associations with such fantastic people. Also, I babbled out loud, "I'm so lucky to have such an outstanding man think so highly of me. I'll be sure to tell him how much he means to me when I get back from Vegas."

Sadly, I never had the pleasure of his companionship again. Even after amassing so much awareness from my thirty day long retrospective writing adventure, I still feel the same unavoidable bereaved sensation over the loss of Padre. I often reflect over how events and acquaintances from my life have been intertwined. Certainly, some episodes of my life were not entirely transformative. However, the preponderance of my memorable events have been conspicuously influential. Indeed, every milestone, mishap, and predicament had its own innate contribution. For a while, I speculated, *If it were only feasible to continue the legacy of those I had surrounded myself with, maybe I actually could deserve their praise.* But then a voice in my head, possibly Padre's or my grandfather's from beyond, countered, *It is very possible you already have.*

This entire quest initiated as a personal search to understand if or why I neglected to come to the aid of others in their time of need.

Somewhere along my path of discovery, I realized that I'd never had power over my grandfather's, Padre's, or Lieutenant Bob's destinies. Consequently, a slew of unexpected and more significant questions emerged. That unforeseen trajectory ultimately delivered the most important answers of my life. As my grandfather had left a piece of himself within my soul, I feel as though Padre did the same. He had suggested the use of the Lord's Prayer as a tool to combat impulsively misguided reactions, but I had previously never paid much attention to the message it contains about forgiveness. But his suggestion to forgive myself finally put things into perspective.

Ironically, a serene acceptance now replaces the hollow angst of my past. My trek has delivered the liberating tranquility of self-absolution. For the first time in my life, I feel as though I am perfectly fine with not being perfect. I actually do not require the validation from others that I had sought during my youth. I accept that I have always possessed the free will to choose my own path, just as we all have such potential power. It was me who drove my life, as each person before me has driven his. Assuming that is true, we all must take ownership of our own imprint on humanity, whether that impression is flattering or not. It was not simply fate directing me as if I were on a railroad's predetermined path. While I looked toward others for strength many times, the impetus to continue had always originated within me. Over the years, I've searched in so many directions for my holy grail, only to find that all the sorcery and enchantment had long ago been implanted deep within me. It is sad, nonetheless, that such profound losses had to be experienced before I came to the appropriate conclusions. Perhaps those sacrifices were necessary to fulfill the overall master plan.

When my grandfather passed away, I learned that nothing worth attaining comes without a price. That high cost forced my recognition that the greatest rewards in my life have been whatever virtues I've managed to accrue. Quite possibly, then, I have emulated my grandfather more than I had given myself credit for. I, too, was confronted with many challenges because I've been an ordinary man who was forced to meet the unique circumstances of my particular life. Eventually, my seeds of wisdom may be all that I'm compelled to pass along. By keeping my final promise to Padre, I may well have done exactly that.

Conceivably, the world does not require me to become another Mahatma Gandhi. If that is true, then perhaps I have been too tough and intolerant of my personal failings. Then again, had I not been as stringent and unrelenting, my life would have been completely altered. As imperfect as I've undoubtedly been, I guess I have been a decent person. Or, according to one extraordinary mentor's opinion, "My life is my message."

The value of one's life is infinite because dividends may last generations.